ELECTIONS IN INDONESIA

For many decades, the Indonesian government had little sympathy with Western notions of elections as events for the transfer of power. Instead, it saw elections as 'festivals of democracy' – occasions at which ordinary Indonesians were given the opportunity to celebrate the country's achievements under the rule of its New Order leadership, as well as to legitimize the continued use of these leaders. The fall of Suharto in May 1998 and subsequent reforms promised to change that.

This book examines and compares two elections in Indonesia – the last New Order election in May 1997 under the authoritarian government, and the first free election in the post-Suharto era in June 1999 – making an important contribution to our understanding of the demise of the New Order, and the directions being taken by the new regime. By exploring a mix of local, cultural, national and political perspectives on these elections, the contributors highlight how intense political rivalries on a local level in the 1997 elections were surprisingly similar to the elections under the reform-minded government in 1999.

By utilizing a multi-layered view of national events, this book unearths new findings on political behaviour and political culture in Indonesia. As the first comprehensive study of local practices in Indonesian elections, *Elections in Indonesia* will appeal to scholars of Southeast Asian studies and those with research interests in new and developing democracies alike.

Hans Antlöv is a programme officer of Governance and Civil Society at the Ford Foundation in Jakarta, Indonesia.

Sven Cederroth is a social anthropologist at the Centre for Asian Studies, Göteborg University, Sweden.

NORDIC INSTITUTE OF ASIAN STUDIES – DEMOCRACY IN ASIA SERIES
Edited by Tak-Wing Ngo
(*Sinological Institute, Leiden University*) and
Hans Antlöv
(*Ford Foundation, Jakarta*)

In recent years an often acrimonious East–West debate has arisen on issues of democracy, human rights, good governance, etc. One aim of this series is to augment traditional political studies with more culturally sensitive treatments so that our knowledge of local interpretations of democracy and political legitimacy is improved. Accordingly, welcome additions to the series will be studies of local political structures and political cultures (and their operation within national political processes), new avenues of transnational interaction, and the meeting between what governments interpret as democracy and local cultural and political realities. In so doing, the series will contribute to the discussion about democracy, democratization and democratic alternatives in Asia, and provide a natural meeting place for scholars working in this field.

INDONESIA AND THE '*THIRD WAVE OF DEMOCRATIZATION*'
The Indonesian Pro-Democracy Movement in a changing world
Anders Uhlin

THE CULTURAL CONSTRUCTION OF POLITICS IN ASIA
Edited by Hans Antlöv and Tak-Wing Ngo

DEMOCRACY AND AUTHORITY IN KOREA
The cultural dimension in Korean politics
Geir Helgesen

HUMAN RIGHTS AND ASIAN VALUES
Contesting national identities and cultural representations in Asia
Edited by Michael Jacobsen and Ole Bruun

ELECTIONS IN INDONESIA
The New Order and beyond
Edited by Hans Antlöv and Sven Cederroth

DEMOCRACY, DEVELOPMENT AND DECENTRALIZATION IN
PROVINCIAL THAILAND
Daniel Arghiros

FROM SUBJECTS TO CITIZENS – BALINESE VILLAGERS IN THE
INDONESIAN NATION–STATE
Lynette Parker

ELECTIONS IN INDONESIA

The New Order and beyond

Edited by Hans Antlöv and Sven Cederroth

RoutledgeCurzon
Taylor & Francis Group
LONDON AND NEW YORK

Nordic Institute of Asian Studies
Monograph Series, No.88

First published 2004
by RoutledgeCurzon
11 New Fetter Lane, London EC4P 4EE

Simultaneously published in the USA and Canada
by RoutledgeCurzon
29 West 35th Street, New York, NY 10001

RoutledgeCurzon is an imprint of the Taylor & Francis Group

© 2004 editorial matter and selection, Hans Antlöv and Sven Cederroth;
individual chapters, the contributors

Typeset in Sabon by
Newgen Imaging Systems (P) Ltd, Chennai, India
Printed and bound in Great Britain by
The Cromwell Press, Trowbridge, Wiltshire

British Library Cataloguing in Publication Data
A catalogue record for this book is available from the British Library

Library of Congress Cataloging in Publication Data
A catalog record for this book has been requested

ISBN 0–7007–1351–4 (hbk)
ISBN 0–7007–1352–2 (pbk)

CONTENTS

NOTES ON CONTRIBUTORS

Hans Antlöv is a program officer of governance and civil society at the Ford Foundation in Jakarta, where he has been on contract since 1998. He has a Ph.D. in social anthropology from the Göteborg University, Sweden. Before joining the Ford Foundation, he worked at the Nordic Institute of Asian Studies and the Centre for Asian Studies at Göteborg University. His present research interest include local politics, leadership, and democratization in Indonesia.

Sven Cederroth is an Associate Professor at the Department of Social Anthropology, Göteborg University, where he is also associated with the Centre for Asian Studies. Between 1988–97 he was a senior researcher at the Nordic Institute of Asian Studies. He has carried out fieldwork on the islands of Lombok and Java in Indonesia, and in Peninsula Malaysia. He is presently completing a re-study of religious practices on Lombok based on his original fieldwork 30 years ago. He has published a large number of books and articles on leadership, religious practices and rural livelihoods.

Syamsuddin Haris is senior researcher at the Center of Political Studies (P2P) at the Indonesian Institute of Sciences (LIPI). He holds an M.A. degree from the University of Indonesia. He is a well-known media contributor to political issues and has published a number of books in Indonesia on elections, democratization, and politics during and after the New Order.

Endang Turmudi is senior researcher at the Center of Social and Cultural Studies (P2K2) at the Indonesian Institute of Sciences (LIPI), where he has worked since 1983. He has a Ph.D. in sociology from the Australian National University. He has written extensively on Islam in Indonesia and, more recently, on the relationship between Islamic practices and politics.

Kaarlo Voionmaa holds a readership in Finnish as a second and foreign language at the Oulu University, Finland. He has an M.A. in general linguistics from Helsinki University and a Ph.D. in linguistics from Göteborg University, where he also has been associated with the Centre for Asian Studies. His current research interests include minority language policies, adult second language acquisition and critical discourse analysis.

GLOSSARY AND ABBREVIATIONS

Abangan   a syncretist Moslem.

ABRI   *Angkatan Bersenjata Republik Indonesia*, the armed forces of the Indonesia Republic. After the fall of Suharto, ABRI was renamed TNI, *Tentara Nasional Indonesia*.

Adat   customary law or tradition, specific for each ethnic group.

Aliran **lit.**   'stream', in political studies defined by Clifford Geertz as a political party surrounded by voluntary organizations as found during the 1950s.

Bapak **lit.**   'father', a man of high status.

Bupati   district head.

DPR   *Dewan Perwakilan Rakyat*, House of Representatives, the Indonesian Parliament.

DPR-D   *Dewan Perwakilan Rakyat Daerah*, Local House of Representatives, either at the provincial or municipal level.

Fatwa   Islamic decree.

Golkar   *Golongan Karya*, lit. Functional Groups, the main electoral machine of the New Order.

GOLPUT   *Golongan Putih*, lit. 'the white group', referring to blank voters.

Hajj (**sometimes** *haji*)   someone who has done the pilgrimage to Mekkah.

Hansip   *Ketahanan Sipil*, the community-based para-military guard force.

ICMI   *Ikatan Cendekiawan Muslim se-Indonesia*, the Association of Moslem Intellectuals.

Istighosah   Islamic ritual carried out by a *tarekat*.

Jurkam   *juru kampanje*, the campaign expert.

KH   *kiai haji*.

Khittah   foundation.

Kiai   Islamic teacher, often with great charisma, heading a *pesantren*.

KISDI   *Komite Solidaritas untuk Dunia Islam*, the Solidarity Committee of the Islamic World.

KORPRI   *Korps Pegawai Republik Indonesia*, the Civil Servants' Corps.

KPU   *Komite Pemilihan Umum*, the post-Suharto General Election Commission.

LPU *Lembaga Pemilihan Umum*, the New Order's General Election Commission.

Masjumi *Madjelis Syuro Muslimin Indonesia*, a modernist Islamic party during the Sukarno-era.

Mega–Bintang the 'campaign coalition' between PDI and PPP during the 1997 election.

MKGR *Musyawarah Kekelurgaan Gotong Royong*, a founding organization of Golkar, since 1998 a separate party.

Mono-loyalitas lit. 'singular loyalty', a 1970 decree mandating civil servants to join Golkar.

MPR *Majelis Permusyawaratan Rakyat*, People's Consultative Assembly, consisting of DRP plus appointed regional and functional members.

NASAKOM *Nasionalis, Santri, Komunis*, the government coalition of nationalists, Muslims and communists during the late Sukarno period.

'New Order' a short-hand description of the Suharto-regime, as opposed to Sukarno's 'Old Order'.

NU *Nahdlatul Ulama*, a mass-based organization for traditional Moslems in Indonesia.

PAN *Partai Amanat Nasional*, the National Mandate Party.

Pancasila lit. 'five pillars' the national ideology consisting of the belief in God, humanitarianism, a united Indonesia, democracy through consultations, and social justice.

Parmusi *Partai Muslimin Indonesia*, a modernist Islamic party formed ahead of the 1971 election after the Suharto government refused to rehabilitate Masjumi.

PBB *Partai Bulan Bintang*.

PDI *Partai Demokrasi Indonesia*, the Indonesian Democratic Party, one of three parties under the New Order, established in 1972 by the merging of five nationalist and Christian parties (PNI, Murba, IPKI, Partai Katolik and Parkindo).

PDI-P *Partai Demokrasi Indonesia Perjuangan*, the Indonesian Democratic Party of Struggle, the party established by Megawati Sukarnoputri after she was ousted from PDI.

Pemangku leader in Lombok responsible for customary law.

Pembangunan development, a cornerstone of the New Order policy.

Pengembosan lit. 'to deflate', the policy of NU not to support PPP ahead of the 1987 election.

Pesantren Islamic boarding school.

PIB *Partai Indonesia Baru*.

PID *Partai Islam Demokrat*.

PK *Partai Kesatuan*.

PKB *Partai Kebangkitan Bangsa*, the National Awakening Party, a party established in 1999, closely associated with NU.

PKI *Partai Komunis Indonesia*, the Indonesian Communist Party, banned in 1966.

PKU *Partai Kebangkitan Umat*.

PNI *Partai Nasionalis Indonesia*, the Indonesian Nationalist Party, established by Sukarno, merged into PDI in 1972.

PNU *Partai Nahdlatul Umat*.

PP *Partai Persatuan*.

PPP *Partai Persatuan Pembangunan*, United Development Party, one of three parties under the New Order, established in 1972 by the merging of four Islamic parties (NU, Parmusi, *Partai Sarekat Islam Indonesia* and Perti).

Priyayi a person of noble birth.

PSII *Partai Sarekat Islam Indonesia*.

PSII-1905 *Partai Sarekat Islam Indonesia-1905*.

PUI *Partai Ummat Islam*.

PUMI *Partai Umat Muslimin Indonesia*.

PUY *Partai Abul Yatama*.

Santri **lit.** a student of a *pesantren*, usually denoting a devout Muslim.

SUNI *Partai Solidaritas Uni Nasional Indonesia*.

Tarekat an Islamic movement based on Sufi mysticism.

TNI see ABRI.

Tuan guru Islamic teacher in Lombok, often with great charisma, heading a *pesantren*.

Ulama Islamic teacher.

Ummat the Islamic community.

Wasiat Islamic decree, often in the form of a last will and testament.

Wetu Telu a syncretic form of Islam in Lombok.

1

INTRODUCTION

Hans Antlöv

The 1999 national election in Indonesia has been heralded as a benchmark for the transition towards democracy. Just two years earlier, the Suharto government, the so-called New Order, had organized its sixth election. Just as in earlier elections, the government party Golkar had won a solid victory, this time receiving more than 75 per cent of the votes in a not very free or fair election. After Suharto's fall and his loyal vice-president Habibie's ascent to power, the main demand of the democracy movement was for new elections. The chapters in this book will examine and compare these two elections in Indonesia, the one organized by the New Order government on 28 May 1997, and the subsequent democratic elections organized thirteen months after the fall of Suharto and held on 7 June 1999. A previous version of this book had already been completed in late 1998, when it was announced that new elections would be held in June 1999. We decided to include these elections, and make it a comparative study. The chapters thus analyse similarities and differences between the two elections. We also discuss how dissatisfaction articulated during the 1997 election contributed to the demise of the New Order government, and the changes the democratic election in 1999 brought to national and local politics.[1]

Why study elections? They provide fascinating insights into political practices for us. On a superficial level, they are to politics what stock exchanges are to economics: ways to measure confidence and assess the 'market'. But elections and politics are more than markets and economics (in spite of what Thatcherites might say!); they also prompt new subjectivity, political assertiveness and self-consciousness. Elections are about morality, governance and authority – notions in the centre of political philosophies. An election, when people put on their best clothes and vote in public (but by secret ballot) for the candidate or party of their choice, is a symbolic commitment that raises the spirit of the voter and of the community, and makes it easier to mobilize for political purposes. Modern national elections have been criticized by agents of strong national identities (such as the proponents of Asian Values) for grafting and imposing liberal values on societies with long and valuable political traditions. In these societies, it is

1

argued, authority is based on kinship or patronage by powerful figures. The challenge that modern elections holds out is the possibility for emerging classes to go beyond legitimacy achieved through hereditary privilege, cognatic succession and charismatic appeal. Elections can thus both legitimize and challenge existing orders. They are complex events that should not be reduced to mere statistical analysis of election results.

The symbolic importance of elections was clearly recognized by the authoritarian New Order government, which organized six general elections. The results as such were not really interesting or important, since the outcome was more or less determined beforehand. Elections in New Order Indonesia were organized in order to provide a degree of international recognition while not constituting a threat to national stability. Through elections, the government could display to the public that it was in control of the country. The regime spent massive amounts of money on mobilizing voters and organizing polls. Elections were known as *pesta demokrasi*, democratic festivals, and their success was measured by how smoothly and uneventfully the campaign and balloting went.

In one of the few systematic treatments of Indonesian elections, Bill Liddle (1996) investigated the elections as a legitimizing factor for the Suharto regime, calling them 'a useful fiction'. His study is a good account of the elite's manipulations and manoeuvring of elections at the national macro level. A 1997 article in *The Economist* replicated Liddle's arguments: 'Elections under Suharto, while raucous and apparently competitive, are not intended to offer a choice between different potential governments. They are intended to return Golkar with as large a majority as possible' (*The Economist*, 26 July 1997, Indonesia supplement, p. 5). Most other commentators are equally unimpressed by the New Order election track record. In the same volume as that in which Liddle examined the New Order elections, Benedict Anderson contributed a comparative study of elections in Thailand, Indonesia and the Philippines in which he simply dismissed the Indonesian elections: 'There is no need here to spend any time on the series of elections since 1971 by Suharto's New Order military regime. They are carefully managed to produce externally plausible two-thirds majorities for Golkar, the government's electoral machine, and a passive parliament without any genuine representative character' (Anderson 1996: 30–31).

Elections in New Order Indonesia thus had very little to do with democracy. But they were politically and symbolically important and are worth studying for this reason alone. Consequently, we find the Anderson quote here – from an otherwise astute observer of Indonesian society and culture – not quite satisfactory (even more so when it appears in a volume on elections in Southeast Asia). From the perspective of democracy we obviously agree with Anderson. As mentioned, the New Order was a manipulative and authoritarian regime, where the result of elections could be estimated in advance. There are two sides to this. First, in the local studies of the

1997 election in this book, we will see the enormous apparatus that was mobilized ahead of the election, and the huge sums of money that were spent on the campaign. If the elections were completely fixed, the government would obviously not have gone to these extremes to make sure that Golkar would win. Besides, Indonesia was never Iraq (as I lay the final hand on this article, in October 2002, Saddam Hussein's Bath party has just received 100 per cent of the votes in the national election). Although the non-government parties the PPP and the PDI were circumscribed in campaigns, they were real choices for people who, when stepping into the ballot station, actually could decide to vote for them. It is therefore a bit too easy simply to dismiss elections as engineered and manipulated – we would much rather focus on how they were engineered and manipulated.

Second, there are other stories to be told if we attempt to see what lies beyond and behind the surface view of the national elections. Even during the rigged elections of the New Order (perhaps especially during the rigged elections!), there was intense political activity on the local level with important consequences for our understanding of politics in Indonesia. Thus, politics are more than elite manoeuvring and the development of political institutions. It is also a question of how people perceive their leaders and how they express their feelings through a variety of low-key and everyday means. Crucial to our view is the interaction between politics, identity and local issues.

Most political science studies in Indonesia have focused on figure-watching and speculations about the future personnel of the regime. We seldom learn what ordinary people thought about the New Order and the elections, or how these sentiments were transformed into political forces. Few studies have told us about what was going on in the countryside and in the townships during campaigns and elections. We hope to fill this gap with the present book. On the local level, elections contain a lot of fascinating issues. We will argue that to grasp Indonesian politics and political behaviour in all their complexities it is not enough to observe politics from Jakarta or to count votes on the macro level. We need also to appreciate how people perceive and interpret national events. National politics often focus on specific local issues (such as the corruption of a party representative), and local politics often refers to national issues (such as what kind of development candidates are promoting). These interlinkages will be highlighted in this book.

We will look beyond the national scene to understand some of the sentiments and values that motivate people's political behaviour. We will take the 1997 election seriously, not simply dismissing it as mere manipulation; and we will not hail the 1999 election as simply 'free and fair', without looking at what actually was going on. On the local level, the two elections were alike in many ways, and carried similar meanings for people: making conscious statements about political preferences. This is obviously not to discount the grandeur of gerrymandering or the large-scale repression that took place during the 1997 elections. On the contrary, we will argue that a study of that

3

election makes for a better understanding of the many ways in which authoritarian rule operated in Indonesia – not only as repression and manipulation, but also related to cooptation, developmentalism and patronage. We can thereby gain a better understanding of how the former government was able to maintain its authority for so many years, and what the local and historical foundations are for the future. A lack of focus on the deep sentiments and voting behaviour of the masses of Indonesian citizens might also explain why the *reformasi* movement of 1998 came as such a surprise to most commentators. Likewise we have no intention of dismissing the money politics and vote manipulation that took place in the 1999 election. It is only through a study of actual practices that we can learn how political systems operate and how they can be improved. As we are finishing this book, Indonesia is gearing up for the 2004 election. Public debate about the future election system is emerging. We hope that the present book will in some small manner contribute to a more informed political debate in Indonesia in the years to come.

It is in the mix of the local, the national, the political and the cultural that the most fascinating details about democratic and political ideals are revealed. If the expected order is not maintained, there can be violent reactions, from the state as well as from the citizens. This goes back to the question of political legitimacy and the quest for moral authority (Alagappa 1995). Elections tell us about the moral basis for political authority, and how it can be mobilized at election time. If we start to investigate the meaning of elections for ordinary people, we might come up with some surprising new findings on political behaviour. By looking at national events through the prism of local issues, and by constructing our understanding of Indonesian politics through empirical studies of local politics, we can extend our knowledge of politics in Indonesia. How do people explain how they vote? What are the obstacles to and motivations for free and fair voting? What do people think when they place their vote in the ballot box? What are the local issues that inform their choices? How do political parties mobilize voters? Questions such as these might provide a corrective to the prevalent view of Indonesian voters as 'political robots' who vote as the authorities or charismatic figures tell them. In general, Indonesian people talk a lot about leadership, they argue over ideology and they discuss the central precepts of governance – all questions that are at the heart of political struggles. The chapters in this volume will claim that elections were arenas of contestation and resistance not only during the democratic election of 1999 but also during the earlier New Order elections (but on a local level).

Electoral politics of the Old and New Orders

This is perhaps a pretentious heading, but what we will do here is to highlight some of the main characteristics of national politics in modern

Indonesia, in order to put the events of 1997 and 1999 into relief. The first national election in Indonesia was held in 1955. This was for forty-four years also the only (relatively) free election in Indonesia, held in the middle of a brief period of parliamentary democracy. Most commentators agree that this was as free and fair an election as was possible in the Third World of the 1950s. It resulted in the creation of four blocks in Indonesian politics: modernist Muslims (Masjumi), traditional Muslims (Nahdlatul Ulama, or NU), nationalists (PNI) and communists (PKI). Clifford Geertz (1965) called this system *aliran* (streams) consisting 'of a political party surrounded by a set of sodalities – that is voluntary organizations – formally and informally linked to it' (1965: 127). Religio-ideological differences and party affiliations became the major axes of social identification, around which political parties built subcultures of organizations. Around the time of the 1955 election all major political parties had competing political groups for organizing women, youth, peasants, workers and so on, all with strong feelings of a common cause and identity. The four large parties shared the majority of the votes.

Social tensions, especially between the Muslims and the communists, increased. In response to this difficult situation, in 1957 President Sukarno disbanded the parliament and soon after proclaimed 'Guided Democracy' – it would take forty years for democracy to return to Indonesia. The country was led by various coalition governments, the NASAKOM cabinets (nationalists, Muslims and communists). Sukarno was, however, finding it increasingly difficult to manage the communist–Muslim–nationalist balance. On a local level, and soon on the national scene, this led to intense social conflicts, with 'rooted' political parties mobilizing local supporters around the country. Dwindling foreign investment, hyper-inflation and domestic economic chaos made the economy turn extremely sour in 1963–65. A showdown was inevitable, and a series of events led to a coup followed by a counter-coup in late September 1965, out of which the anti-communist Lt General Suharto emerged as new commander-in-chief and eventually president.

Indonesia under Suharto was more than a plain military regime that achieved acquiescence through repression and terror. There was also a highly developed ideological apparatus centred around notions of political stability, economic development and *Pancasila*, the national ideology.[2] For more than thirty years, economic growth and political stability formed the core around which politics was spun. Pressures from a weak civil society towards reforms were dismissed, and criticism of official policies was perceived as disloyalty or subversion. Civil and political liberties suffered, and democratic institutions functioned in name only, creating an image of political stability and communal harmony to spur foreign investments. A political system was created based on hierarchy, centralization and coerced compliance. The powerful executive branch reached out to each and every village in Indonesia. The 1945 constitution did not protect the separation of powers between the executive, the legislative and the judiciary. The result was an authoritarian and centralized state. The relationship between state and society was characterized by a strong central accumulation of power and a paternalistic governance system. Public policy formulations were strongly monopolized by civil servants, high-ranking military officers, and a small number of state-sponsored think tanks.

For a long time, Indonesia prided itself in not being a regular parliamentary democracy. Former presidents Sukarno and Suharto both consciously promoted the idea of a specific Indonesian version of democracy. Sukarno used the concept *Demokrasi Terpimpin* (Guided Democracy), and Suharto built his new polity around the ideas of *Demokrasi Pancasila*. Suharto meant to return to the original ideas of 1945, which he argued had been corrupted over time by Sukarno. Indonesia, it was argued, had its own understanding of power and politics, which justified the restrictions on political liberties. Since common people were servile and obedient they should not be bothered with ideological matters. Politics should be left to the state. According to an official regulation by the People's Consultative Assembly in 1971, the population was a 'floating mass' (*masa mengambang*). People should not concern themselves with politics except during the brief national campaign each five years. As we will see in various chapters in this volume, political practices did not necessarily support these notions.

During its first years, elections were not a top priority for the New Order regime. The elections that were promised for 1968 were postponed. At first the economy had to be stabilized and politics controlled. As discussed further by Haris in Chapter 2, there were two reasons behind finally holding the promised elections in 1971. The first had to do with international pressures. Western anti-communist governments were the main sponsors of New Order Indonesia (the USA, West Germany, Japan), and it was important for them to show publicly that Indonesia at least had the institutions, if not the practice, of democracy. The second reason was internal. The New Order came to power on top of a wave of popular movement. The first years of the New Order, in the late 1960s, have been described as the 'honeymoon period'. In the early 1970s, it became important for the government not only to display their international commitment to democracy but also to address the domestic concerns of the legitimacy of the New Order.

The real issue of the first and subsequent elections was never to elect a new government. Right from the start, the elections were to be *pesta demokrasi* (festivals of democracy – although this particular concept was first used in 1982), and were largely ritual in character. In the first election in 1971, Golkar won a comfortable 67 per cent of the votes. In the following series of five-year elections this figure varied between 64 and 76 per cent. New Order elections, as already noted, were thus not about free choice. A successful election was rather a peaceful election, without violence. Such an election was an important legitimating factor, since it showed the regime's capacity to maintain stability – and attract foreign investment.

The political system was radically restructured after the 1971 election. In the remaining New Order elections, only three political parties were allowed to compete for votes. Of these Golongan Karya (Golkar) became the state's political body and Suharto's electoral vehicle (Reeve 1985 remains the best study of Golkar's early years). President Suharto was a life-long patron of its Executive Committee. Golkar's self-image was that it was a stabilizing and dynamic force in Indonesian society, and as such was responsible for the impressive economic growth. Golkar was not a real party. *Golongan Karya* literally means 'functional groups' and Golkar was defined as a social-political group. As such it was allowed to organize itself in the countryside. Other parties were not.

Presidential Instruction no. 6 of 1970 outlines this policy. Although this instruction (later to be known as '*mono-loyalitas*') only banned party membership for the very top layer of civil servants, it also contained the statement that 'civil servants in carrying out their office may not carry out political activities which are not in accordance with their status as civil servants' (quoted in Reeve 1985: 288). This was interpreted to mean that civil servants were not to be party-political and that they were allowed to join political parties only with the explicit approval of their superiors. But since Golkar was not a political party, the policy did not affect it. In fact, as we shall see, civil servants and local leaders were encouraged to support Golkar.

Golkar acted to monopolize ideological discussions in between elections. Someone once said that it was not the ruling party, but the ruler's party. This is an important distinction, since Golkar was not responsible for government policy. Golkar's initial function was to depoliticize politics, that is, to defuse potential political conflicts by providing a strong united front for the New Order. With an increasingly sophisticated citizenry, Golkar increasingly played the role of funnelling and controlling political demands. During the 1980s and into the 1990s, Golkar became more inclusive and pro-active in responding to demands from below. It also started to become more like a regular party through allowing membership (initially it was based only on the functional groups).

Golkar spread its membership base by recruiting local members. To manage this, the party mobilized the authority of community leaders and local notables and turned them into what Antlöv in Chapter 6 calls 'clients of the state'. In exchange for their loyalty, leaders and officials were given privileged treatment and access to power and material resources. Golkar created a national network of loyal clients that could be mobilized at elections – one important factor in their electoral achievements.

Two other parties were created after the 1971 election. *Partai Persatuan Pembangunan* (PPP) was formed in 1972 by means of a state-rigged coalition of a number of Islamic parties. Until 1984 its symbol was the *kabah* of Mekkah (thereafter the party carried a star as its symbol), and it recruited mainly Islamic voters (although not always successfully so, see Turmudi's chapter). As a Muslim party, the PPP had only limited support in Christian and Hindu areas, such as Minahasa and Bali. The second political party, *Partai Demokrasi Indonesia* (PDI) was a similar coalition of Christian and nationalist parties. The PPP and the PDI both existed under heavy restrictions, and cannot be considered as opposition parties in any real sense. They were not allowed to have separate party programmes and their leaders had to be approved by government officials. Criticism of the government and of the president was illegal. Parties and individuals could thus not really oppose Golkar, since it was the government party. The PPP and the PDI can therefore better be characterized as non-government parties. They did not have access to government patronage and state resources. Neither of the two parties was permitted to organize below the district/municipality (*kabupaten/kotamadya*) level, and they were allowed to campaign only immediately before national elections. Thus, while the 'social-political group' Golkar was strongly present in all Indonesian villages, the PDI and the PPP could not even organize in the countryside.

Golkar voters were recruited through co-opting, patronage and mass-mobilization. The main political messages were those of economic development and political stability. Promises of progress and investments were an integral component of all campaigns. Political space for the PPP and the PDI was extremely limited. As Haris writes in Chapter 1: 'Long before they started the campaign, and long before people put their ballot in the box, the political system was construed so as to make it virtually impossible for the PPP and the PDI to obtain any substantial support'. At certain times and places the PPP and the PDI could build on strong personalities (see Turmudi's chapter for a story about the PPP in East Java in 1987), but many of the votes were more votes against Golkar than pro-PPP and PDI (Antlöv 1995: 202).

With the growth of an educated middle class in the 1980s and 1990s, aspiring critical thinkers and leaders within civil society no longer saw the New Order as the only possible regime in Indonesia. Cracks started to appear. When Sukarno's daughter Megawati Sukarnoputri was elected chairman of the PDI during a turbulent congress in 1994, the party's image was boosted. However, in an even more turbulent congress in May 1996, the government orchestrated the ouster of Megawati as the party chairman. Her supporters refused to recognize the new chairman, and occupied the PDI's headquarters in Jakarta. During the summer of 1996, supporters of Megawati arranged an open-speech forum in front of the PDI's headquarters. On 27 July 1996, the police attacked the headquarters, an attack which forced

Megawati's supporters to take to the streets. Subsequent street fighting led to the death or disappearance of several PDI supporters. It marked the start of two turbulent years.

Between December 1996 and March 1997 there were riots against the police in Tasikmalaya, against the Chinese in Rangkasbitung and finally violent clashes between the Dayaks and Madurese transmigrants in West Kalimantan, events which led to the death of several hundred, possibly thousands, of people. One common factor in the riots was the youth. Groups of fairly well-educated but unemployed and frustrated youths were the most visible participants in the riots. These were the people who traditionally had also been most active in election campaigning.

Campaigns and elections, 1997 and 1999

The government therefore decided to circumscribe the 1997 campaign: there would be no rallying on open trucks, and permissions for meetings would be restricted. In hindsight, the new regulations were not very successful, mainly because campaigns had been the only permitted outlets for political steam in an otherwise controlled environment. It was not possible to take away this last bastion of popular resistance. On 28 May 1997, Indonesia held its seventh national election.[3] For the sixth consecutive time, the position of the government party Golkar and its patron Suharto was reinforced, and the New Order could put the result into the files as yet another great democratic festival. The elections received considerable global attention. The restrictions on free campaigning, balloting and monitoring were criticized. The erupting campaign violence was widely broadcast by the international media. More than two hundred people were killed in campaign-related accidents and rioting. New coalitions emerged in the wake of the government attack on Megawati's PDI office. Supporters of Megawati joined the campaign of the Islamic party PPP, while Megawati herself went public with her decision to cast a blank vote. On the other hand, Abdurrachman Wahid, at that time the charismatic leader of the largest Muslim organization, the NU (and later president of Indonesia), who a few years earlier had established the Democratic Forum, a pro-democracy network, surprisingly joined Golkar meetings with Siti Hardijanti 'Tutut' Rukmana, Suharto's daughter, a move which provided a boost for Golkar. In the election, the PDI was virtually eradicated, causing much commentary. Would the demise of the PDI lead to a new two-party system? What long-term effect would the campaign violence have on Indonesian society? Would Islam become an even stronger political force? And once again, what would happen to the New Order regime after the ageing Suharto ceased to be its leader?

Just a year later, we knew the answer to the last question, at least. On 21 May 1998, after a tumultuous six months characterized by a financial meltdown, violent student demonstrations, state's, counter-violence and finally the employment of elite divisions, Suharto had no choice but to leave the future of Indonesia in the hands of his trusted vice-president, Habibie. We will not write the story of the transition here; many books have been and are being written about the political game in Jakarta during 1998.[4]

One of the immediate demands of the pro-democracy movement was for new elections, well ahead of the scheduled 2002 elections, this time with the proviso that they were held democratically. The new elections were held just a year later, on 7 June 1999. Compared with the New Order elections it was, on paper at least, a very different affair. In 1997, representatives of the PPP and the PDI had supervised the election, organized by the government. This time the political parties organized the elections, supervised by independent election monitors and supported by national elections commissions. There were 119 accredited national organizations and twenty international election-monitoring institutions in Indonesia (Pax Benedanto *et al.* 1999: 31).[5] Tens of thousands, if not hundreds of thousands, of independent election observers monitored the election in almost every single polling station in Indonesia. No less than forty-eight parties competed in an election described by most commentators and international observers as relatively free and fair, given the urgency with which it took place.

On the local level, another important difference between the elections during the New Order and those in 1999 was the role played by community leaders, the 'clients of the state'. In all New Order elections these local leaders had played a crucial role in rallying voters behind Golkar, but in the 1999 election they were prohibited from playing a formal role. Presidential Decree no. 5/1999 stated soberly that civil servants were no longer allowed to join political parties – and this time it meant Golkar as well, which had been registered as a political party in late 1998. This decree literally signified the end of *mono-loyalitas* of civil servants and their compulsory support of Golkar. If in 1997 Golkar was identified with the New Order and portrayed as the source of all development, in 1999 the party was portrayed by the opposition as the root of all evil in the country. At least on the populous island of Java and in larger cities, the party received little or no support for its programme. However, as is shown in Cederroth's chapter and argued by Haris, Golkar was still able to mobilize much of its resources. Golkar was and remains by far the richest party in Indonesia, and this was shown during the 1999 campaign, more obviously in the outer provinces than in Java. Perhaps this was one reason why Golkar was so successful outside of Java – the election surprise. They managed to emerge as the second largest party in the country. Despite the fact that in many places (especially in Java) they were even prevented from carrying out proper campaigning, they could still draw on old political loyalties. The Golkar campaign focused on national unity and economic development, in an era in which regional conflicts were rocking the country and the economy was severely injured. In the turbulence of democratization and deep economic recession, the message of unity and development 'as usual' (meaning during the New Order) was reassuring.

Nationally, the party that Megawati Sukarnoputri had established ahead of the elections, the Indonesian Democratic Party of Struggle (PDI-P) won a comfortable victory in the country, although not a majority. Like no one else, Megawati was able to mobilize the masses, rallying them around her father and against the New Order. She personified everything positive in the new democratic era, and needed only to show herself to gain support. The PDI-P campaign portrayed a vision of a future: sentiments that were extracted from participants in the mass rallies and campaigns built strong mutual bonds and feelings of joint community among PDI-P followers. An imagined enemy was construed, the 'status quo forces', represented by the established leadership, especially Golkar.

If the PDI-P and Golkar were the success stories of the 1999 election, the Islamic parties were the main losers. During the New Order, the government was perceived by Islamists as suppressing basic Islamic fundaments. Radical Islamic movements were banned, and organizations were prohibited from having Islamic principles as their sole foundation. The lack-lustre government support for Islam is perhaps nowhere better symbolized than when President Suharto in the mid-1980s inaugurated an anti-extremist Islam museum (the *Museum Waspada Purbawisesa*, inside the compounds of the Armed Forces Museum on Jalan Gatot Subroto in Jakarta). In the late 1980s, the New Order changed its strategy; President Suharto went on the pilgrimage and became *Haji* Mohammed Suharto. The Association of Moslem Intellectuals (ICMI) was established a few years later, and B.J. Habibie, then Minister of Research and Technology, was appointed as its first chairman. But there was still strong criticism from some Islamic leaders that the New Order government was not serious in promoting Islamic principles and instead used conservative Islam as a political tool to muster support for Golkar. The PPP failed to organize a meaningful opposition towards the government party Golkar. So there were great hopes among Islamic leaders in 1999 that Islamic parties would be able to capitalize on the growth of conservative Islam and regain the political ground they had lost. But they lost quite badly. The only Islamic party that managed to get more than 2 per cent of the votes was the PPP, the reformed New Order party. As discussed by Haris and Turmudi in their contributions, the main reason for their failure was the split among so many Islamic parties, most of which had almost identical programmes. Of the forty-eight registered parties in 1999, seventeen had Islamic names, principles or symbols (the two larger parties, the PKB and the PAN, had secular-nationalist platforms, although with Islamic leadership).

One of the issues in 1999 was whether the return to democratic elections also would mean the return of *aliran* politics, that is, voters clustering within a few strong 'social forms' that could also mobilize voters in between elections, the system that so characterized the 1955 elections. One of the reasons that people were looking at the *aliran* patterns is that the 1999 election took place in a period of increasing social tensions, just as in 1955. There were tensions between various regions in Indonesia (with Papua, East Timor and Aceh the most well-known, but also regions such as Riau and Kalimantan demanding fairer treatment) but there were also intense social conflicts within and between communities. There were systematic (ideological, religious or ethnic) killings in East Java, West Kalimantan, West Timor and in the Moluccas. However, the conclusion of the chapters in the present volume is that this 'aliranization' has not yet happened, if we by this mean parties acting as social movements, each with their own organizations. The main reason for this is that the political parties in Indonesia today do not have the skill (or political will) to organize communities in the way that the much more politicized parties did during the 1950s. In other words, politicians today are simply not as good at building ideological vehicles as they were forty years ago. Political parties in Indonesia are shallow, and depend on religious sentiments and leadership. As in many parts of the world, the new political parties in Indonesia are ephemeral clubs of intellectuals, without effective grassroots. Perhaps the only exception to this is the former state party Golkar, and this factor may perhaps foretell its return in upcoming elections.[6]

We might, however, see the return of *aliran* politics in another sense of the word, that of strong religiously based ideologies. In the 1950s the distinction was between *santri, abangan* and *priyayi*, but perhaps that now needs to be revisited. Endang Turmudi and Sven Cederroth portray the large gap that existed between the PPP and the PDI during the New Order, in which the differing basic worldviews and accompanying norms and values made it very difficult for a voter to move from one party to the other. Golkar, which was a 'depoliticized' party, could capitalize on this and draw dissatisfied voters from both the PPP and the PDI, although both PPP and PDI members were critical of Golkar. It was better for a dissatisfied PPP supporter to vote for Golkar rather than the PDI, and vice versa. Much of the voting behaviour during the New Order was thus based on 'protest voting': people voted for Golkar (or the PPP or the PDI) not necessarily because the party was attractive but because the other parties repelled them. In the 1999 election, similar patterns could be found in East Java (Turmudi) and Lombok (Cederroth). Modernist Muslims in Jombang refused to vote for the PKB or the PPP, since they were led by families with traditionalistic leanings. The old rivalry between modernist (*santri*) and traditionalist (*abangan*) Muslims, as formalized by the intense competition between Muhammadiyah on the one hand, and NU and to some extent the PDI-P on the other, as well as between their influential chairpersons, Amien Rais (who was elected chairman of the People's Consultative Assembly), Abdurrahman Wahid (who was elected president of Indonesia in 1999 and later ousted), and Megawati Sukarnoputri (vice-president under Wahid, later replacing him as president) took on a new turn when the three leaders settled into their new posts.

Overview of the book

It is obviously impossible in a small book like this to discuss all aspects of elections under the New Order and the issues in democratizing Indonesia. We have therefore chosen to focus specifically on two themes which we believe highlight our main concern with the interaction between local factors and national politics, as outlined here. The two themes are the politics of Islam (Turmudi and Haris) and national elections in villages (Cederroth and Antlöv). There are two additional chapters that act as introduction to these themes, providing the setting and background (Haris and Voionmaa).

Syamsuddin Haris's first chapter (Chapter 2) provides a more detailed overview of how the election system worked under the New Order. He shows how Golkar emerged as the *anak mas*, the 'favourite child' of Suharto and was turned into his electoral vehicle. The election system was structured and then manipulated in such a way that Golkar was strengthened and the other political forces disempowered. Political leaders on all levels were forced to join the party. The government frequently intervened in the internal governance of the PPP and the PDI. Haris concludes that long before the PPP and the PDI started their campaigns, long before people put their ballots in the box, the political system had been constructed so as to make it virtually impossible for these non-government parties to obtain any substantial support. He shows in some detail how this was done.

The next two chapters focus on Islamic election politics. Endang Turmudi's chapter (Chapter 3) shows, by means of a case study from Jombang (the heartland of Islam in East Java) how Islamic politics during the New Order were manipulated by the government in order to diminish the potential for Islamic unity and secure the electoral success of Golkar. Local religious leaders were recruited into Golkar, sometimes by not very democratic means, and leaders remaining outside were put under strong pressure. The PPP was not allowed to present itself as an Islamic party, and it had no clear direction or leadership. Leaders with political aspirations would by necessity have had to join Golkar, and this also included Islamic teachers and officials. Ahead of the 1987 election, the largest Islamic organization in Indonesia, the NU, decided to withdraw their support for the PPP and allow supporters to vote for other parties. In the 1997 election, the PPP succeeded in gaining a larger proportion of the national vote, but many of those voters were mainly anti-Golkar and not necessarily pro-PPP. However, in Jombang, the PPP could still win 44 per cent of the votes. The reason for this was the strong support for the PPP from local religious leaders, the *ulama*, caused by their disappointment with Golkar policy.

This trend was partially related to the general 'Islamification' of society during the late New Order, but more importantly, Jombang *ulama* (Islamic teachers) could draw on people's disappointment with both national and local developments. This changed drastically in 1999, however, when the exclusively Islamic parties received less than 10 per cent of the total votes in Jombang.

This theme is discussed by Syamsuddin Haris in Chapter 4, in which the main focus is on the failure of the Islamic parties to attract voters in the 1999 election. He identifies the main reason for this as the high degree of fractionalization among the Islamic parties. Around twenty parties competed for Islamic votes. There was also a high degree of self-righteousness and over-confidence: one of the problems for Islamic parties in 1999 lay in the misguided outlook and self-perception among the Islamic leaders concerning the relationship between Islam and the state on the one hand and the relationship between the Islamic leaders and their followers on the other hand. This self-deception eventually resulted in the choice of the wrong solutions, as reflected in the formation of such a large number of Islamic political parties with scarcely any differences in their programmes and political platforms. The outcome was a fully divided constituency.

The Chapters 5 and 6 are local studies of two Indonesian villages, one in Lombok (Cederroth) and one in West Java (Antlöv). The main thrust of these chapters is to investigate in some detail how the campaign and elections were carried out: the initial strategic party meetings, voter recruitment, accompanying threats, campaigning, voting and the reporting of the result. The aim of these anthropological chapters is to provide a balance to many other political science studies that focus on national politics, statistically analysing the result. The two chapters outline the methods used by the New Order government to monitor, limit and discipline local politics. One of the more important of these methods was the use of the traditional authority of community leaders. Through state patronage, the community leaders became representatives for the government party Golkar. The pressures put on people to join Golkar were strong indeed. But when the two authors discuss the 1999 elections, an important difference emerges. In the West Java village (which was typical of many villages in Java), the PDI-P and other parties were able to break the monopoly of Golkar. Drawing on sentiments of joint action, of mass mobilization through utilizing rituals, and powerful symbols (such as former President Sukarno), the PDI-P won a comfortable victory in West Java. However in Lombok (and outer Indonesia more generally), the Golkar elite was able to maintain its traditional hold over the voters. Cederroth argues that the type of power struggles characteristic of the traditional petty kingdoms in Lombok continue, now within the guise of modern political parties. In Cederroth's area of study, patron–client relations and traditional loyalties remain strong, and Golkar cleverly drew its own strengths from these. However, in both these chapters, as well as in

Turmudi's study of the *ulama* in Jombang, the role of powerful figures shines through as a main theme in determining political affiliation.

The final chapter by Kaarlo Voionmaa discusses the nature of the media discourse during the 1997 and 1999 elections, and focuses especially on the lack of detailed discussion in the national media about public policies and party ideologies. In an analysis of *The Jakarta Post* during March and April 1999, Voionmaa finds that the discourse was very much confined to discussions about formal procedure and leadership figures. In fact, according to Voionmaa, it seems that both the two largest parties, the PDI-P and Golkar, actively tried to shift the public discourse away from ideological issues. It is ironic, argues Voinonmaa, that the PDI-P, the party that most strongly objected to public debates, was the one that received the most votes. But with the important role given to leadership and mass mobilization during the campaign, we should perhaps not be too surprised to learn this. Voionmaa also compares the discourse in 1999 with that of the campaign in 1997 and finds many similarities. Although the media in 1999 were free to write whatever they wished, media contributors had difficulties in moving beyond the old practice of reporting what party leaders had said, without much analysis. In the articles analysed, Voionmaa could not find a single piece of investigative journalism. This is a limitation, and one that could impede the development of a system of checks and balances, a prerequisite for democratic governance.

Taken together, it is our hope that the chapters in this book will provide fresh data on and challenging pictures of the complexities of recent national elections in Indonesia. Through the various case studies, we will see the importance of local factors (both leadership and sentiments) for an understanding of the election results in 1997 and 1999. We will see how national elections have become enmeshed with local politics, and how elections in many ways should be understood as continuations of traditional power structures. The challenge for Indonesia (and many other modernizing countries) is how to link the modern invention of liberal elections, in which 'free and fair' elections are novel institutions, with traditional political systems. In this volume, we highlight some of the underlying structures that determine politics in Indonesia. By doing so, we hope to raise the challenge of how to create a better political system for Indonesia.

Notes

1 This publication is the result of a comparative research project on 'Discourses and Practices of Democracy in Southeast Asia', led by the Centre for Asian Studies at Göteborg University, Sweden, and funded by SAREC. Our counterpart in Indonesia was the Centre for Southeast Asian Studies (*Kajian Asia Tenggara*) at the Indonesian Institute of Sciences (LIPI) under Professor Taufik Abdullah.

2 *Pancasila* is the national ideology of belief in God, humanitarianism, a united Indonesia, democracy through consultations and social justice.

3 For further details see: Ariwibowo, Aloysius Arena and Adirsyah, H.A. (1997) *Pemilu 1997: Antara Fenomena Kampanye Dialogis dan Mega–Bintang*, Jakarta: Penakencana; Eklöf, Stefan (1997) 'The 1997 General Election in Indonesia', *Asian Survey*, 37(12); *Evaluasi Pemilu Orde Baru: Mengapa 1996–97 Terjadi Pelbagi Kerusuhan? Menyimak Gaya Politik M. Natsir*, Bandung Mizan/Jakarta: Laboratorium FISIP UI; Haris, Syamsuddin (1998) *Menggugat Pemilihan Umum Orde Baru: Sebuah Bunga Rampai*, Jakarta: Obor; Haris, Syamsuddin (1999) *Kecurangan dan Perlawan Rakyat Dalam Pemilihan Umum 1997*, Jakarta: Obor; Kristiadi, J. (ed.) (1997) *Pemilihan Umum 1997: Perkiraan, Harapan dan Evaluasi*, Jakarta: CSIS (Centre for Strategic and International Studies); Srengenge, Sitok (1998) *Surat Rakyat Tentang Pemilu 1997*, Jakarta: ISAI.

4 Because of the magnitude of literature published in Indonesia, I only list books published in English: Edward Aspinall, Herb Feith and Gerry van Klinken (eds) (1999) *The Last Days of President Suharto*, Clayton: Monash Asia Institute; Arief Budiman, Barbara Hatley and Damien Kingsbury (eds) (1999) *Reformasi: Crisis and Change in Indonesia*. Clayton: Monash Asia Institute; Kees van Dijk (2001) *A Country in Despair: Indonesia between 1997 and 2000*, Leiden: KITLV Press; Stefan Eklöf (1999) *Indonesian Politics in Crisis: The Long Fall of Suharto 1996–1998*, Copenhagen: Nordic Institute of Asian Studies; Geoff Forrester (ed.) (1999) *Post-Suharto Indonesia: Renewal or Chaos*. Leiden: KITLV Press/Singapore: ISEAS; Geoff Forrester and R.J. May (eds) (1998) *The Fall of Suharto*, New South Wales: Crawford House; Richard Mann (1999) *Fight for Democracy in Indonesia*, Jakarta/Toronto: Gateway Books; Chris Manning and Peter van Diermen (2000) *Indonesia in Transition: Social Aspects of 'Reformasi' and Crisis*, Singapore: ISEAS; Adam Schwartz and Jonathan Paris (eds) (1999) *The Politics of Post-Suharto Indonesia*, New York: Council on Foreign Relations Press; Bilveer Singh (2000) *Succession Politics in Indonesia: the 1998 Presidential Elections and the Fall of Suharto*, London: Macmillan/New York: St Martin Press.

5 See: Pax Benedanto, Ignatius Haryanto and E. Pudjiachirusanto (1999) *Pemilihan Umum 1999: Demokrasi atau Rebutan Kursi*, Jakarta: Lembaga Studi Pers dan Pembangunan; Susan Blackburn (ed.) (1999) *Pemilu: the 1999 Indonesian Election*, Clayton: Monash Asia Institute; Indra Ismawan (1999) *Money Politics: Pengaruh Uang Dalam Pemilu*, Yogyakarta: Media Pressindo; Mulyana W. Kusuma and Juri F. Ardiantoro (1999) *Transisi Demokrasi: Evaluasi Kritis Penyelenggaran Pemilu 1999*, Jakarta: KIPP; William R. Liddle (2000) 'Indonesia in 1999: democracy restored', *Asian Survey*, 40(2), 2000; Sebastian Pompe (1999) *De Indonesische Algemene Verkiezingen 1999*, Leiden: KITLV Press; François Raillon (2000) 'Indonesie 99: desintegration', *Archipel*, no. 59; Takashi Shiraishi (2000) 'Whither Indonesia', *Bulletin of Concerned Asian Scholars*, 32(2); Hadi Soesastro (1999) 'The 1999 election and beyond', *Bulletin of Indonesian Economic Studies*, 35(2); Hermawan Sulistiyo and A. Kadar (2000) *Uang Kekuasan dalam Pemilu 1999*, Jakarta: KIPP, 2000; Charles U. Zenzie, 'Indonesia's new political spectrum' (1999) *Asian Survey*, 39(2).

6 This would be identical to what we have seen in Eastern Europe, where communist parties have been able to renew themselves and even return to power.

References

Alagappa, Mutiah (1995) *Political Legitimacy in Southeast Asia: The Quest for Moral Authority*. Stanford, CA: Stanford University Press.

Anderson, Benedict R. O'G. (1996) 'Elections and participation in three southeast Asian countries'. In R.H. Taylor (ed.), *The Politics of Elections in Southeast Asia.* New York: Woodrow Wilson Center Press, pp. 12–33.

Antlöv, Hans (1995) *Exemplary Centre, Administrative Periphery: Rural Leadership and the New Order in Java.* Richmond, Curzon Press.

Geertz, Clifford (1965) *The Social History of an Indonesian Town.* Cambridge, MA: MIT Press.

Liddle, R. William (1996) 'A useful fiction: democratic legitimation in New Order Indonesia'. In R.H. Taylor (ed.), *The Politics of Elections in Southeast Asia.* New York: Woodrow Wilson Center Press, pp. 34–60.

Reeve, David (1985) *Golkar of Indonesia. An Alternative to the Party System.* Singapore: Oxford University Press.

2

GENERAL ELECTIONS UNDER THE NEW ORDER

Syamsuddin Haris

As a 'non-indigenous' political institution expected to represent the ideals of the newly formed republic, the first general election of 1955 in Indonesia was welcomed with great enthusiasm by all but the traditional elite. This was made evident by the overwhelming number of parties and candidates who expressed their intention to participate as contestants. A national election was a novel institution in Indonesia's political life. There had been local elections for village headmen since the early nineteenth century, and during the late 1940s the Dutch had held elections in some of their puppet states, but by and large, Dutch colonial rule had allowed very limited political participation. The 1955 election was held during what was the short-lived era of parliamentary democracy (1950–57). It was a democratic and open election. No fewer than 172 political parties and individuals were registered, although 'only' twenty-seven political parties and one single individual eventually succeeded in making it to the DPR (*Dewan Perwakilan Rakyat*, or House of Representatives).[1] Four of the contending parties, that is, *Partai Nasional Indonesia* (PNI), *Madjelis Syuro Muslimin Indonesia* (Masyumi), *Nahdlatul Ulama* (NU) and *Partai Komunis Indonesia* (PKI) emerged as the top winners. Out of the 257 DPR seats that were being contested, the PNI and Masyumi secured fifty-seven seats each, NU forty-five seats and the PKI thirty-nine seats. In terms of participation, close to 90 per cent of Indonesians with suffrage cast their ballots.

Despite fears that mass unrest might occur during the time leading up to the general election as well as during the election itself, it turned out that the competition among the political parties, which stemmed from their ideological rivalries and political claims, did not hatch any large-scale clashes. Apparently, the people were able to accept the differences in terms of ideologies and political streams ('*alirans*') as a logical consequence of the diversity that characterized the Indonesian nation. Such differences did not result in people being trapped in conflicts among themselves. Thus, Indonesia stated to the world that it could manage the most important political institution in the modern nation-state.

However, the result of the 1955 election failed to provide the political stability for which there was a dire need as the young country tried to improve its national economy. There were sharp disagreements between President Sukarno and the political parties, and between the PKI and the Islamic parties. Cabinets collapsed as a matter of routine, and new governments were formed. Sukarno was pushing for a 'four-legged' cabinet comprised of a coalition between the four top winning parties of the 1955 election. However, some of the political parties, especially Masyumi, did not wish to see the PKI getting a foothold in the cabinet. As bystander, the military, particularly the army, saw the conflict between Sukarno and the parties as a great opportunity to exert a more important role in politics. This desire stemmed from the army's dissatisfaction with the practice of parliamentary democracy. At the time there were widespread insurgencies in some regions in which the elites of various political parties were involved. Furthermore, in the national parliament there were continuing debates between parties that tended to favour changing the constitution – giving the army an uncertain future.

Pushed by the military, Sukarno in 1959 issued a Presidential Decree which ordered a return to the 1945 Constitution, dissolution of the national parliament and the introduction of a political system, Guided Democracy, that was to become famous.[2] The new, three-pronged political system consisting of the President (Sukarno, who by then was quite authoritarian), the military and the PKI was the antithesis of the earlier parliamentary democracy model, which had been characterized by the active roles of plural political parties. However, Guided Democracy was doomed when a number of military officers attempted a coup on 30 September 1965. The failed coup attempt was blamed on the PKI and Guided Democracy – for which Sukarno was largely responsible – and it provided an unprecedented momentum for the army to spearhead a new political order, which later was considered a synthesis of the two previous delinquent political orders, liberal and Guided Democracy.

So the 'New Order' was born, out of tumult and chaos, with parties and ideologies severely injured, both structurally and in popular perception. General elections during the so-called New Order were consistently won by the state's own party, the Functional Group (*Golongan Karya*, Golkar), an alliance of non-party state organizations that had been formed by the military and eventually became the extension of the bureaucracy.[3] Golkar's role can only be understood in the context of the consensus reached between the military, the technocrats and the bureaucrats. The main losers included civilian politicians, parties with Islamic orientation, radical nationalists who supported Sukarno, and the leftists – particularly the communists. It was not surprising that, during the early period of the New Order, after 'eliminating' supporters of the PKI, the government proceeded to crush ex-Masyumi Islamic groups (radical modernist Muslims whose leaders had been involved in separation movements in the late 1950s) as well as 'non-loyalists' belonging to the PNI. All of this had been accomplished by the time the 1971 election was held. The Islam-based political forces, as well as the nationalists, henceforth became political minorities in all subsequent elections: 1977, 1982, 1987, 1992 and 1997.

Against this backdrop, this chapter will attempt to recreate the politics of the general elections during the Suharto era. It seeks first and foremost to shed light on the reasons behind Golkar's consistent landslide victories in the elections despite public outcry for changes in the election system and in the political format in general. It will also try to uncover the reasons why criticisms of the People's Consultative Assembly (MPR) and the House of Representatives (DPR) did not diminish despite the fact that after each election the members invariably came to office with better qualifications – at least in terms of their general educational background. It will focus on finding the answers to these questions through a descriptive analysis of New Order elections; it will seek an understanding of the structure and process of the elections – the position held by the government, the people and the political parties, as well as an understanding of the issues of representation, the balance of power, and the performance of both the MPR and the DPR during the New Order.

Political restructuring in the early New Order

During the early years of the New Order, political and economic reforms got first priority and there were two issues, especially, that came into the focus of the New Order economists and technocrats as they embarked on renovating the political and economic life of the nation. First, there was an urgent need to rehabilitate the economy which had been marked, among other things, by a crippling three-digit per cent inflation rate towards the end of the Guided Democracy era. Second, the experience of being under an unstable administration with constant changes in government cabinets had been traumatic. To address these issues, the New Order technocrats sought to build and restructure the political mechanisms. The objective was to achieve political stability in the hope that it would improve economic life.[4]

For the New Order reformists, the political instability and the economic hardships of the early 1960s were the results of two factors. First, the heterogeneous community of Indonesia was not ready for the modern democracy that the country's leaders were trying to adopt in the 1950s. Second, there was the ideological manipulation by Sukarno that left behind an 'unfinished revolution'. For the reformists, the military elite and pragmatic bureaucrat-technocrats of the emerging New Order, cultural plurality did not necessarily lead to a fruitful ideological and political mix. On the contrary, political pluralism, defined as the polarization of political parties, was viewed as the main reason for separatism and political turmoil.

These factors posed threats to the political stability and thereby to national integration. For decades, these political traumas were widely socialized as lessons from Indonesian 'national history'. This was done not only through formal education in the schools but also through the courses on *Pancasila* (the state ideology) that for decades had to be taken by civil servants, employees of state-owned business enterprises and newly enrolled students – from primary school to university level – as well as leaders of political and community organizations, merely correcting the mistakes that Sukarno had made.

In the economic sphere, by using the concept of modernization based on the developmentalism school of thought adopted from Western scholars, the New Order exponents launched campaigns for a new ideology that was aimed at producing a total correction to all the misconduct of the preceding political orders (Moertopo 1974). It was not surprising that the new ideological slogan that was launched was 'to adhere to *Pancasila* and the 1945 Constitution in a truthful and consistent manner'. In other words, the New Order regime claimed itself to be the saviour both of the national ideology of *Pancasila* and of the 1945 Constitution.

Based on this intention, a restructuring of the political and economic sphere – with the chief objective of achieving stability – was promoted to the international world, especially to the anti-communist Western states, as a way for gaining support and attracting foreign investment. Therefore, as is common in newly established regimes, the first agenda of the New Order government included a promise to carry out a general election. This was initially scheduled to take place on 5 July 1968. To pave the way for this exercise the government worked at the end of 1966 on a legislation package consisting of three draft bills that were meant to provide a legal basis for the election in particular and for political restructuring in general. The three bills were: (1) a bill on general election; (2) a bill on political parties, functional groups and mass organizations, and (3) a bill on the structure and position of the MPR, the DPR and the Regional Councils/District House of Representatives (DPRD).

'The national consensus'

At the outset, the military would have preferred district-based elections, as was recommended for instance during the important Second Army Seminar on 25–31 August 1966. The seminar also recommended a domicile requirement for each legislator candidate; that political organizations and mass social organizations should adopt *Pancasila* as their sole ideological basis; the right for members of the armed forces to elect and to be elected; the requirement that only 'social forces' based on *Pancasila* would be allowed to run the country, and finally that the MPR should reach a new national consensus on *Pancasila*.

These recommendations were rejected by the political parties, who still preferred the proportional election system that had been applied during the 1955 election. Due to pressure from the armed forces and Suharto, a compromise ensued, later known as 'the national consensus'. It was seen as the way out of the debate in the interim parliament on the three bills, a debate that had been dragging on for more than two years (1967–68). There were signs of an impending gridlock – which again would have launched Indonesia into a period of political uncertainties. These developments led to a postponement of the first election to July 1971. Still the debate was so drawn out that the passing of the bill on political parties, functional groups and social organizations actually had to be suspended until after the 1971 election – only the election law itself was passed in time.

The main points in the compromise or national consensus that directly affected the general election were:

1   the election system was to be based on simple proportional representation;
2   in return the President would be allowed to appoint a hundred members of the armed forces to the House, making the total number of seats 460;
3   the domicile requirement was withdrawn;
4   the number of appointed MPR members would be one-third of the total number of members;
5   the number of represented constituents was also taken into account, but each district or municipality was guaranteed at least one seat in the DPR;
6   election districts were on the provincial level; and
7   there should be a balance between the number of legislators representing Java and the outer islands (Notosusanto 1985).

With regard to the structure and position of local parliaments, it was agreed that the number of appointed military members of the local parliaments at the provincial and district level would be one-fifth of the total number of members.

The fact that one-third of the members of the MPR were to be appointed as were a hundred armed forces members to the DPR, and also 20 per cent armed forces members to the regional parliaments, coupled with a reduction in the number of elected members in the DPR met with a lot of criticism during the early New Order days. Not only were the arrangements considered undemocratic, but they were also perceived as an effort to perpetuate the political structure characteristic of Sukarno's Guided Democracy (Samsuddin 1972: 52–58). As far as elections were concerned, the criticism was well founded, since the appointment of such a significant number of the House members necessarily would lead to a reduction in the importance of the election procedure itself. At the same time, the appointment of such a substantial number of military officers to the national and regional parliaments not only expanded the socio-political role of the armed forces but also clearly demonstrated their extraordinary position – their dual function – in the political format now being established by Suharto. By and large, the new consensus benefited the President and Golkar, which had the funds and the political apparatus to establish branches all over Indonesia. Since the government could control local legislators and governments, the DPR's regional representatives were also strongly in favour of Golkar. And since the Armed Forces were a part of the 'Greater Golkar Family' and Suharto was the Commander-in-Chief, they would never oppose him.

Elections and the search for a new political format

In the 1971 election ten political parties participated. Eight of these were old parties that had survived the Guided Democracy period. One was a new modernist Muslim party, Partai Muslimin Indonesia (Parmusi), which had been formed after the government had refused to rehabilitate Masyumi.[5] And then there was the Functional Group (Golkar), which had been designed so as to become the extension of the military and the main force within the New Order.

The 1971 election resulted in an absolute victory for Golkar and its patron Suharto that allowed the government to argue that it had now 'successfully' demonstrated the failure of the parties inherited from previous political orders. Not only that, the government could now also convincingly argue for the urgency of restructuring the party system as a necessity to achieve the New Order goals of political and economic stability. Therefore, a new format comprising only two political parties and Golkar (which was a 'functional group' and not a political party) had to be accepted by the political public, although it was admittedly the New Order government itself that had initiated the fusion among the political parties. Thus, after the 1971 election, a political restructuring along these lines was begun. The existing political parties were assembled into two groups. These were on one hand the 'material–spiritual' group comprising the PNI, Murba, the IPKI, Partai Katolik and Parkindo, and on the other the 'spiritual–material' group comprising parties with an Islamic orientation – NU, Parmusi, PSSI and Perti. The first group was later named the 'Democratic Development Group' and the latter the 'United Development Group'. In the beginning of 1973, the parties that had been gathered together into these two groups chose to merge. The first group then became known as the Indonesian Democratic Party (*Partai Demokrasi Indonesia*, PDI) and the second as the United Development Party (*Partai Persatuan Pembangunan*, PPP).

The government's next agenda was to present once again the bill on political parties, functional groups and mass organizations that had been turned down by parliament in 1969. The bill was now passed as Law No. 3 of 1975 on Political Parties and Functional Groups. With the ratification of this law, the legal framework for allowing only three parties – the PPP, Golkar and the PDI – to participate in the subsequent elections had been secured. There are four aspects of this that set the framework for the new but undemocratic elections under the New Order.

First, as already noted, there was the restriction on the number of political parties that could take part in elections. Therefore, people were not only deprived of their right to form new political parties, but their choice was limited to the three government-recognized parties. In practice, partiality, bureaucratic discrimination and the instilled phobia against 'political parties' caused voters in the rural areas, especially outside Java, to choose only Golkar. It became almost traumatic to vote for the PPP or the PDI, and it was associated with risk, as the chapters by Antlöv and Cederroth in this volume show.

Second, to add salt to the wounds, the government was in total control of the parties. Its ability to control them resulted in the so-called policy of 'political development'. The government, through the Ministry of Home Affairs, acted as the political tutor to the parties. In practice, the political development policies provided the government with a valid means for intervention in and engineering of the internal life of the PPP and the PDI, such as interfering in party congresses (Syamsuddin Haris 1997b: 58–68). In addition, it enabled the government to filter out unwanted and critical politicians. An example was the government's interference in the internal rift within the PDI in the mid-1990s. This ended with Megawati Sukarnoputri being ousted from the party leadership through a conspiracy between elements of the military and the government. This was perhaps the final evidence of the absurdity of the policy – and arguably the one that soon afterwards led to its demise. But during the 1970s, 1980s and 1990s, the government interfered again and again in the internal affairs of both the PPP and the PDI.

Third, a depoliticization of the general public was launched. At the district and municipality levels there were restrictions severely restricting party organizations and activities. As long as such restrictions were seen as a means for eliminating ideological and political conflicts at the community level, they were often favourably received. In practice, however, the restrictions only affected the PPP and the PDI, while the government-backed Golkar was able to utilize the hierarchical structure of the bureaucracy as a conduit for the socialization of its programmes to the rural population.

Fourth, the enforcement of the official principle of 'mono-loyalty' (*mono-loyalitas*) in the government bureaucracy inhibited government employees from becoming members and functionaries of the political parties. Again, in practice, the restriction affected only the PPP and the PDI, since government employees were even forced to become members of Golkar. It seems that it was the distinction between the attributes *Partai* and *Golongan*, respectively, that was needed to preserve what was seen as an almost 'sinful legacy' of the political parties. The discrimination by the bureaucratic apparatus – who dominated the election committees – against the PPP and the

PDI caused severe injustices in a political system that had very little to do with democracy. Long before they started the campaign, and long before people put their ballots in the box, the political system was construed so as to make it virtually impossible for the PPP and the PDI to obtain any substantial support. In the following, I will show how this was achieved.

The structure and process of general elections

Generally speaking, the process of every general election in Indonesia under the New Order consisted of thirteen stages that spanned a period of eighteen months. The process began when the voters were registered, and ended when the newly elected members of the DPR and DPR-D took their oaths. The stages were as follows:

1 registering voters;
2 determining the number of DPR members to be elected in each election district;
3 filing the names and symbols of the participating parties;
4 nominating the legislative candidates;
5 screening of the candidates;
6 finalizing the list of the candidates;
7 announcing the names of the candidates;
8 campaigning;
9 casting of the ballot;
10 counting the votes;
11 announcing the results of the election;
12 allocating seats and determining the elected candidates; and
13 endorsing the elected legislators.

Some six to nine months after the general elections, the MPR, which consisted of the DPR plus regional and functional members, would convene to unanimously re-elect President Suharto. Since this was a strictly formal procedure that had nothing to do with real elections, I will not deal with the presidential 'election' here.

The Election Committee

The entire election process was organized by an Election Committee whose members were predominantly government officials. Law No. 15 of 1969 on the General Election was amended three times (1975, 1980 and 1985) and finally replaced in 1999. Despite these revisions, there were no substantive modifications in comparison to the original law. The law underscored that general elections in Indonesia were the responsibility of the President and the MPR. As the organizer of the election, the government established an Institute of General Elections (*Lembaga Pemilihan Umum*, or LPU). This institute was headed by the Minister of Home Affairs and was responsible for carrying out the elections. The LPU in its turn then established election committees that were responsible for the elections from the national level all the way down to the village level. These were the Indonesian Election Committee at the national level (*PPI*); Regional Election Committee 1 (*PPD tingkat I* – provincial level); the Regional Election Committee II (*PPD tingkat II* – district and municipality level); the Regional Registration Committee (*Pantarlih* – district and municipal level) and finally some 65,000 Organizing Committees (KPPS – sub-district and village level). In order to supervise the elections each committee had a subcommittee responsible for monitoring the election. These were, respectively, the National Election Monitoring Committee (*Panwaslakpus*), the Provincial Election Monitoring Committee (*Panwaslakda* at the provincial level), the Regional Election monitoring Committee (*Panwaslakda* at the district and municipality level) and the Sub-district Election Monitoring Committee (*Panwaslakcam* at the sub-district level).

The head of the Institute of General Elections as well as those of the organizing committees and the supervisory committees were always government officials appointed *ex officio*, a fact which caused much heated debate. The Minister of Home Affairs headed the LPU and the PPI, governors chaired the provincial PPD, district heads and mayors chaired the district PPD, down to the village committees which were chaired by the village headmen. These officials, according to the doctrine of *mono-loyalitas*, were *ex officio* Golkar cadres, activists or functionaries. The Minister of Home Affairs was a member of Golkar's Central Advisory Board. The governors were usually the chairmen of Golkar's regional advisory council and so forth. At every level of the election organizing committees, government elements were dominant while the political parties, the PPP and the PDI, were represented by only a few committee members. At the lowest levels, that is, *Pantarlih* and *KPPS*, neither the PPP nor the PDI were represented. These committees consisted solely of government officials whose interests were, of course, to ensure that Golkar would win. In a similar manner, from the top of the national level down to the sub-district level the election monitoring committees (*Panwaslak*) were led *ex officio* by government officials at their respective levels. The National Election Monitoring Committee (*Panwaslakpus*) was headed by the Chief Justice, *Panwaslakda* was headed by the Chief Judge of the district high court, and so on. Again, all of these officials were Golkar members.

The structure of the election committee was another source of debate, since the law on political parties and functional groups in fact prohibited government officials or government employees from becoming members – not to mention becoming functionaries – of the political parties and of Golkar without the approval of their superiors. In practice, the restriction only affected officials who wished to become members, functionaries

26

or legislators of the PPP and the PDI. By virtue of their membership in the Civil Servants' Corps (KORPRI), every government employee automatically became a Golkar member regardless of his own political orientation. Every government employee was a KORPRI member, and for them the only route to channel their political aspirations was through Golkar.

Due to weak social control, non-functioning representative institutions, and a strong dominance of the government in the organizing committees, frequent incidents of cheating, poll rigging and violation of the direct, open, free and confidential principles of the general elections were claimed (but never officially filed). One main source of injustice in the New Order elections was obviously the obligation of every government official to ensure the victory of Golkar. There was usually a target score that should be reached, and the result was almost always announced less than twenty-four hours after the balloting – and this in a country with thousands of inhabited islands and more than one hundred million registered voters! The structure of the government's domination and the subjective partiality towards Golkar not only resulted in political discrimination by the bureaucracy against non-government parties but also eliminated any possibility of fair competition among the contestants. During the 1997 election, for example, Golkar garnered above 80 per cent of votes in all election districts outside Java (except for Aceh). In the provinces of Jambi, Bengkulu, Lampung, Bali, East Nusa Tenggara, North Sulawesi, Southeast Sulawesi and South Sulawesi, Golkar even managed to win more than 90 per cent of the votes. Given that only twelve months later, violent anti-government riots would shake the country and force Suharto to step down, it seems unlikely that 90 per cent reflected any true intention of the voters (if it even reflected how people had voted).

Screening of candidates

One of the objectives of elections is to choose representatives who will articulate the aspirations and the interests of voters through popular and responsive institutions, both at the national and the regional levels. Under the New Order, elections were held to choose people's representatives who would join the DPR (national level), the DPR-D *tingkat I* (provincial level) and the DPR-D *tingkat II* (district and municipality level). At the national level in the three first elections (1971, 1977 and 1982) there were a total of 260 elected legislators and in the two following elections (1987 and 1992) the number had increased to 400. In all these five elections, the number of appointed members from the armed forces was one hundred. During the last New Order election, in 1997, there were 425 elected legislators, and 75 appointed members from the armed forces.

Officially, any citizen who met the requirements could become a legislator. However, in practice, the names of the candidates appearing on the lists were drawn up by the party elite without any direct involvement of the constituents. The government determined whether or not a person could serve as a legislator, with the help of a special screening body, popularly known as '*litsus*' or special examination. The screening involved obtaining a clearance from the armed forces that the nominated candidates had no connection with the banned Indonesian Communist Party. In reality – and this led to criticism from the public – the screening body was often used by the government apparatus to ward off outspoken candidates who might criticize the government. In several cases, respondents who had undergone the *litsus* reported that the questions they had to answer were nonsensical and were unrelated to the PKI. The questioning officers' intent was to find faults with the non-Golkar candidates who were being screened (Syamsuddin Haris 1997a).

Formally, the names of the legislative candidates were nominated by party functionaries at the district level. However, the ranking, including the order in which the names appeared on the list, was still determined by the central committees of the parties – which were controlled by the government. Voters had no way of selecting and determining the legislators who would represent them in the parliament. Since the parties were not based on active membership, people living in a constituency could neither influence candidates nominated by their favoured political party, nor would they know their capabilities. Furthermore, in the case of Golkar, the candidates were mostly those who had access to the party leaders and the government. Favouritism in nominating candidates could not be avoided.

With such a recruitment process, it is not surprising that the majority of the candidates were those with a close relationship to the party elite and with proven loyalty to the politics of the New Order government. This was clearly demonstrated by the list of nominees from Golkar. The majority of the candidates were bureaucrats or former bureaucrats, celebrities, client businessmen and children, wives, in-laws and relatives of officials or former officials – both civilian and military.[6]

The Election Law was supposed to guarantee that each district had at least one representative in the House. However, since any domicile requirement was absent, the majority (52 per cent) of the candidates nominated by Golkar for the 1997 House of Representatives, for instance, resided in Jakarta and its suburbs (sometimes they were not even born in the district they allegedly represented). During the 1987 and 1992 elections, the percentage of Jakarta residents in the list of Golkar nominees for the legislative body exceeded 60 per cent (Syamsuddin Haris 1993: 56–69). Who represented the farmers, fishermen, workers and other voices of the poor and marginal?

Campaigns

So far we have discussed the regulatory framework, and we have seen how many aspects of this were deliberately manipulated by state agencies and clients. It should therefore come as no surprise to learn that there were injustices also during the brief campaign period.[7] The New Order government always mobilized its entire apparatus and used all its facilities to support and ensure victory for the ruling party, Golkar. Officials and politicians at all levels campaigned for Golkar, while the corps of civil servants – after mobilizing the grassroots – filled the fields and streets of Golkar's campaigns. To provide accommodation and transport, each government office contributed funds, vehicles and other facilities. Suharto's cronies furnished virtually unlimited funds to cover whatever Golkar needed to secure the victory. There was no mechanism to assure accountability for the use of political funds during the campaign period, since this was not required by the Election Law or other related laws. Therefore, it was literally impossible to measure the extra funding that Golkar accumulated, in addition to the officially allocated funds that all three groups received from the state budget. There were no public records of how these funds were spent, since most of it went to vote buying and to pay local officials for their loyalty.[8] Participants in Golkar's campaigns got paid for being present during campaigns, in addition to receiving free transportation, meals and a T-shirt or army-style cap.

In contrast, PDI and PPP members had to spend their own money when attending their parties' campaigns. Hardly any business people had the courage or the willingness to donate funds to the PPP and the PDI. Still, these two non-government parties did receive a limited amount of donations from independent entrepreneurs who did not rely much on government facilities and protection. However, the number of such sponsors was small.

Let us end this section on campaigning with a brief note on ideology and the messages contestants proclaimed during campaigning. Not much can actually be said about this topic, since the elections were not really competitions between parties and contenders with different ideological standpoints. The elections, as far as the government was concerned, were between Golkar versus non-Golkar, stability and economic development versus chaos and demise. Golkar generally emphasized the need for continued economic development, political stability and national unity. The PPP focused on the urgency of political justice, economic fairness and social justice in general. The PDI stressed the need to improve the condition of the poor and the urgency for bringing changes to the New Order political life and democratization. But people did not really choose between these. Despite the promises, most political analysts agree that there was no significant correlation between the grandeur of the campaigns, the political messages and the number of votes the parties would receive at the polls. The impressive campaigns of the PDI in Jakarta during the 1992 election, for instance, were not followed by a victory for the party in that election area. Similarly, the teeming campaigns of the PPP, which had 'greened' the whole city of Jakarta during the 1997 campaigns (the PPP had green as its official colour, Golkar yellow and the PDI red), did not lead to its victory. Campaigns, in reality, were 'people's festivals', moments that granted a little more freedom to the people on the street. During the campaigns, they were able to ride motorcycles without wearing helmets, or dance in the middle of the city traffic, follow their unique creativity, and do other things that they were normally not allowed to do – instead of listening to government indoctrination. Elections were festivals, but they were not democratic.

The poll and the vote counting

Most observers tend to agree that on the election day itself there was relatively little cheating or manipulation, at least to be observed on the surface. For the casual observer, Indonesian elections under the New Order might look professionally organized, and fairly democratic. However, the fact of the matter was that pressures, intimidations and threats had been made long before the voters arrived at the polling station. In many rural areas, especially outside Java, most people would not have the courage to vote for the PPP or the PDI, as it would be viewed as a rebellious act against the government (see the chapters by Antlöv and Cederroth). If people failed to vote for Golkar, this could lead to various kinds of discrimination in attaining bureaucratic services, such as not being issued ID cards or letters of recommendation. Worse, they could even end up being accused of subversion. In Aceh or East Timor, they could be charged for being affiliated with the 'outlaws'; in Irian Jaya they could be accused of being sympathizers of the Free Papua Organization, and in other parts of the country such 'betrayers' could simply be accused of affiliating with the banned Communist Party. Such kinds of intimidation, pressures and threats were internalized well for years under the New Order so that on the day of the ballot the voters simply tried to live with their powerlessness – and do what was expected of them as 'good *Pancasila* citizens'.

However, following the actual balloting, rigging and manipulation were common, particularly when the results were brought from the polling stations (where votes were counted) to the village office, and then from the villages to sub-district offices. The study by Alexander Irwan and Edriona (1995) notes that violation of the election principles mostly occurred at the KPPS on the village level. Charges were based not only on evidence and cases, but the counting process itself was unaccountable. The counting of the ballots was done entirely by members of the bureaucracy whose task it was to clear the way for Golkar's victory. While it was true that the PDI and the PPP had representatives to witness the counting process at the polling stations, they – as regulated by the Minister of Home Affairs-cum-Chairman of the General Election Institute – were usually not given a copy of the summary of the results of the vote counting although they were required to sign it.

From this description it should be clear that the position of the people and the mass organizations, including the non-government political parties, was very marginal in the political format of the New Order. As far as the political parties were concerned, it was a fact that the voters' choice was limited only to the three contestants – they had no other alternative. The voters were to elect and approve the names of the legislative candidates that had been selected unilaterally by the elite of the political parties (and the government through the screening mechanism) with no way of disagreeing.[9] After the counting of the votes had been completed by the government, without the presence of any independent election monitors, the two non-government parties – and the general public – simply had to accept the final results announced by the LPU and the PPI.

Election results

Given the election format described here, it is fairly obvious that the two non-government parties would be unable to compete with Golkar. It is even justifiable to say that the elections in the New Order era served only to demonstrate the power of Golkar and its domination. Golkar succeeded in maintaining its vote at above 60 per cent at every election under the New Order, the lowest being 62.1 per cent at the 1977 election and the highest being 74.3 per cent at the 1997 election. At the same time, neither the PPP nor the PDI ever reached a vote of 30 per cent (see Table 2.1).

Nevertheless, Golkar's consistent victories in the six elections were not reached without efforts. Despite the fact that Golkar was backed by all levels of the bureaucracy (civilian as well as military), that it had the largest number of affiliated mass organizations, that it was relatively homogeneous in terms of ideology, and that it had almost unlimited resources, the ruling party had to work hard to secure its position, especially in Java, Bali and

Table 2.1 Election results (per cent)

Parties	1971	1977	1982	1987	1992	1997
PPP	27.11*	29.29	27.78	15.97	17.00	22.43
Golkar	62.80	62.11	64.34	73.16	68.10	74.51
PDI	10.09*	8.60	7.88	10.89	14.90	3.06

Source: Institute of General Elections.

Note
* The total percentage of votes obtained by Islamic parties (NU, Parmusi, PSII and Perti) who merged into the PPP and the total percentage of votes obtained by the PNI, the IPKIP Murba, Partai Katolik and Parkindo who merged into the PDI.

Aceh. In the 1977 election, the PPP, which capitalized on the spirit of 'political Islam', was able to garner the largest number of votes in both Jakarta and Aceh. The competition was so tough that R. William Liddle, for example, describes the second election during the New Order rule as the rivalry between Islam and the government (Liddle 1978: 175–185). Based on this experience, the government subsequently increased its attempts to co-opt civilian political and religious leaders. This resulted in the heightening of internal conflicts both within the PPP and the PDI, particularly when the 1982 and 1987 elections were approaching. As a result, the PPP suffered a loss of votes in the 1982 election. The party was unable to secure a victory in any of the provincial election districts, although at the district and municipality level it won in at least twenty-six districts (Syamsuddin Haris 1991: 122).

The fall of the oil price in the world market in the early 1980s did not deter the government from rearranging and strengthening the corporative political format of the New Order. At any rate, the government increasingly needed the active participation of 'the people' to boost the state's foreign exchange reserve and sustain the economic growth. However, when it came to politics, the government continued to consolidate itself for the next election. For this purpose, a package of five bills was presented by the government to the parliament in 1984. The five bills that were passed by the DPR in 1985 were

1   Amendment to the Election Law;
2   Amendment to the Law on the Structure and Position of People's Consultative Assembly, House of Representatives and local parliaments;
3   Amendment to the Law on Political Parties and Golkar;
4   Law on Mass Organizations; and
5   Law on Referendums.

The new additions to the Law on Political Parties and Golkar and to the Law on Mass Organizations required all parties and mass organizations to adopt *Pancasila* as the sole ideology. As already mentioned, this was actually one of the recommendations made by the Second Army Seminar in 1966. Furthermore, through the Law on Referendums, the government reduced the possibility of the political forces and the people making changes to the 1945 Constitution, although Article 37 of the constitution clearly allowed that to happen. Thus, the contents of the package were intended to provide the government with more power to control and suppress the non-government political parties, mass organizations and the public in general.

Therefore, in subsequent elections, Golkar emerged as a hegemonic power, while the non-government parties lost power in their competition with Golkar. Before the 1987 election, NU decided to withdraw its support for the PPP following the extended rifts among its elite (see Endang Turmudi's chapter in this volume). Consequently, the Islamic party suffered the biggest loss in votes throughout the history of the New Order; it now managed to pick up only 16 per cent of votes. On the other hand, the PDI indirectly benefited from the internal problems of the PPP, and its votes jumped from 8 per cent in 1982 to 11 per cent in 1987.

The 1992 election was marked by a new phenomenon as the rivalry shifted from Golkar versus the PPP to Golkar versus the PDI. In a clever move, the PDI's elite at that time recruited two of Sukarno's children – Guruh Sukarnoputera and Megawati Sukarnoputri – before the New Order fifth election. This step, which was taken by Surjadi, the general chairman of the PDI, not only enlivened the party's campaigns but also raised its votes significantly – from 11 per cent in 1987 to 15 per cent in 1992. Quite unexpectedly, and without approval from the government – which had plotted to have the more accommodating Budi Hardjono in the post – Megawati was overwhelmingly, and with very strong support from the grassroots, elected as the next party chairman during the extraordinary congress of the PDI in Surabaya in 1993.

Government concern over this PDI phenomenon seems to have been the motive behind the ousting of Megawati in the following party congress in Medan in June 1996. This move was fully backed by the military and the central government. As a result, the government-backed the PDI, now again under Soerjadi managed to secure only 3 per cent of votes in the 1997 election down more than 11 per cent from its result in 1992. At the same time, Golkar won an overwhelming victory with 74.5 per cent votes, the highest share it has ever had during the New Order. But it was to be a pyrrhic victory.

Role and function of the elected DPR

Let us briefly look at the consequences and political implications that such a flawed electoral system had on the composition and function of the parliament. Most important is that the legislators became representatives of their respective political patrons and parties rather than of their constituents. The election format, whereby the recruitment was done by the political parties, did not make it possible for the legislators to represent their constituents. This is even more so in the case of legislators from the Golkar faction; most of them having had their permanent residence in greater Jakarta, even though they were listed under their 'home' provinces. As mentioned, most of them are bureaucrats, celebrities, client–business people and relatives of government officials or former officials, rather than 'people's representatives'. This tendency became stronger as the elite of the political parties increasingly felt it safer to collaborate with the government rather than to partner the voters.

The parliaments elected under the New Order did not function as legislative bodies, conduits for popular aspirations or as the 'checks and balances' mechanism for the executive branch. Members of the parliament were politically impotent, as expressed in a joke in which it was claimed that their job specification was to 'come, sit down, be silent, and get paid' (4D: *datang, duduk, diam, duit*). They were for all practical purposes only rubberstamping executive decision-making. To my knowledge, since 1971 not a single piece of legislation had originated in the parliament. All draft bills were initiated and drafted by the executive, and then handed over to the parliament for approval, a procedure which usually was swift. The parliament did not control the executive, on the contrary. By means of various policies and mechanisms, such as screening, political development, special examination and recalling, the government was fully capable of controlling the House. The parliament was so dependent on the government that when President Suharto came up with the idea that the soon-to-be-appointed legislators should first attend a special crash course before they came to office, members unanimously agreed. This balance of power between the representatives of the government and those of the non-government parties did not provide any opportunity for the latter or for critical legislators (there were actually one or two!) to deviate from the mainstream politics of the incumbent power (see Table 2.2).

Table 2.2 Allocation of seats at the DPR 1971–97

Factions	1971	1977	1982	1987	1992	1997
Government						
Golkar	236	232	242	299	282	325
Armed forces	100	100	100	100	100	75
Subtotal	366	332	342	399	382	400
Non-government						
PPP	94*	99	94	61	62	89
PDI	30*	29	24	40	56	11
Subtotal	124	128	118	101	118	100
Total	460	460	460	500	500	500

Source: Institute of General Elections and *Kompas*, 24 June 1997.

Note
* The total percentage of votes obtained by Islamic parties (the NU, Parmusi, the PSII and Perti) who merged into the PPP and the total percentage of votes obtained by the PNI, the IPKI, Murba, Partai Katolik and Parkindo who merged into the PDI.

Conclusions

From the beginning the election system implemented by the New Order had deep and irreparable problems. These were related to a number of factors: the decision of the political elite to grant the armed forces and Golkar a privileged position as the official extension of the regime; the restriction in the number of parties that could take part in an election; the depoliticization and the deflation of the political parties in the rural communities; the subjective mono-loyalty that affected the government bureaucracy; and finally the right of the government to interfere in the internal affairs of the non-government parties in the form of a supervisory policy that was implemented in the name of 'political development'. These factors turned elections under the New Order into nothing more than a legitimating mechanism for the state to endorse Golkar's victory and to maintain the power of the New Order – 'useful fictions' as William Liddle has called them (see Chapter 1). With an election format characterized by a restricted participation by the people, discrimination, unfairness and limited opportunity for competition among election contestants, in addition to an election process that was entirely under the control of the bureaucracy – which had the sole interest of championing Golkar and defending their power – it was virtually impossible for Indonesia to become a more democratic society. The election format created political stability and relatively high economic growth, but the elections increasingly became a mechanism through which the government could renew its legitimacy as opposed to an opportunity for the people to articulate their interests.

However, it was the government's partiality towards Golkar and the unfair process that seems to have been one of the causal factors behind the demise of the New Order in 1997–98. It started with the street fighting after Megawati was forcefully ousted as party chairwoman of the PDI in July 1996. The dissent then continued with riots that escalated, particularly in different areas of Java, during the 1997 campaign. An uncounted number of official and private properties were burned down or destroyed by angry masses. Since some of this was triggered by the arrogance demonstrated by the bureaucracy, it was not surprising that many of the targets of the mass anger were state apparatuses (the military and the police), the offices of the police precinct, the offices of sub-districts and village offices, in addition to other government institutions.

At the heart of elections is a process of checks and balances, a system through which popular legitimacy can be won and maintained. However, since this system was flawed in Indonesia, it can be argued that the elections under the New Order actually contributed to the downfall of the regime. For a long time, the absence of a sizeable middle-class population, an acute polarization among social organizations, a lack of strong civilian leaders and a diversity of views on the change itself hindered radical political change. But during the 1990s the foundation had been laid for the growth of dissent, both in terms of increasing regime decay (corruption, power abuse, state violence), and by providing the skills and sentiments necessary for students and activists finally to challenge the government. And interestingly, it was the 1997 election that was the catalyst.

Notes

1 For a more in-depth discussion on the 1955 general election, see Alfian 1971 and Feith 1956.
2 For the best study of the period of transition to Guided Democracy, see Lev 1960.
3 For more detailed studies of Golkar, see Nisihara 1972; Bahasoarl 1981; Boileau 1983; Reeve 1985 and Suryadinata 1992.
4 One of the best descriptions of the birth of the New Order was written by Mas'oed 1989. For the 'official' version of the New Order, see Moertopo 1974.
5 For more on Parmusi and the government's refusal to rehabilitate Masyumi, see Ward 1970.
6 D&R Magazine of 1 February 1997 calculated that there were at least 45 House candidates from Golkar who were close relatives (children, wives, in-laws, etc.) of officials or former officials.
7 During the 1971 election, the campaign period lasted for 60 days. During the subsequent elections, the period was shortened to 45 days, 35 and, finally in 1992 and 1997, 21 days.
8 There are, as I am revising this in 2001, ongoing court cases involving funds from state institutions such as BULOG and Jamsostek allegedly being used for questionable purposes, including funding the Golkar campaign in 1997.
9 Although voters could file objections to the candidates, it was only a formal procedure. During the 1997 election, LPU and PPI admitted that they had received hundreds of letters of objection directed against a number of candidates, but almost 99 per cent of the names nominated by the three parties remained unchanged.

References

Alfian (1971) *Results of 1955 General Election for House of Representatives.* Djakarta: Leknas-LIPI.
Bahasoarl, Awal (1981) 'Golongan Karya: Mencari Format Politik Baru' [The functional groups: looking for a new political format.] *Prisma*, no. 12, December.
Boileau, Julian M. (1983) *Golkar Functional Group Politics in Indonesia.* Jakarta: CSIS (Centre for Strategic and International Studies).
Feith, Herbert (1956) *The Indonesia Election of 1955.* Ithaca: Cornell Modern Indonesia Project.
Irwan, Alexander and Edriona (1995) *Pemilu: Pelanggaran Azas Luber* [Elections: violating the free and fair principles.] Jakarta: Pustaka Sinar Harapan.
Lev, Daniel S. (1960) *The Transition to Guided Democracy in Indonesia 1957–1959.* Ithaca: Cornell Modern Indonesia Project.
Liddle, R. William (1978) 'Indonesia 1977: the New Order's second parliamentary election'. *Asian Survey*, 18(2).

Mas'oed, Mochtar (1989) *Ekonomi dan Struktur Politik: Orde Baru 1966–1971* [Economy and political structure: the New Order 1966–1971.] Jakarta: LP3ES.

Moertopo, Ali (1974) *Strategi Politik Nasional* [National political strategy]. Jakarta: CSIS.

Nisihara, Masashi (1972) *Golkar and the Indonesian Election of 1971.* Ithaca: Cornell Modern Indonesia Project.

Notosusanto, Nugroho (ed.) (1985) *Tercapainya Konsensus Nasional 1966–1969* [Achieving a national consensus 1966–1969.] Jakarta: Balai Pustaka.

Reeve, David (1985) *Golkar of Indonesia. An Alternative to the Party System.* Singapore: Oxford University Press.

Samsuddin, A. (1972) *Pemilihan Umum 1971: Seri Berita dan Pendapat* [The general elections of 1971: news and views.] Jakarta: Lembaga Pendidikan dan Konsultasi Pers.

Suryadinata, Leo (1992) *Golkar dan Militer. Studi tentang Budaya Politik* [Golkar and the military: a study on political culture.] Jakarta: LP3ES.

Syamsuddin Haris (1991) *PPP dan Politik Orde Baru* [PPP and New Order politics]. Jakarta: Grasindo.

——(1993) 'DPR: "Wakil Daerah" tanpa Mandat Rakyat Daerah' [Regional representatives without regional mandate.] *Jurnal Afkar*, no. 2, April–June.

——(1997a) 'Pembinaan Politik, Demokratisasi, dan Pembentukan "Civil Society": Problematik Kepartaian Indonesian di Bawah Order Baru' [Political control, democratization and the formation of a civil society: problems of Indonesian political parties under the New Order.] *Jurnal Ilmu Politik* no. 17.

——(ed.) (1997b) *Pemilihan Umum di Indonesia: Telaah atas Struktur, Proses dan Fungsi* [General elections in Indonesia: a study of their structure, process and functions.] Jakarta: PPW-LIPI.

Ward, Ken (1970) *The Foundation of the Partai Muslimin Indonesia.* Ithaca: Cornell Modern Indonesia Project.

3

PATRONAGE, *ALIRAN* AND ISLAMIC IDEOLOGIES DURING ELECTIONS IN JOMBANG, EAST JAVA

Endang Turmudi

There were troubles in Indonesia when the 1997 election was approaching. Socio-religious conflicts had received much international attention and there were questions about Suharto's health – and the increasing greediness and ambition of his children. Violence had become more open, as in the July 1996 crushing of Megawati Sukarnoputri's faction of the Indonesian Democratic Party. The government needed a show of force, and went all out to make sure that Golkar – the New Order's elector machine – would win its largest majority ever. Political pressures and intimidation were fairly openly carried out, destroying people's political initiative and imagination. In many parts of Indonesia, people felt threatened not to vote for the two other parties, the PDI and the United Development Party (PPP – Partai Persatuan Pembanguan). Golkar won in all regions in Indonesia and received a majority of the national votes, accounting for more than 74 per cent.

One of the exceptions to this story is Jombang, East Java. Here, Golkar did not win a two-thirds majority ('only' 51.7 per cent). For religious and ideological reasons, devout Muslims supported the Islamic party, the PPP, despite strong pressure put upon them by local government officials and Golkar activists who promoted Golkar as the natural choice for Muslims. The role of religious teachers (*ulama*) was crucial.[1] There was a 'religious calling' which encouraged people to vote for the party. Supported by *ulama* organized within Nahdlatul Ulama (the NU), Muslim voters regarded the support for an Islamic party as their religious duty in upholding Islam. This pattern of electoral behaviour in Jombang has been relatively constant since the 1977 election, except for the 1987 election when internal conflicts between *ulama* provoked devout Muslims to support Golkar.

This chapter aims to highlight the electoral pattern in Jombang, focusing specifically on Islamic political behaviour. It discusses the factors that influenced the political allegiance and electoral behaviour of devout Muslims, and analyses the dynamics of local politics, especially in the 1987, 1997 and 1999 elections. One of the main themes will be an analysis of political polarization among supporters of Islamic parties in Jombang, and the continuation of Islamic politics from the New Order to the democratizing regime.

The devout Muslim or *santri*[2] society in Jombang has for a long time had a strong tendency to use Islamic political parties as vehicles to convey their aspirations, pursue their political interests and to realize the ideals of Islam generally. This orientation derives from their understanding that support of Islamic parties is a religious obligation. The two dominant factors that characterize Jombang society and affect people's political attitudes are the existence of a well-developed *pesantren* tradition[3] and the widespread practice of *tarekat*.[4] The *pesantren* are centres of learning and *da'wa* (preaching), while *tarekat* are sufi orders through which Muslims practise religious rituals by performing special *wird* (litany comprising Qur'anic excerpts repeatedly recited).[5] Whereas the primary activity of the *pesantren* lies in educating the *santri*, the *tarekat*'s activity focuses on building *batin* (the inner life of a person), which means that both contribute to the development of Islam in the society and the moulding of the individual's and the community's religiosity. These two features might suggest that Islamic life in Jombang flourishes, but this does not mean that Jombang is dominated by devout members of society since there are also a substantial number of Javanese whose practice of Islam is minimal. This situation has resulted in the emergence of two tendencies with regard to politics, one of which is more Islamic and another which is more secularly orientated. This tension has characterized politics in Jombang for decades, and will form the focus of this chapter.

Islam and political parties, 1955–87

In the 1955 general election, Islamic voters in Jombang (and around the country) gave their support to the NU and Masjumi, which were then the two largest Islamic political parties. The NU, representing traditionalistic Islam, won fourteen out of thirty-five seats in the local parliament, while Masjumi, which represented modernist Muslims, won three seats (Ward 1974: 167). Since most *ulama* in Jombang were members of the NU in the 1950s, the NU could obtain the majority of votes in 1955. A kaleidoscope of parties, including the nationalists and the communists, won the remaining seats. It needs to be noted here that not all Muslims support Islamic political parties, not only because Islam affects them differently but also because they have different understandings of what they have to do with regard to politics as a secular domain. To understand the different orientations among Muslims in Indonesia, it is relevant to see Geertz's (1965) framework, which relates religiosity on Java to people's (relative) political support. Geertz (1959, 1960, 1965) categorized religious orientations among Muslims into three kinds of subcultures, marked by differences in political behaviour. He called this '*aliran*' – ideological stream. Although his categorization of *santri, priyayi* and *abangan* has been criticized, it nevertheless depicts the intensity and quality of Islam's influence on the ethos of cultural groupings and shows how a certain religious outlook can establish a certain political orientation. Among the three categories, it is only the *santri* who are strongly influenced by Islam, who have made use of Islam as a guide for their lives and who use Islamic political parties as a vehicle to realize their secular and religious ideals. This framework explains why the *santri* 'leaned towards' Masjumi and NU as the two main Islamic political parties during the 1950s, while the *abangan*, who were represented by a large number of rural Javanese and who are more syncretic in their Islam, tended to support the Indonesian Nationalist Party (PNI) or the Indonesian Communist Party (PKI). The framework also depicts why the *priyayi*, who were white collar civil servants of noble descent, by and large were supporters of PNI or (only occasionally) PKI. The political manoeuvre set in motion through this *aliran* system condensed the four political parties into two blocks: one Islamic block represented by Masjumi and the NU and another nominal or syncretic block, including non-Muslims, represented by PNI and PKI. During the New Order government, the *aliran* system did not work well because of the changes in political constellations. We will return to how this actually played out during elections in Jombang.

The emergence of the New Order and the presence of Golkar in the 1971 general election changed this tendency among Muslim voters quite radically. The two large Islamic parties experienced a drastic decrease (see Table 3.1). Golkar activists used all means available to win the election, ranging from asking powerful community figures to stand by their side during meetings to intimidating people. The *ulama* as informal leaders for Muslims were subjected to intimidation by being approached by state officials who asked them to support Golkar; and they could not hold any *pengajian* (religious gathering) unless they received approval from the local police office, which was usually hard to obtain unless they were loyal to Golkar, of course. Some *ulama* and NU activists who remained loyal to Islamic parties were imprisoned before the 1971 general election. It was not very hard for police officers to accuse a person of a crime and take him or her to jail.

Generally speaking, the 1971 general election saw great political pressure on *santri* society. Many people did not dare to express their support for Islamic parties. The decrease in the share of votes for Islamic parties at the national level in the 1971 election was very significant. With the exception of the NU, all other Islamic parties lost the support of Islamic voters. It seems that members and sympathizers of Masjumi, an Islamic party which was banned by Sukarno in 1959 and which was not allowed to take part in the 1971 election, did not give their support to any of the other Islamic parties. The Parmusi, which was claimed by its activists as the Masjumi

Table 3.1 Percentage of votes by political parties in Jombang elections, 1971–97[a]

Year of election	PPP	Golkar	PDI
1971	42.9[b]	52.0	5.0[c]
1977	40.6	56.2	3.1
1982	40.6	53.1	6.2
1987	25.7	62.8	11.4
1992	31.4	45.7	22.8
1997	43.8	51.7	4.3

Notes

a Since the party composition was so different in 1955 and 1999, it does not really make sense to compare them with New Order elections. I will return to the 1999 elections later.

b This percentage is based on the vote shares of four Islamic parties taking part in the 1971 general election: that is NU, Parmusi, SI and Perti. PPP was a merger of these parties, and broadly represented the same constituency.

c This percentage is based on the vote shares of PNI and the smaller Christian parties in the 1971 general election. The PDI was a merger of these parties, and broadly represented the same constituency.

successor, was unable to mobilize Muslim enthusiasm to support the party, and received only 5.4 per cent of the national vote (compared to Masjumi which obtained around 20.9 per cent in the 1955 election).[6] This significant decrease in votes for the Islamic parties was balanced by a significant increase for Golkar, which won the election in almost all regions in Indonesia. Even though it was its first general election, Golkar managed to secure almost 63 per cent of the vote. In Jombang, Golkar gained 18 seats out of 32 in the local parliament.

It is important to note that although at the national level, the NU's result in the 1971 general election remained impressive, strong pressure on its members by government officers and Golkar's activists supported by the military reduced its vote share in Jombang. The NU obtained 13 seats, while the other Islamic party, Parmusi, obtained only 1 seat (two other Islamic parties, Perti and Sarekat Islam, did not receive any seats in this election).

On the national level, there was no competition between political organizations. The Suharto government, as we will see, engineered the elections so that their results were predictable. However, since 1971 general elections in Jombang have always been marked by competition between the PPP and Golkar, oscillating in their vote results. Table 3.1 shows that the PPP's decrease in the 1977 general election, compared to the votes shares of Islamic parties in the 1971 general election, was balanced by an increase in Golkar's vote share, while the former's decrease in the 1987 election was balanced by the latter's increase. Furthermore, the increase in the PPP's share of votes in the 1992 general election was balanced by Golkar's decrease. Except for the 1992 election, PDI was a marginal party in Jombang. It would seem that votes in Jombang were divided between the PPP and Golkar.

There are two noteworthy results that I will spend some time to explain in the next sections: the drastic decline of the PPP in 1987 and its drastic increase ten years later, in 1997.

The 1987 election: 'deflating' Islam

In the 1987 election the PPP lost almost a third of the votes in Jombang that it had received in the last election five years earlier. In 1985 the largest coalition partner of the PPP, NU, had launched its policy of 'back to *khittah*' – back to the original 1926 fundamentals. Under pressures from and manipulations by the Suharto government, the NU declared that it would return to its position as a 'socio-religious organization' as conceptualized when it was established in 1926. Although the NU was the biggest component of the PPP when the party had been created in 1972, the 'back to *khittah*' policy meant that the organization formally dissociated itself from the PPP. However, the NU did not forbid its members to be active in politics, it was simply not a constituent part of the PPP any longer. As we shall see, many NU members went to Golkar.

Most *ulama* in Jombang, especially those who controlled a *pesantren*, followed the 'back to *khittah*' line because they had been NU members. It was very difficult for an *ulama* with a different standpoint to openly oppose an NU decision. The NU had been used by *ulama* as a network through which problems of their *pesantren* were discussed. In addition, the *ulama* established Rabitah Ma'ahid al-Islami, an organization under the NU umbrella which coordinates *pesantren* and through which the *ulama* maintain a kind of solidarity which directs them to follow the NU's decisions. For these *ulama*, therefore, the application of the 'back to *khittah*' policy was an important duty. They believed that they had to make NU members in general understand that the NU was no longer formally part of the PPP, although this proved to be a very difficult task because of the long established link with the PPP.

In the same year – 1985 – all social organizations in Indonesia, including the PPP and NU, had to change their ideological basis to the national ideology of *Pancasila*. The PPP symbol was changed from the *Ka'bah* to a star, and its party programme was revised. Since *Pancasila* is secular and allows religious pluralism, the PPP could no longer present itself as an Islamic party. The main appeal of the party, being Islamic, therefore disappeared.

Furthermore, there were leadership conflicts within the PPP. As the biggest component of the PPP, the NU was represented by a large number of politicians in the leadership of the party, and many PPP members of parliament were derived from the NU faction. This NU dominance, however, was challenged when the chairman from a competing modernist Islamic faction within the PPP was appointed as the PPP chairman in the late 1970s. The new chairman marginalized NU representatives in the party, and replaced them by colleagues from his own modernist Islamic faction, a situation which not only incurred disappointment from NU members in general but also resulted in a general NU dissociation from the party.

This discontent caused NU elites and activists to support a campaign in 1987 to undermine the PPP. This policy became known as *penggembosan* (literally, to deflate as in deflating a tyre; meaning to weaken). The *penggembosan* was manoeuvred nationally in order to withdraw NU support from the PPP, thereby weakening the party. In Jombang, Muslims were told to leave the party since the PPP was not a good party for NU members. The argument was clear: since the PPP was no longer an Islamic party, it was no longer compulsory to support the PPP. The resulting sharp decrease in votes was obviously in the direct interest of the Suharto government, whose advocates were quick to draw the dissatisfied voters into Golkar.

There was however a minority of NU leaders and *ulama* who disagreed with the NU's 'back to *khittah*' policy, and wanted the NU to continue its political cause. The NU had to continue to be involved in politics, since that was the vehicle for pursuing Muslim struggles. This view was held by a minority of *ulama* and their followers, such as some within the *tarekat* Jam'iyah Ahli Thoriqoh Al-Mu'tabarah An-Nahdliyah. Within this *tarekat*, two forms of political allegiance emerged. The first consisted of those NU *ulama* and members who continued to support the PPP, and thus disapproved of the *penggembosan* policy. Their continued support for the party was possible since in essence the NU did not prohibit its members from continuing to be affiliated with the party. According to them, what the NU did with its policy was to dissociate itself formally from the PPP. But it allowed its members to affiliate with any political party, including the PPP. The second group were those NU *ulama* and members who changed their support from the PPP to Golkar. This group insisted that support for Golkar was a national necessity. It was this group which promoted the *penggembosan* movement. This group was supported by a few *ulama*, especially those that held formal local NU leadership.

These various poles of interpretations and consequences of 'back to *khittah*' (support the PPP, support Golkar, remain outside altogether) produced wider local conflicts. The attitude of most formal NU leaders in Jombang disappointed many *ulama* and NU members in general who still continued to support the PPP. These NU leaders, supported by various local *ulama*, tried to weaken the PPP by their policy of *penggembosan*. Three of the four large *pesantren*[7] in Jombang gave public support to the *penggembosan* and encouraged Muslims in Jombang not to vote for the PPP in the 1987 general election. Another large *pesantren* in Jombang, the *Pesantren Darul Ulum*, had been supporting Golkar publicly since 1977 when its leader, *Kiai*[8] Musta'in, had 'defected' to the state party. The *ulama* of this *pesantren* did not have any problems with the NU's policy of 'back to *khittah*'. Although *ulama* of the three larger *pesantren* (*Pesantren* Tebuireng, *Pesantren* Denanyar and *Pesantren* Bahrul Ulum), publicly discouraged Muslims from supporting the PPP in the 1987 general election, this did not mean that all their *ulama* adopted the same line. *Kiai* Syamsuri Badawi of the *Pesantren* Tebuireng, for example, was a PPP national candidate for parliament and his candidacy produced a reaction from the head of his *Pesantren*, Yusuf Hasyim (but in this case he was supported by his *santri* who had articulated their interests through the PPP). There was also a PPP candidate for local parliament among the *ulama* family in the *Pesantren* Bahrul Ulum, a situation which created hidden internal conflicts among the *ulama* family following the 1987 general election.

These leading *ulamas*' decision to encourage Muslims to support the government party, Golkar, was made prior to the 1987 general election in the *Pesantren* Denanyar, located in the western part of Jombang. It should be noted, however, that the decision was reached only after long discussions. One young *ulama*, for example, initially said that he did not agree with the decision of 'encouraging NU members to vote for the government's party', but he surrendered after being convinced by a senior *ulama* who claimed that in politics everything was possible. He was then asked to convince Muslims in his district to support Golkar, and during the campaign these PPP critics encouraged their followers to support Golkar. These *ulama* and NU politicians felt that the NU was disadvantaged in comparison to other factions within the PPP, and they used 'back to *khittah*' and NU dissociation from the party to weaken it by conducting *penggembosan*. The leadership of the NU in Jombang tended explicitly to support the politics of *penggembosan*, thereby dividing the support of devout Muslims, NU members in particular, for the first time among various political parties.

However, a *wasiat* (literally 'last will and testament') of a great *ulama* in Jombang, Adlan Ali, significantly influenced Muslims to continue supporting the PPP. The *wasiat*, pronounced during the 1987 campaign, asked Muslims to continue to support the PPP since it was 'the house of Muslims'. The *wasiat* actually supported an earlier *fatwa* (religious decree) of *Kiai* Syamsuri Badawi, a great *ulama* of Jombang, suggesting that '*umat Islam wajib mendukung PPP*' (Muslims are religiously obliged to support the PPP) pronounced in 1986. A similar *fatwa* had also been delivered by *Kiai* Bisri Syansuri a decade before, obliging Muslims to support the PPP during the 1977 election. If *Kiai* Bisri Syansuri's *fatwa* was intended to increase the PPP's share of the vote, *Kiai* Syamsuri Ba's *fatwa* and *Kiai* Adlan Ali's[9] *wasiat* were aimed at preventing the PPP's share of the votes from decreasing since they were pronounced in the context of the decrease in the NU's *ulama* support for the PPP.

These *wasiat*s and *fatwa*s were not only politically but also socially important, since they were pronounced in the second half of the 1980s, a time when

Muslim society in Jombang (and especially NU members) was bewildered by the political situation marked by the conflict among leading NU figures. With these *wasiat*s and *fatwa*s, a large part of NU society in Jombang was reminded of the moral necessity to 'return to their house' (i.e. to support the PPP).

As we have seen, *penggembosan* was successful in reducing the PPP's national share of votes from 26 per cent in the 1982 election to 15 per cent in 1987, while in Jombang the PPP's vote decreased from 41 per cent in 1982 to 25 per cent in 1987. It is thus evident that the launch of the 'back to *khittah*' policy in 1984–85 had changed the pattern for existing political parties in Jombang. The tacit support of the *penggembosan* movement by some *ulama*s' encouragement to vote for the government party was a significant factor in turning away more than one-third of PPP supporters from the party. Although the *penggembosan* movement was not a formal policy of the NU, it was nevertheless sustained by the tacit support of *ulama*s in the mainstream of the NU, locally as well as nationally.

Some NU members who took an interest in politics were also unsympathetic towards the new leadership of PPP. Many *ulama* in the NU mainstream and their followers throughout Indonesia considered that PPP political leadership needed to be weakened since it was deemed as being unfairly disadvantageous to the NU, the largest component of the party. Naro, the new PPP chairman elected in 1978, discriminated against the NU and cultivated a feeling of hostility among PPP faction members. According to an informant, the political actions of Naro were neither derived from an *ikhlas* (honest) perspective nor from a desire 'to struggle for Islam'. Rather they were characterized by selfish interests. He suggested that the differences in the group characteristics of the former PPP components – NU, Parmusi, Perti and Sarekat Islam – did not necessarily need to be forcefully diminished. In fact this was probably impossible. What needed to be done was to cultivate the same perspective on the necessity of supporting the Islamic struggle through politics. Naro, however, the informant added, did not try to create such a situation but rather sharpened the differences.

The 1997 elections: challenging Golkar

The 1997 general election meant a strong return for the PPP – indeed they even challenged Golkar in Jombang and received almost the same amount of votes. Even five years earlier, in the 1992 general election, the PPP in Jombang had succeeded in increasing its vote to some 31 per cent, or an increase of about 22 per cent from its all-time low result in the 1987 election. Briefly, the main reason for the 1992 result was that many NU members who had voted for Golkar in the 1987 general election were now becoming dissatisfied. Golkar had promised to keep its door open for the NU's politicians, and to increase Islam's political role, but none of this had happened. Many former PPP supporters thus returned to vote for the party again.

This tendency was further strengthened in the 1997 election (the last election under the New Order). There were many factors that contributed to create a conducive environment for the further increase of the PPP vote, some national, others local. In addition to the demise of *penggembosan*, conflicts among *ulama* in Jombang before the 1997 general election had pushed some leaders to revise their attitude with regard to the PPP. *Ulama* who had encouraged Jombang Muslims to leave the PPP in the 1987 general election now returned to give their full support for this party in the 1997 general election. *Hajj* Yusuf Hayim, the leader of *Pesantren* Tebuireng and a senior politician with a national reputation (and as we recall, one of the leaders behind the *penggembosan* in 1987), did not engage in any political activity which could be classified as disadvantageous to the PPP in 1997. Significantly, he gave his full support to the PPP at an important speech in a *Halal Bihalal* held by the PPP in February 1997.[10]

This shift in political allegiance can be attributed to two factors. First, it needs to be remembered that the *ulama*s' 'gut' preference had always been that they were supporters of the PPP. Not only was the party the one that conveyed an Islamic political message, it was also the party they had brought into being in 1973. Second, the *ulama* realized that their presence in Golkar only benefited the government, and not their own personal good or that of the larger Islamic *ummat*. It was felt (probably correctly) that the Golkar elite used the *ulama* only as vote-getters to increase their party's share of the vote in the election. In addition, there was no reason to weaken the PPP as they had done before since now all its leaders in Jombang were people with an NU background, their colleagues[11] (Naro had left the chair after the 1987 election and the new leader was closer to the NU). This change in attitude influenced former PPP supporters who had voted for Golkar in 1987 and 1992 to return and again vote for the PPP in the 1997 general election.

Another factor that contributed to the increase of the PPP result in the 1997 general election was the national conflict and disintegration within the PDI. The fragmentation among PDI members and sympathizers was the result of a conflict between its leadership at the national level. This had led to the creation of two groups of national leaders in the party, one led by Megawati Sukarnoputri (the daughter of former President Sukarno) and one led by the government-sanctioned candidate Surjadi. The forceful occupation of the central PDI office in Jakarta in July 1996 by the Surjadi faction – a takeover which was supported by the army – had incurred unsympathetic responses from the PDI's members and sympathizers. Although Surjadi's leadership was legitimized by a PDI congress (rigged by the government) held a few months later in Medan (six months ahead of the national elections), the new party leadership did not receive much support from PDI members at the grassroots level. Many members and sympathizers continued to give their loyalty to the toppled Megawati. Since a large number of pro-Megawati PDI members had felt disadvantaged by Surjadi and therefore did not vote for the PDI in the 1997 election, the party in Jombang lost no less than seven of the eight seats it had obtained in the 1992 general election.

It has been argued that many of the PDI votes went to the PPP rather than to Golkar, not as Islamic votes but as protests against the government. This assumption is supported by the fact that there were political manoeuvres by dissatisfied PDI leaders to induce their supporters to vote for the PPP in the 1997 general election. PDI members also expressed their disappointment with the Surjadi faction by displaying '*Mega–Bintang*'[12] posters at PPP campaigns, a symbol of collaboration between supporters of Megawati and the PPP and of the hostility of the former towards Surjadi.

However, this assertion does not necessarily hold true for Jombang. Several PPP activists in Jombang with whom I spoke doubted whether former PDI supporters really had voted for the PPP in the election. First, the PDI supporters, who, generally speaking, are secular nationalists (Ramage 1995), were unlikely to support the PPP because they do not like the *santri*. In spite of its *Pancasila* basis, and the criticism from within of watering down the Islamic message, the PPP was still perceived by outsiders as an Islamic party. Hence the aversion of the PDI supporters, who are Javanese syncretists, to supporting the PPP was due to ideological reasoning. Accordingly, it is understandable that although the leaders of the PDI in Jombang asked their members to give their support to the PPP, the latter's campaigns were not attended by the PDI's members and supporters, since it is traditionally very rare that supporters of one political party attend a campaign held by other parties.[13] At this point it was more likely that these PDI members voted for Golkar than the PPP, since the former was more secular in its politics.

If, in fact, most PDI members and sympathizers in Jombang voted for Golkar in the 1997 general election, then it follows that the increase in the PPP vote share must have come from former Golkar supporters. There was no emotional attachment or religious legitimacy that could force NU members who had supported Golkar in previous elections to continue supporting the government party, and it was therefore not hard for them to change their support in 1997. In addition, the PPP was a party created mainly by NU leaders, and it was thus very likely that NU members had strong emotional attachments to the party. As we have seen, this attachment was also supported by a *fatwa* from 1986 suggesting that it was *wajb* (a religious obligation) to support the party. Apart from these factors, NU members were encouraged to leave Golkar and support the PPP because of dissatisfaction with Golkar's national politics. Social and political riots preceding the 1997 general election in regions with a strong NU presence such as Situbondo, Tasikmalaya and Pekalongan had targeted NU members. The riots incurred an antipathy from

Muslims, especially NU members and sympathizers, against the government, since it was deemed that not only had the government been unable to stop the riots but perhaps it had even been organizing them.

In spite of the good result for the PPP, a number of *ulama* in Jombang continued publicly to support Golkar. These *ulama*, according to a reliable source, organized several *istighosah*,[14] funded by the district chairman (*bupati*) of Jombang.[15] These *istighosah* highlighted the good relationship which NU leaders and the *bupati* had long established, but they were very political since they aimed to influence NU members to give their support to Golkar. This time there was no direct *penggembosan* by NU *ulama* as had been the case ten years earlier. But there were other steps taken by the *ulama* to disadvantage the PPP. For instance, the political manoeuvres by the national chairman of the NU, Abdurrahman Wahid, provided opportunities for the Suharto's daughter, Siti Hardiyanti Rukmana (one of several Golkar national chairpersons), to visit NU *pesantren* and attend *istighosah*.

Similar *istighosah* were conducted by the leader of the Jam'iyah Ahli Thoriqoh Al-Mu'tabarah Indonesia centred in the *Pesantren* Darul Ulum.[16] This stream of *tarekat*, formerly led by *Kiai* Mustai'in, had long been affiliated with Golkar. In its big *istighosah* preceding the 1997 general election, the leader of this *tarekat* asked the members to support and give their vote to Golkar while threatening (religiously) those who ignored his request. As loyalty and obedience to the leader in the *tarekat* is absolutely required, 'it would hence be wrong', the leader suggested, 'if followers did not follow their *tarekat* leader in politics'.

The *bupati's* support for these religious activities indicated his eagerness to assist Golkar during the election. The *bupati* and the Golkar leaders in Jombang were really satisfied with the *istighosah* since these activities were attended by a large number of important leaders, guaranteeing Muslim support for Golkar. As the relationship between the *ulama*, not to mention the leader of the *tarekat*, and members of society has been marked by the latter's obedience, the leader's support for Golkar would induce Muslims to support the government party. That was why the *bupati* felt that he did not need to put more pressure upon people in Jombang in this election and was not even bothered when he learnt that there were some people from 'Darul Ulum University' involved in KIPP's (an independent and arguably anti-Golkar election monitoring committee) activities.

Most, if not all, Golkar activists throughout East Java carried out political activities which worked to the disadvantage of the PPP and the PDI. This was done before and even on the day of the election, for instance by distributing rice early in the morning on election day. In return for the rice the people were asked to vote for Golkar. In other regions of East Java, such political manoeuvres incurred strong negative responses from PPP supporters and sympathizers. In Sampang, for instance, government buildings were burnt, an event triggered by rumours of the death of a PPP *ulama*, allegedly killed by a security officer.

However, the *bupati* did not have reason to be quite so satisfied with these activities since he had misunderstood the polarization of the *ulama* leadership in Jombang. As mentioned before, the *ulama*s in Jombang were divided into three groups, that is those in the formal NU leadership, those in the Jam'iyah Ahli Thoriqoh Al-Mu'tabarah Indonesia centred in the *Pesantren* Darul Ulum, and those in the Jam'iyah Ahli Thoriqoh Al-Mu'tabarah An-Nahdliyah centred in Cukir. If the *ulama*s in the NU leadership leaned toward support for Golkar, and those in the former *tarekat* were loyal Golkar supporters, the *ulama*s in the latter *tarekat* were actually PPP supporters. The *bupati* received support from the first two groups, but he did not realize the strong influence of the *ulama*s in the third group. In addition he also did not understand that although all *ulama*s in Jombang were NU members, the *ulama*s were part of an independent entity which in some occasions ran politics contradictory to the NU's. As most Muslims in Jombang are followers of *ulama*s, NU was often powerless in inducing their political intentions if they were not supported by the *ulama*s.

Since the decision by Muslims on how to vote was not dependent on the NU and only two groups of *ulama*s gave their full support to Golkar, PPP leaders did not worry about the Golkar manoeuvres. In addition, there was another group of *ulama*s who did not give their support to Golkar. 'The situation is different from that in the previous [1987 and 1992] elections', one of the PPP leaders suggested. 'In the 1997 general election, most PPP members and sympathizers knew what they had to do, and no *ulama* tried to influence their decision to vote for a particular party'. According to him, PPP supporters could not be influenced by the *ulama*s in the NU's leadership because ever since the 1987 general election, when their politics had been pro-Golkar and contradicted that of devout Muslims, they had lost some of their credibility. In addition, the reference by NU members, especially by the *tarekat* followers in Jombang, was not the *ulama*s with leadership positions in the NU, but *Kiai* Makki Ma's'um and *Kiai* Khoerul Anwar, the leaders of the *tarekat*, both of whom had consistently given their support to the PPP.

Both Golkar and the PPP used religious gatherings and *istighosah* to deliver their political messages. These media were very effective. Not only did the audiences come from the group affiliated with a specific political party, but also the messages were legitimized by religious arguments. In the *istighosah* during April 1997, for instance, all *ulama*s of the Jam'iyah Ahli Thoriqoh Al-Mu'tabarah An-Nahdliyah recommended that the audience vote for the PPP, basing their recommendation on religious grounds. The same arguments were used by the *ulama*s of the Jam'iyah Ahli

Thoriqoh Al-Mu'tabarah Indonesia, who encouraged their members to vote for Golkar.

Islamic voting behaviour during the late New Order

We have seen that some Muslims in Jombang felt compelled to support the PPP because it was seen as an Islamic political party and because the *ulama*s encouraged them to support it. These religious reasons were derived from their understanding that Muslims should affiliate with an Islamic party and give their support to it in the general election since 'to support' is among the religious obligations which they should honour – in short, politics and religion should not be separated. The political line which must be pursued, according to this view, was therefore characterized by an Islamic frame-work, a situation which indicated a tight connection between religious orientation and political behaviour. This would suggest that Islam had a strong position in Jombang. Religious ideas were behind and influenced the political behaviour of leaders and adherents generally. This religiously moti-vated political orientation had been established as a result of the Muslims' grasp of Islamic values and their understanding of Qu'ranic precepts. Moreover, it was sustained by the Muslims' view that there could be no separation between secular and religious activities. Politics and Islam were like two sides of the same coin: Islam is the idea, while politics is a means for realizing and applying such an ideal to real life in the society.

These ideas were displayed in 1987, when some Muslims in Jombang refused to vote for Golkar, despite the fact that the PPP had changed its ideological basis from Islam to *Pancasila*. They continued to support the PPP since the party had an historical relationship with Islam and because they recognized that the party continued to struggle for their interests. The NU's dissociation from the PPP in 1985, which was a political decision to change the electoral behaviour of Muslims, had limited influence on Islamic voting behaviour. What I am arguing here is that what influenced them to support the party was not their NU association but the 'Islamness' of the PPP.

The support of Muslims for the PPP in late New Order elections was closely related to the Islamic political ethos which had and still has a strong influence on the attitudes of Javanese Muslims. This ethos placed Islam as the dominant idea that continuously reminded Muslims to behave accord-ing to its values. Islam was a driving force that engendered feelings of dis-comfort among those who ignored it. Some examples of this can be found among those who continued to support the PPP regardless of the pressure or even threats. A young man of 20, for example, suggested that he felt that he had to support the PPP because all his family and friends, as well as other people in his village, did so. Although he had no ideological reason to support the PPP – he did not mention its relation with Islam and he did not come from a devout family – he felt ashamed to support other parties.

His attitude was manifested by his voting for the PPP in the election.[17] This case is one among several examples which indicate that the 'Islamic' political ethos continues to be strongly embedded and influences Muslim political behaviour. It has become 'representative consciousness', that is the consciousness which has been formed through shared historical experience and understanding of the society on the existing socio-political situation. This consciousness formed a great moral pressure on this young Javanese, as well as for many other in Indonesia and propelled him to support the PPP.

The 1999 election – *aliran* rivalry

Of the 48 parties that were registered nationally to take part in the 1999 election, 27 registered and campaigned in Jombang (only those parties that registered locally were allowed to campaign; voters could give their votes to any of the 48 parties). Most of these parties were small and only a handful received significant support from the people of Jombang. Of the 8 parties that received seats in the local parliament, the reformed *Partai Demokrasi Indonesia Perjuangan* (PDI-P) and *Partai Kebangkitan Bangsa* (PKB) reached the highest number of seats, 16 and 12, respectively. The New Order parties, Golkar and the PPP received 4 and 3 seats each, and the rest of the seats were shared between the PAN (two seats) and the PBB, the PNU and the PKP (one seat each) (Table 3.2).

This change in the formal structure of Indonesian politics was possible only after Suharto stepped down. The establishment of the PKB by NU *ulama*s on 23 July 1998 in Jakarta meant that the support given by NU members and sympathizers in Java and Madura to the PPP and Golkar was withdrawn. As the 1999 election results reveal, a majority of NU members in Jombang seem to have supported the PKB, resulting in a significant decrease in the PPP's and Golkar's share of the votes. The PKB was successful in gathering all factions of NU members and its *ulama* involved in the local politics in Jombang, and thereby succeeded in receiving a vote share comparable to that which the NU had received in the 1971 election.

Table 3.2 Results of the 1999 elections in Jombang

Rank	Political party	Votes	Seats
1	PDI-P	270,773	16
2	PKB	195,291	12
3	Golkar	72,012	4
4	PPP	54,637	3
5	PAN	27,688	2
6	PBB	6,068	1
7	PNU	4,227	1
8	PKP	7,520	1

There are two main reasons that explain Muslims' support for the PKB. First, in Jombang the PKB was seen as an Islamic party, in spite of its elites always emphasizing that the party was 'nationalistic' in character, a key-word for promoting *Pancasila* and not Islamic precepts as its legal foundation. This 'Islamic' perception derives from the fact that the party was led by Islamic leaders with an NU background. As discussed in the previous section, Muslims' attachment to Islamic parties is strong since it is supported by religious legitimation. Muslim support for the PPP in the past was thus based on the fact that it was seen as an Islamic party, and they felt that they were expected to support it because such support was subsumed under 'performing a religious duty'. The same applied to the PKB.

Second, the PKB was established by NU *ulama*s involved in the NU leadership. Since the PKB was only one of more than fifteen Islamic parties taking part in the 1999 general election, the involvement of NU *ulama*s in the formation of the PKB was an important factor. This induced support from NU members and increased the NU's strength, a situation similar to that in the 1955 and 1971 general elections, when the NU constituted a separate political party. Most *ulama*s of the Jam'iyah Ahli Thoriqoh Al-Mu'tabarah An-Nahdliyah who previously had constituted the backbone of the PPP chose to support the PKB in the 1999 election. Followers of this sufi order, led by the important Abdullah Sadjad, were encouraged to vote for the PKB; only an insignificant number remained loyal to the PPP. The same applied to *ulama*s of the Jam'iyah Ahli Thoriqoh Al-Mu'tabarah Indonesia, who in 1987 and 1992 had voted for Golkar. Although there were no *ulama*s of this sufi order involved in the establishment of the PKB – since they were affiliated with Golkar and since their *mursyid* (chief leader) was a Golkar member of the local parliament – a significant number of their followers voted for the PKB.[18] The reasons given were based on the religious orientation of the party and its formation by NU *ulama*s. This seems to suggest that their support for Golkar in the previous general election was not merely because they followed their *ulama*s' political lead, but because there was no 'real' Islamic political party,[19] a situation which indicated that there was no difference between the PPP, Golkar and the PDI, so that, in their opinion, they had no moral obligation to support any particular political organization.

The party that received the largest share of votes in Jombang was the PDI-P (the Indonesian Democratic Party of Struggle). That party, led by the daughter of former President Sukarno, was also the national winner of the election. In Jombang the party received its support from the nationalists and *abangan* (syncretists), formerly supporters of the PDI and Golkar. They now voted for the PDI-P because they had been sympathizers of the nationalist party, PNI, established by Sukarno in the 1950s. The political ideology of PNI had been adopted by the PDI when this party was established in 1973. The same held true with former PNI sympathizers who had been affiliated with Golkar and continuously supported this political organization after they received political pressure to do so from the 1971 general election and onwards.[20]

From the discussion here, it is clear that the higher share of votes for the PDI-P and the PKB in the 1999 general election was balanced by a decrease in votes for Golkar and the PPP. While most former Golkar supporters switched to the PDI-P and the PKB, those who had voted for the PPP changed to the PAN and the PBB as well as to the PKB. The support for the PAN and the PBB derived from Muslims with a Muhammadiyah background (a competing modernist religious organization that until recently was led by Amien Rais, the present speaker of the People's Consultative Assembly, who had established the PAN before the 1999 election). These Muhammadiyah supporters felt dissatisfied with the PPP, since most of the leaders of the reformed PPP came from families with an NU background. Rather than voting for the PPP (not to mention the PKB!), these Muhammadiyah members supported other Islamic parties, such as the PAN and the PBB whose leaders were modernist Muslims.

This voting pattern suggests the emergence of an ideological polarization similar to that of the 1950s (also seen during the New Order, although less transparent). In other words, attachment to *politik aliran* remained strong. As in the 1950s, politics could incur conflicts between various groups of party supporters at the grassroots level since they were imbued with ideological fanaticism. *Aliran*, according to Geertz (1965), was more than a mere political party and more than a mere ideology: it was a set of interconnected social forms which acted to group large masses of people into a generalized category. If the *aliran* system in the 1950s was represented by four big political parties, that is, the PNI (nationalists), Masjumi (modern Islam), the NU (traditional Islam) and the PKI (communists), the same *aliran* were in 1999 represented by the PKB, the PBB and the PDI-P. These three parties had their own traditional supporters. The PKB can be seen to represent the former NU party, while the PBB and the PDI-P inherited the ideologies of Masjumi and the PNI, respectively.[21] People supported and voted for certain parties not because they had good candidates but because they had a similar culture and ideology to their own. NU members in Jombang gave their political support to the PKB because the party was established by the NU's *ulama*, while Muhammadiyah members gave their votes to the PAN and the PBB because these parties were established by Muhammadiyah leaders. Because of the traditional rivalry between Muhammadiyah and Nahdlatul Ulama, there was no cross-voting between these parties. The same held true for PDI-P supporters, who are mostly derived from former PNI sympathizers.[22] As already noted, PNI had been a political party of the nationalists that stood in opposition to Islamic parties such as the NU and Masjumi.

The 1999 election marked the return of Islam into Indonesian politics from which it had been banned after the introduction of the 'sole ideology' policy in 1985 which had forced political and other organizations to adopt *Pancasila* as their only ideological foundation. Although formally the PKB is a secular party, it nevertheless represents the biggest Islamic constituency because its supporters derive from the NU (with perhaps forty million supporters). Because of this Islamic character many *ulama* and *santri* gave their support to the PKB. In Jombang two influential *ulama*, *Kiai* Aziz Masyhuri and *Kiai* Makki Ma'shum were among those who pioneered the formation of the NU party. They were both involved in the national meetings preceding its establishment.[23]

The results of the 1999 election indicate the return of competition and rivalry between the Islamic and nationalist blocs. The former is represented by the PKB, the PPP, the PAN, the PBB and the PNU and received 12, 3, 2, 1 and 1 seats, respectively, while the latter is represented by the PDI-P and Golkar which received 16 and 4 seats, respectively. The competition between the NU and PNI in the 1955 election in Jombang seems now to be continued through the tacit competition between the PKB, led by NU politicians, and the PDI-P, which is led by former PNI supporters. This competition of course expresses the dynamic of local politics, and the 1999 election could be a good start for pushing the process of democratization to run at a faster pace.

Conclusions: *ulama* patronage, *aliran* and ideology

There are two significant factors that over the past decades have influenced Muslim electoral behaviour in Jombang: Islamic precepts and religious leadership. Although they are closely related, I have argued that we must make a distinction between them, since sometimes the decree of an Islamic leader ('vote for Golkar') can contradict a person's religious convictions ('religion and politics cannot be separated, therefore I must vote for an Islamic party').

Islam has long predisposed its members to hold certain political attitudes. The required attitude should be expressed by the support of Islamic parties as vehicles to realize Islamic ideals. Thus, it was expected of all Muslims that they should support the PPP during the 1987 and 1997 elections, because at the time the PPP was the only Islamic party. To support this party was seen as a religious necessity, and it was difficult for Muslims to deviate from these expectations, because Islamic values and norms constantly informed their shared experience.

In this sense Islam became the basis for Muslim electoral behaviour, and Muslim voting for the PPP was based on the fact that it was an Islamic political party. In 1985 when the PPP was forced to change its ideological base to *Pancasila* and thereafter was no longer perceived as an 'Islamic' party, many *ulama* and *santri* withdrew their support and chose to vote for

Golkar. Other factors entered into the political equation, such as intimidation, state patronage and privileged access to government power and funds, cleverly engineered by the New Order government. In 1999, Muslim support again returned to Islamic parties, but now became more differentiated.

The second factor that influenced Muslim electoral behaviour in Jombang was the *ulama*s, and especially those informal leaders of Islamic *pesantren* schools who are organized in the NU. Their political leads are copied by Muslims, so that changes in Muslim politics in Jombang can be attributed to changing political attitudes among some *ulama*s. *Ulama*s occupy highly prestigious positions. Their leadership is not confined to moulding Muslims' religiosity but also includes struggling for the interests of the *ummat* (the Islamic community) through politics. As the *ulama*s are charismatic leaders with devoted followers, their strong influence in Muslim politics depends on the fact that some of them are also politicians who occupy important positions in the party. In the NU tradition, senior *ulama* are usually placed on the advisory board whose decisions direct the party's policy at large. Because of that situation, many of them were listed as candidates for parliament. To mention a few from Jombang, *Kiai* Makki Ma'shum, the leader of the Jam'iyah Ahli Thoriqoh Al-Mu'tabarah An-Nahdliyah was elected as a PPP member of the local parliament, while *Kiai* Bisri Syansuri became a PPP member in the House of Representatives in Jakarta.

The diminishing Muslim support for the PPP in 1987 can be attributed to the changing politics of some *ulama* following the introduction of the NU's 'back to *khittah*' policy in 1985. This policy, which led to the NU's dissociation from the PPP, caused many Muslims to support other political organizations. The instruction that it was a religious obligation for Muslims to support the PPP was cancelled by the very same *ulama*s who had announced it a decade before. The diminishing Muslim support can also be attributed to the change in the PPP's base from Islam to *Pancasila* in 1985. This change in *ulama* politics gave rise to divisions in Muslim political life in Jombang, and several groups emerged with different political orientations. Thus the Jombang Muslims (most of whom were NU members) were given a chance to affiliate with any political party. This situation, I would argue, was favourable for democratization, since the Muslims were no longer restricted by a dominant religious perspective with regard to politics.

This change in the *ulama*'s political perspective, which took place in 1987, created a conducive environment for the development of a diverse political culture among Muslims in Jombang. But it also incurred internal fragmentation within the *santri* society. The change had divided the political support given by NU members, and opened new conflicts. The NU members' support has, ever since, been divided between those supporting the PPP and those supporting Golkar. Those NU *ulama* and their followers in the Jam'iyah Ahli Thoriqoh Al-Mu'tabarah An-Nahdliyah continued to support the PPP, while those in the formal NU leadership changed to

Golkar (although some people told me they felt it was sinful to affiliate with this government party because it was secular).

The success of the PKB in Jombang in 1999 was attributed to the support given by the NU *ulama* and their followers. A large number of NU *ulama*s who in previous elections had supported Golkar and the PPP now gave their support to the PKB. Unlike the PPP, which is a merger of four Islamic parties, the PKB is regarded as the NU's political vehicle, which made the NU's members feel obliged to support it. Most *ulama* supported the PKB because it was established by the NU's leading *ulama*, including the charismatic Abdurrahman Wahid, grandson of the founder of the NU and later to be elected president of Indonesia. It was this perspective that made NU members in Jombang support the PKB, although many of its politicians suggested that the PKB was an open and inclusive party, actually meaning secular and nationalistic in character. Thus the presence of the PKB changed the existing political polarization among the NU's *ulama*s and their followers as well as their support for political parties. In Jombang they were well united within the PKB.

This situation, however, has brought about new political polarizations in Jombang. The *santri*, most of whom had previously supported the PPP and Golkar, now changed their support to the PKB, while the *abangan* changed their support from Golkar to the PDI-P. These changes resulted in a decrease for Golkar, which since the 1971 general election had always received a majority of the seats in the local parliament, as well as for the PPP, which had long been regarded as representing the devout Muslim's political interests. Golkar, as a kind of middle-of-the-road, safe, catch-all party was no longer needed. The 'de-politicization' of Golkar stood in stark contrast to the radical politics of the post-Suharto era. The current political scene in Jombang indicates a return to the *aliran* structuring of politics. Muslims supported Islamic parties not because of their party programme, but because they had similar ideological orientations to their own. It was hence morally very problematical for an NU member to vote for any party (including Islamic)[24] other than the PKB and the PPP. The same tendency held true for members of Muhammadiyah who voted only for the PAN and the PBB. This ideological demarcation has also limited the non-*santri* community, which in Jombang was likely to vote for the PDI-P, the party that ideologically represents *abangan* politics. And so the rivalry continues, both nationally and locally in Jombang. But that is another story.

I have argued in this chapter that PPP votes during the New Order were to a large extent influenced primarily by voters' perceptions of Islamic ideas, and only secondarily by the influence of *ulama*s. A good Muslim will follow an *ulama*'s request and his political lead, but more important than that, he has certain basic principles that guide his actions. If a conflict arises between what Muslims believe to be the right Islamic action to take and their *ulama*'s advice, the Jombang case shows that most Muslims will choose the former. From this it follows that in order to understand Islamic voting behaviour in Jombang (and more generally in devout Islamic communities), we need to separate religious preferences from the *ulamas'* influence. It would seem that Muslims in Jombang actually decided on their own to vote for an Islamic party. When *ulamas* then asked them to support a party, they only triggered what the voters already had in mind. However, if the request of the *ulamas* contradicted their own choice of Islamic party, the Muslims would predominantly continue with their own choice. In this sense, Islamic ideas exert a stronger influence than the *ulama* in affecting political behaviour. As this study of national elections in 1987, 1997 and 1999 in Jombang demonstrates, it is Islam that influences Muslims' political behaviour, not the religious teachers.

Notes

1 The *ulama* are culturally important figures and informal leaders with supreme religious authority among Muslims (cf. Dhofier 1982). Through their charisma, imbued with religious legitimacy, the *ulama* can induce political action. They therefore play a significant role in getting support from the Muslim society since *ulama* generally are charismatic figures whose authority is greatly acknowledged.

2 A *santri* is a student at a *pesantren*. *Santri* society means the devout part of Muslim society (see Geertz 1960 and 1965).

3 *Pesantren* commonly means traditional Islamic boarding schools. It is the oldest system of Islamic learning in Indonesia. Before the modern education system was introduced by the Dutch, the *pesantren* was the only educational institution available. In present day Jombang many *pesantren* are modern in character.

4 The *tarekat* is a widespread religious movement based on Sufi mysticism. *Tarekat* is embraced widely both in Jombang and in neighbouring districts. The term '*tarekat*' derives from the Arabic *tariqa*, which literally means the mystical path to approach Allah. Members of the *tarekat* perform Islamic rituals that place them closer to Allah.

5 There are two big groups of *tarekat* in Jombang. The first is the Jam'iyah Ahli Thoriqoh Al-Mu'tabarah An-Nahdliyah, while the other is the Jam'iyah Ahli Thoriqoh Al-Mu'tabarah' Indonesia. These groups are derived from the same source and practice the same *tarekat*. Initially, it was the Jam'iyah' Ahli Thoriqoh Al-Mu'tabarah' which organized people practising *tarekat*. The division occurred when different political orientation emerged among its leaders preceding the 1977 general election, a conflict we will return to later.

6 The same decrease was experienced by the nationalist parties among which PNI received only 6.9 per cent, whereas the party had been the biggest of the four parties obtaining 22.3 per cent of the national vote in the 1955 general election.

7 As centres of learning and preaching, *pesantren* function not only to provide students with Islamic studies but they also provide political legitimacy for those members of society affiliated with them.

8 A *kiai* is a traditional *pesantren* teacher, often with great charisma and a loyal following. It is an ascribed title and many great *ulamas* have the honorific *kiai*.

9 Adlan Ali was the leader of the Jam'iyah Ahli Thoriqoh Al-Mu'tabarah An-Nahdliyah, while Syamsuri Badawi at that time was one of the PPP candidates for parliament at the national level. They gave their religious advice

(*fatwa* and *wasiat*) following NU's dissociation from PPP. Bisri Syansuri was NU's president; he delivered his *fatwa* when NU was still an important component of PPP.

10 Interview with Hafidh Ma'shum, 18 October 1997.

11 As mentioned before, the reason why many NU *ulama* and politicians in 1987 had weakened PPP was the political manoeuvres conducted by Naro, the PPP national leader, who came from a different PPP faction, to marginalize NU politicians within PPP.

12 '*Mega*' is a nickname for Megawati, while '*bintang*' (star) is the symbol of PPP. Since the change in the top leadership of the PDI from Megawati to Surjadi was followed by a conflict, its followers did not give their support to Surjadi's PDI which took part in the 1997 general election. *Mega–Bintang* was hence a political action by Megawati followers to weaken the PDI (of Surjadi), by giving their support to the PPP, at least during the campaign season.

13 According to one informant there was a group displaying a Mega–Bintang poster during PPP campaigns in Jombang. As happened in PPP campaigns in other cities, the poster gave an impression of collaboration between PPP and PDI members and supporters attending the campaign. It was, however, found that those people who displayed the Mega–Bintang poster in the PPP campaign in Jombang were in fact *santri* from a Jombang *pesantren* and PPP supporters – no PDI members, to my knowledge, joined the rally.

14 *Istighosah* is actually a religious ritual. The term is commonly used for a ritual carried out by the *tarekat*. According to an informant, this 'political *istighosah*', however, was not carried out by *tarekat* followers (some NU members were not involved in the *tarekat*).

15 Interview with Hafidh Ma'shum, 18 October 1997.

16 Interview with Sukamto, 18 June 1998.

17 This young Javanese Muslim realized in advance that his decision to vote for PPP might work against him, since the village head had threatened not to give him an ID card if he did. However, despite such pressures he still voted for PPP, even though this resulted in the cancellation of his plans to move to Kalimantan to get a job (because without an ID card he could not leave the village).

18 Interview with Zubaidi, one of the local founders of the PKB, 17 June 1998. It should be noted here that I was not present in Jombang during the election. The present post facto analysis is based on voting results and interviews with key actors. It is more sociological than political or ethnographic in character.

19 See the discussion on the influence of Islam on electoral behaviour in the previous section.

20 When the PKI was banned in 1965, its members gave their support to Golkar in the 1971 general election, not only because this political organization was a place of safety for them but also because it had been impossible for them to support Islamic parties due to their hostility toward *santri* society for ideological reasons. The same held true for PNI members after some of the national leaders were identified as socialists, a situation that made the PNI's share of votes decrease significantly nationally and locally in the 1971 general election. It is often assumed that the families of former PKI and PNI members were forced to vote for Golkar; many of them became supporters of the PDI-P in the 1999 general election.

21 We should perhaps add Golkar here, but since it is a newer 'populist' party, it did not really have a counterpart in 1955.

22 In spite of these tensions, there were no explicit clashes between the PDI-P and the PKB supporters during the 1999 campaign in Jombang. The parties' supporters always gave support to each other when they conducted campaigns preceding the election. According to one observer, every time the PKB held

a campaign there were always some people in the audience carrying the PDI-P's symbol and flag, and vice versa.

23 *Kiai* Aziz Masyhuri is the leader of *Pesantren* Denanyar whose involvement in NU has been acknowledged, while *Kiai* Makki Ma'shum is the *mursyid* (leader and teacher) of the Jam'iyah Ahli Thoriqoh Al-Mu'tabarah An-Nahdliyah. The latter told me one day that he would bring all his followers in the *tarekat* to support the PKB. However, in the end this did not happen because he finally decided to support the PPP in the 1999 election (although he had been present during the PKB's founding), thereby further dividing the Islamic vote.

24 Perhaps especially not another Islamic party, given the religious rivalry.

References

Binder, Leonard (1959) 'Islamic tradition and politics: the Kyai and the Alim'. *Comparative Studies in Society and History*, 2, 250–256.

Bruinessen, Martin van (1994) *NU: Tradisi, Relasi-Relasi Kuasa, Pencarian Wacana Baru* [NU: tradition, power relations and the search for a new discourse.] Yogyakarta: Lkis.

Dhofier, Zamakhsyari (1982) *Tradisi Pesantren: Studi tentang Pandangan Hidup Kyai* [From the 1980 PhD dissertation 'The Pesantren tradition: a study of the role of the Kyai in the maintenance of the traditional ideology of Islam in Java'], Australian National University, Canberra. Jakarta: LP3ES.

Fathoni, Khoerul and Muhammad Zen (1992) *NU Pasca Khittah: Prospek Ukhuwwah dengan Muhammadiyah* [NU after returning to Khittah: the prospects for cooperation with Muhammidiyah.] Yogyakarta: Media Widya Mandala.

Feith, Herb (1970) 'Introduction'. In Herb Feith and Lance Castle (eds), *Indonesian Political Thinking, 1945–1965*. Ithaca: Cornell University Press.

Gaffar, Afan (1992) *Javanese Voters: A Case Study of Election under a Hegemonic Party System*. Yogyakarta: Gadjah Mada University Press.

Geertz, Clifford (1959) 'The Javanese *Kyai*: the changing role of a cultural broker'. *Comparative Studies in Society and History*, 2, 250–256.

——(1960) *The Religion of Java*, Chicago: Chicago University Press.

——(1965) *The Social History of an Indonesian Town*. Cambridge, MA: MIT Press.

Haidar, M. Ali (1994) *Nahdatul Ulama dan Islam di Indonesia: Pendekatan Fikh dalam Politik* [Nahdlatul Ulama and Islam in Indonesia: an Islamic legal approach in politics.] Jakarta: Gramedia Pustaka Utama.

Hammond, J.L. (1979) *The Politics of Benevolence: Revival Religion and American Voting Behaviour*. Norwood: Ablex Publishing Corporation.

Hefner, Robert W. (1987) 'Islamizing Java? Religion and politics in rural East Java'. *The Journal of Asian Studies*, 46(3), 533–553.

Liddle, William R. (1978) *Pemilihan Umum 1977: Suatu Tinjauan Umum* [The 1977 general election: a general study.] Yogyakarta: Kelompok Study Batas Kota.

Mansurnoor, I. Arifin (1990) *Islam in an Indonesian World: Ulama of Madura*. Yogyakarta: Gadjah Mada University Press.

Panitia Pemilihan Daerah Tingkat II Jombang [Regional Election Commission, Jombang] (1977) 'Daftar Hasil Penghitungan Suara di Kabupaten Jombang' [The result of the vote count in Jombang.] Jombang.

——(1987) 'Catatan Penghitungan Suara Daerah Tingkat II dalam Pemilu 1987' [Regional votes in the 1987 general elections]. Jombang.

——(1992) 'Catatan Penghitungan Suara Daerah Tingkat II dalam Pemilu 1992' [Regional votes in the 1992 general elections]. Jombang.

Partai Persatuan Pembangunan (Pimpinan Cabang Jombang) [Jombang Branch of Partai Persatuan Pembangunan] (1982a) 'Daftar Perbandingan Hasil Pemilu 1971, 1977 dan Pemilu 1982' [Comparing the results of the general elections in 1971, 1977 and 1982.] Jombang.

——(1982b) 'Hasil Penghitungan Suara Pemilu 1982 di Kabupaten Jombang' [The result of the vote count of 1982 in Jombang.], Tanggal 10 Mei 1982. Jombang.

Ramage, Douglas E. (1995) *Politics in Indonesia. Democracy, Islam and the Ideology of Tolerance*. London: Routledge.

Samson, Allan A. (1978) 'Conception of politics, power, and ideology in contemporary Indonesian Islam'. In Karl D. Jackson and Lucian Pye (eds), *Political Power and Communication in Indonesia*. Berkeley: University of California Press.

Turmudi, Endang (1995) 'Ulama dan Politik: Suatu Telaah atas Perubahan Politik Masyarakat Pedesaan' [Ulama and politics: a study of rural political change.] Paper presented in a seminar organized by the Indonesian Student Association and the Indonesian Embassy, Canberra, 20 May.

——(1997) 'The Tarekat Qadiriyah Wa Naqsyabandiyah in East Java and Islamic politics in Indonesia'. *Southeast Asian Journal of Social Science*, 26(2), 65–84.

——(1998) 'Demokratisasi dan Polarisasi politik Lokal: Kasus Jombang, Jawa Timur' [Democratization and the polarization of local politics: a case study of Jombang, East Java.] Paper presented at the seminar held at Centre for Social and Cultural Studies, Indonesian Institute of Sciences, Jakarta, 1 July.

Ward, Ken. E. (1974) *The 1971 Election in Indonesia: An East Java Case Study*. Monash Paper on Southeast Asia No. 2. Melbourne: Centre of Southeast Asian Studies, Monash University.

4

POLITICIZATION OF RELIGION AND THE FAILURE OF ISLAMIC PARTIES IN THE 1999 GENERAL ELECTION

Syamsuddin Haris

When the democratic elections were held in Indonesia 1999, the Islamic parties had great hopes. After so many years of forced coercion into the government-controlled PPP, religious leaders and associations were finally free to organize themselves in their own way. No more would the New Order straightjacket limit the imagination of voters. Islamic leaders were confident that they would be able to garner an absolute majority of the votes. The PPP leaders, for example, were fully convinced that they would be able to maintain the percentage of votes (22 per cent) that they had amassed in the 1997 election, while the leaders of another Islamic party, the Justice Party, were as confident that their party would be able to win 10–15 per cent of the ballots in the 1999 election. There were seventeen exclusively Islamic parties competing in the election, in addition to several other parties with exclusive Islamic leadership but secular-nationalist platforms. Given this pre-election enthusiasm and confidence, it came as quite a shock to Muslim leaders when the seventeen parties together only managed to secure some 17 per cent of the votes. Only a single party (PPP) was able to get more than 2 per cent of the votes, and they still fared far below their result in 1997 – the remaining sixteen parties receiving less than 7 per cent together.

The poor performance of the majority of Islamic parties came as a big surprise to many, and most of all to the parties themselves. The small percentage that these parties managed to secure represented a devastating failure for the Islamic leaders, who had been very hopeful that the reform era would bring a momentum for the revival of Islamic parties after they had been politically marginalized by the New Order for more than thirty years. In this chapter I shall analyse the reasons for the failure of the explicitly Islamic parties to gain massive support from Muslims. I will seek to identify the various historical, internal and external factors that could be responsible for the poor performance of the Islamic parties.

For analytical purposes, in this chapter the parties considered Islamic are those that explicitly contain 'Islam' in their names, philosophies or symbols. Based on this understanding, the seventeen political parties in 1999 were the *Partai Persatuan Pembangunan* (PPP), the *Partai Bulan Bintang* (PBB), *Partai Keadilan dan Persatuan* (PK), the *Partai Sarekat Islam Indonesia* (PSII), the *Partai Sarekat Islam Indonesia-1905* (PSII-1905), the *Partai Masyumi Baru*, the *Partai Politik Islam Indonesia 'Masyumi'*, the *Partai Persatuan* (PP), the *Partai Ummat Islam* (PUI), the *Partai Indonesia Baru* (PIB), *KAMI*, the *Partai Nahdlatul Umat* (PNU), the *Partai Solidaritas Uni Nasional Indonesia* (SUNI), the *Partai Abul Yatama* (PUY), the *Partai Islam Demokrat* (PID), the *Partai Kebangkitan Umat* (PKU) and the *Partai Umat Muslimin Indonesia* (PUMI). Neither the *Partai Amanat Nasional* (PAN) nor the *Partai Kebangkitan Bangsa* (PKB) are included here, since they both have a secular platform (although they were headed by and recruited most of their votes from the modernist Muhammadiyah and the traditionalistic Nahdlatul Ulama (NU) mass-based organizations, respectively). I am aware that some readers would also want to include these parties in the Islamic fold. They did indeed compete for Islamic voters, but since they had a secular and plural base and did not exclusively reach out to the Muslim community, I have chosen to keep them outside the present analysis (but even if we do include the PAN and the PKB, the nineteen parties only received some 37.4 per cent of the votes, in a country where 90 per cent of the population is Muslim).

Except for the PPP, which managed to rise to the 'big-five' league, all other exclusively Islamic political parties failed to obtain a significant number of votes. The *Partai Bulan Bintang* (PBB), considered the descendant of the defunct *Partai Masyumi*, managed to secure 1.9 per cent of the ballot, while the *Partai Keadilan dan Persatuan* (PK) won 1.4 per cent. Except for these three parties, the remaining Islamic parties were all 'decimal parties', that is, they were unable to secure even 1 per cent of the votes (see Table 4.1). Several other Islam-orientated parties, such as the *Partai Nahdlatul Ummah* (PNU), the *Partai Persatuan* (PP), the *Partai Sarekat Islam Indonesia* (PSII), the *Partai Politik Islam Masyumi* (Masyumi) and the *Partai Kebangkitan Umat* (PKU) managed to secure a single seat in the national parliament, the House of Representatives. The remaining Islamic parties failed to get even a single seat.

This was the second multi-party election in Indonesia. The first was held in 1955 and at that time the Islam-based political parties fared better, even though they still failed to win an absolute majority. Then, the accumulated vote of the Islamic parties was around 43 per cent.[1] Thus, even in 1955 many of the Muslim voters gave their votes to non-Islamic parties, both the nationalist-secular parties such as the *Partai Nasional Indonesia* (PNI) and those with a socialist orientation such as the *Partai Komunis Indonesia*

Table 4.1 Results of 1999 general election for Islamic parties

Party	No. of votes	Percentage	No. of seats
PPP	11,329,900	10.72	58
PBB	2,049,700	1.94	13
PK	1,436,560	1.36	7
PNU	679,179	0.64	5
PP	551,028	0.52	1
PPII Masyumi	456,718	0.43	1
PSII	375,920	0.36	1
PKU	300,064	0.28	1
KAMI	289,489	0.27	0
PUI	269,309	0.25	0
PAY	213,979	0.20	0
PIB	192,712	0.18	0
SUNI	180,167	0.17	0
PSII 1905	152,820	0.14	0
Masyumi Baru	152,589	0.14	0
PID	62,901	0.06	0
PUMI	49,839	0.05	0

(PKI) and the *Partai Sosialis Indonesia* (PSI). The failure of the Islamic parties to gain a majority could also be observed during the first general election under the New Order in 1971. This election can be seen as a limited multi-party election, and it is generally seen as plagued by fraud, rigging and intimidations. At that time, the participating Islamic parties – the NU, Parmusi, PSII and Perti – managed to accumulate around 27 per cent of the vote (Samsuddin 1972).

When the four Islamic parties that participated in the 1971 election two years later were forced by the government to go through a political restructuring programme and merge into the *Partai Persatuan Pembangunan* (PPP), there was hope among the Islamic politicians that a major Islamic political force would emerge in the country. However, since general elections during the New Order period were designed to allow the government party Golkar to come out as the sole winner, the PPP, which used Islam as its banner, only managed to win 29.3 per cent of the votes in the first election after the fusion (1977). In that election, the majority of voters gave their votes – or were told to give their votes – to the pragmatic and secular-orientated Golkar. In the subsequent New Order elections, especially after *Pancasila* had been officially adopted as the uniform philosophy for all parties in 1985, the PPP's performance declined to 27.8 per cent in 1982 and then to a mere 16 per cent in 1987. It then rose slightly to 17 per cent in 1992 and to 22 per cent in 1997. In Chapter 2 of this volume, I described in some more detail how the political system in Indonesia was manipulated so as to make it virtually impossible for any party other than Golkar to win the elections. I shall return to some of these factors later, since they are related specifically to the Islamic political forces.

The failure of Islamic parties: internal factors

Let us now turn our attention to the 1999 election. Internally, there were three main issues that Islamic leaders put forward in relation to the interaction between their religion and the state. First, there was the historical aspect, which stemmed from a conviction (based on real experience) that Muslims had made a dominant contribution to the formation of the Indonesian identity, its proclamation as a nation-state, and the efforts to defend it as a free country during the 1945–49 revolution. Second, there was the theological issue, the belief that Islam was not a mere religion in the narrow sense but a set of teachings that should govern all aspects of human life, including the state and politics. However, on a broader level and no matter how much Muslim leaders claim that Islam is a total system, nowhere can any empirical evidence be found to support this claim. No country in the modern era, including those that are commonly regarded as 'Islamic states', has succeeded in implementing such a totality in its political reality. The Muslim communities in a number of Islamic states in the Middle East, for instance, have long sought a proper way out of the chains imposed by their monarchic Islamic systems, which are undemocratic and not accommodating towards the political aspirations of their citizens. Third, there was the sociological reality that Islam is the religion adopted by the majority of the Indonesian people, and that therefore this social majority should also become the political majority. Based on this belief, the New Order political format failed (or did not even try) in making a political majority out of the social majority and in making Islam the determining factor that influences political processes.

These three big issues seem to influence the outlook and the perception of the Muslim leaders regarding the 'normative position' of Islam and the Muslim community in the nation-state. It is the struggle to secure this 'normative position' that has characterized the rise and fall of the interactions between Islam and the state since the 1945 proclamation of independence. During the parliamentary era the Islamic parties stood opposed both to the rightist secular force of the PNI and the leftist secular force of the PKI, and later during the New Order era they were pitted against the opportunistic coalition consisting of Golkar, the military and the government bureaucracy. The rise and fall of Islamic parties, both during the parliamentary democratic era, at the beginning of the New Order era, during the New Order era, and even in the post-New Order era, can be viewed in terms of a continued pursuit of this 'normative position'. Thus, the reason that the Islamic leaders re-created all the Islamic political parties after the fall of the New Order seems to be what they referred to as the 'ideals of the Islamic struggle' or the 'struggle of the Muslim community' to realize their normative position.

However, it is crucial to remember that what is referred to as 'Islamic struggle' or the 'interests of Islam' are in themselves highly biased concepts, and they were therefore interpreted differently, even often distorted, by various Islamic leaders. In reality, the concept of the 'interest of Islam' was understood in its narrow sense to mean an opportunity for the Islamic leaders to hold public positions, both inside and outside the government – including in legislative institutions, such as the House of Representatives (DPR) and the provincial and district parliaments (DPRD). Amien Rais, Muhammadiyah's leader who later became a leading reform figure and chairman of the PAN, for example, said that the quest for political representation was a serious matter that had to be fought for by the Indonesian Muslims. According to Amien Rais, political representation should be reflected in a power structure dominated by the Islamic community (quoted in Arief Afandi 1996). Frequently, there was no question as to whether such a political representation might be sufficient to guarantee an improved position for Islam and the Muslims in the political constellations. This question would become even more relevant should the opportunity to snatch political positions be obtained through 'non-Islamic' ways or through an application of the principle that the 'end justifies the means', as it was used by Suharto in garnering support from the Islamic community, through establishing the ICMI (Association of Muslim Intellectuals) and forcing compliance in the early 1990s.

Therefore, if the Islamic leaders set out to form Islamic political parties in order to resolve the three issues mentioned here, I would argue that they were in fact trying to set up a new trap for their followers. This is so because the Indonesian Islamic community is so diverse. Some are 'nominal' Muslims, while others may be characterized as doctrinal followers. The nominal Muslims, also known as *abangan* in Clifford Geertz's categorization, tend to cast their votes for political parties with a secular orientation. Not only that, among the more doctrinal Muslims there are widely varying political orientations. Deliar Noer (1988), for example, grouped the political orientations of the doctrinal Muslims into four categories: (1) a group with a strong commitment to Islam – although it is not clear what is meant by an 'Islamic commitment'; (2) a group that is willing to cooperate with the authorities; (3) a group that sees Islam merely as a 'teaching for society', and finally (4) Muslims who refuse to link Islam with politics. Based on his study of the general elections in the Probanti region of Yogyakarta, Afan Gaffar (1992: 120–131) found that there are also different levels of devoutness amongst the *santri*s (students at traditional Muslim schools), ranging from those who do not regularly practice their religious rituals to those who most consistently and piously fulfil God's commands. Furthermore, he claims that the lower the level of devoutness of the *santris*, the smaller the probability that they will vote for an Islamic party. All this naturally leads us to the question: how will the Islamic parties be able to amass significant support when the political orientations of the Muslims themselves are so fragmented? The answer in 1999 was to build a wide array of political parties – one for every taste, if you wish.

Thus, the failure of the Islamic parties from one election to the next, including 1999, was understandable if one takes into account this fragmentation of the political orientations of the Muslims. The failure of these parties actually reflects the misconception among the Islamic leaders that they are representing the Muslims and that they have a complete understanding of Muslim aspirations, and consequently the right to act on their behalf.

The failure of Islamic parties: external factors

Aside from the internal factors, the failure of the Indonesian Islamic parties was also caused by various external considerations. These include the changes – or at least the shifts – in the political orientation of the Muslims that were the results of the socio-economic transformation that took place over more than three decades under the New Order government. On the one hand, the New Order economic development, which focused on growth and expansion, resulted in severe economic gaps. On the other hand, it also created a great opportunity for many Muslims to achieve social mobility.

Social mobility among the Islamic community, particularly among the middle class, could have meant great news to the Muslims in Indonesia in general. However, their social mobility did not imply any strong orientation towards Islamic politics. On the contrary, the 'new Islamic middle class' strengthened the position of the state vis-à-vis the aspirations of other Islamic communities. In other words, the expanded socio-economic opportunities that became available to the upwardly mobile Muslims seemed merely to give the government a justification to claim that the New Order state was concerned with the progress of Islam in Indonesia.

The north coast of Java is an exception to this. In this area, the middle class tended to strengthen the position of the community of Islamic entrepreneurs, a group who formed the basis for the PPP in the area. The PPP was regarded as an alternative political party for delaying the secularization and capitalization of the state, which was seen as taking place through a coalition between the opportunistic Golkar, Chinese businessmen and local administrations. This was the reason why the PPP won a majority of votes during the 1997 election in several districts (see Turmudi's case study of Jombang in the present volume).

In the meantime, a reorientation of views took place among Islamic intellectuals and scholars as they examined the relationship between Islam and the state in particular and between Islam and politics in general. Regardless of the fact that Islam was regarded as a 'total discipline', a group of Islamic scholars led by Nurcholish Madjid argued that this totality did not have to be achieved through formal means, such as an 'Islamic state' or an 'Islamic political party'. This reorientation of the thinking was reflected in new slogans such as 'Islam yes, Islamic political party, no', slogans which have been popular since the 1970s (see for instance Madjid 1987). Against this background it was not surprising that a large number of the young and educated who came from more radical Islamic student movements had no aspirations to join Islamic parties. On the contrary, they were more interested in securing positions on the executive committee of Golkar, the ruling party, by which they would have the opportunity to become favoured candidates for legislative positions. Others from these groups joined the bureaucracy and enjoyed political and economic benefits from the authoritarian and corrupt political format built and maintained by the New Order regime.

A shift in orientation was also observed among traditional Muslims belonging to the NU. In the early 1980s it became clear that NU politicians had failed in their ambition to dominate the leadership of the PPP, a fact which prompted NU leaders to review their political involvement in this party. The turning point occurred in 1984, when the NU's congregation at the twenty-seventh NU *Muktamar* (Congress) in Situbondo, East Java declared a return to the organization's *khittah* (foundation) of 1926 (Kuntowijojo 1997: 199–200; see also Turmudi in this volume). The NU withdrew from practical politics overnight, and the PPP lost its major political support group.

Aside from the issue of political secularization in general, the leaders who formed the new Islamic political parties in 1999 failed to notice the increasing 'Islamization' among secular political parties and the flexibility shown by the New Order state in accommodating the aspirations and the interests of the Islamic communities. Regardless of the widely held opinion that Golkar is a direct continuation of the authoritarian New Order, one cannot deny the fact that Islamization has also taken place within this political group, albeit perhaps superficially. The formation of various *Lembaga Dakwah* (Islamic missionary institutions), such as Majelis Dakwah Islamiyah (MDI), is a good example of these efforts. It seems that the secular parties had recognized that the majority of Indonesian Muslims were to be found among those who were called 'nominal Muslims', Muslims who were not completely practising the teachings of Islam, or among the 'secular Muslims', those who reject any form of political formalism of Islam. Therefore it was not surprising to see that the largest support for secular parties, both the PNI (1955) and Golkar (1971–97) came from the Muslim community. During the last election, the one held in 1999, main support for the PDI-P also came from the Muslim community, although instances of non-Muslim legislature candidates had the opportunity to deflate the support to a certain extent.

On the other hand, although the New Order state did not allow any scope for the resurrection of 'political Islam', in almost all fields outside the political arena the Suharto regime did its best to accommodate the interests of the Islamic communities, especially in the context of what Kuntowijoyo calls '*Islam ibadah*', or 'ritual Islam' (Kuntowijojo 1997). In the field of education, for example, the New Order state built a large number of religious schools from the elementary level (*madrasah ibtidaiyah*) up to the tertiary level (*Institute Agama Islam Indonesia*, IAIN or Indonesian Institute for the Islamic Religion). In addition, there were missionary and social activities that were embodied in the formation of *Majelis Ulama Indonesia* (MUI, or 'Indonesian Council of Ulamas') and celebration of Islamic holidays in the State Palace or at the *Istiqlal* State Mosque. There were also activities sponsored by *Yayasan Amal Bhakti Muslimin Pancasila*, or The Pancasila Muslim Foundation for Charity, through which active subsidy of the construction of various places of worships for Muslims across Indonesia took place. Similar efforts were made by the New Order regime in passing the Law of Religious Court (1989) and in the Presidential Instruction on the Compilation of Islamic Laws (1991). President Suharto himself undertook the pilgrimage to Mecca, the *haj*, and then took the first name Mohammed. Many critics have claimed that these efforts were made by the New Order regime simply to embrace (or co-opt) the Muslim communities in Indonesia. Nonetheless, these efforts have also been responsible for changing the way many Muslims view Islamic political parties in particular and political Islam in general.[2]

This list of external factors not only led to a reorientation of the Muslims' views on the relationship between their religion and the state, but also had an impact on the way they regarded the Islamic parties. A part of the Muslim community no longer thought of the Islamic parties as a forum that would represent their political aspirations and interests. This tendency to disregard the Islamic political parties became even stronger when it became clear that the number of such parties was so large, while at the same time each leader kept claiming that his particular political party was the most 'Islamic' of all.

Politicization of religion and political opportunism

In addition to the factors mentioned here, there has for some time been a very strong tendency among the leaders of Islamic organizations and the politicians from the Islamic parties to claim that their presence in the midst of the national issues implied a representation of the Muslims' aspirations. Muslim leaders (the *ulamas* and the *kiais*) often position themselves as the legitimate interpreters of the reality experienced by their followers. However, ever so often they would be trapped by the politicization of religion or religious missions, especially when facing the momentum of a political event such as a general election. In the 1999 election in Pekalongan, Central Java, for example, the teachers of Islam who all belonged to the traditionalistic NU but were supporters of different parties, namely the PKB and the PPP, each used religious messages to justify the presence of, and to underscore the merits of, their respective parties. This led to a number of mass clashes between the groups belonging to either of the two parties. All of the Islamic leaders claimed that they were acting on behalf of their community, which as a matter of fact they could not do since the concept of an Islamic community presumes a cohesive, homogeneous and unified Islamic community. The objective reality is that the Indonesian Muslim community is very diverse in terms of culture, ideology and political orientation.

This tendency to politicize religious teachings and messages is by no means a new phenomenon. During the New Order era, ironically, the politicization of Islam was conducted not only by secular political parties such as Golkar and the PDI, but by the Islamic parties themselves. Before the 1977 election, for example, KH Bisri Sjamsuri, *Rois Aan* (chairman) of the *Syariah Pengurus Besar Nahdlatul Ulama* (the NU's central board) issued a *fatwa* or 'ruling' that voting for the PPP was an obligation for every Muslim, male or female (Dhakidae 1981 and Turmudi in the present volume). However, when the elite within NU, including the religious teachers, were pushed out of the list of PPP candidates for the parliament drawn up before the 1987 election, the ruling (which when issued was claimed to be based on a religious interpretation) was modified to read 'NU members and followers are not obligated to vote for the PPP. They are allowed to vote for Golkar and the PDI' (quoted in Syamsuddin Haris 1991). This latest ruling was also issued by the *Rois Aan* of the NU's central board, a position then held by KH Achmad Siddiq.

At the level of practical politics, the reality posed a threat to the Islamic parties since all claims on behalf of the interests of Islam would eventually result in a politicization of the religion. This means that there would be a strong tendency to reduce what would actually be 'Islamic objectives' to the interests of certain groups, parties and communities. This would lead to an abuse of the messages of God or the Prophet in order to justify the positions and views held by certain political parties. In the end, narrow-minded and parochial loyalty to a particular political party would take the place of the religion's universal values, which would actually bridge these interpretative discrepancies. The issue of a female candidate for president in 1999 can be seen as the most relevant example in this regard. Supporters and admirers of Megawati Sukarnoputri cited religious rules to convince the public that Islam basically did not question the gender of a candidate suited to become its national leader (see for instance the polemic in the daily *Kompas*, 20 August 1999). On the other hand, those who were against Megawati also cited God's sayings to support their belief that Islam would never give approval to a female leader. The debates in *pesantrens* and the media were heated.

In the end this politicization was the cause of physical clashes between fellow NU members – the PKB and the PPP – in Pekalongan and Jepara in the period leading up to the 1999 election campaign period as well as during the campaign itself. The two groups called each other 'infidels', attacked each other, burnt houses belonging to members of the other group and caused severe physical and psychological damage among themselves. The religious leaders who supported the PPP claimed that their political party was 'more Islamic' than the PKB. The same claim was made by the leaders from the PKB front. During this period many *santris* left their boarding schools because the leader and owner of the school had a different political aspiration.[3]

On a national level, this tendency among the supporters, as well as the elites, of the various Islamic parties to attack one another minimized the possibility of forging alliances between the parties. The politicization of the religion caused disappointment among the Muslims, whose interests these parties were supposed to defend. At the same time it was still fresh in the public's memory how many of the Islamic leaders had used their position as public figures to support the New Order regime. An example of this can be seen, for instance, in how the *ulama*s of the *Majelis Ulama Indonesia*, (MUI, or Indonesian Council of Ulamas) during the Suharto period frequented the palace of the regime.[4] Consider also the actions of the leaders of the radical-fundamental *Komite Solidaritas untuk Dunia Islam* (KISDI, or the Solidarity Committee of the Islamic World),[5] who eloquently used Islam to justify the amiable relationship between its elites and the corrupt New Order regime, which, as I tried to argue earlier, was seen by some Islamic leaders as anti-Islam. As a result of the entrapment of the religious politicization, there was hardly any particular issue or programme specifically proposed by the Islamic parties during the campaign. Among the Islamic parties themselves, there was almost nothing that could help the public distinguish one party from another. In general, the political programmes promoted by the Islamic parties in 1999 did not differ from the programmes presented by the secular parties, the PKB and the PAN, which were parties with Islamic masses as their basis but which refused to use Islamic symbols. Even the programmes of the non-Islamic parties, such as the PDI-P and Golkar, did not differ significantly from those of the Islamic parties. Therefore, it came as no surprise that some Islamic parties such as the KAMI, the PUI, the PAY, the PIB, the SUNI, the PSSI 1905, Masyumi Baru, the PID and the PUMI (See Table 4.1) failed to garner a sufficient number of votes to secure even a single seat in the DPR. Often, the masses that attended their campaigns were more interested in viewing the musical concerts than listening to the programmes being proclaimed by the campaign masters of the political parties (in fairness, this was also true of most non-Islamic parties as well. See the chapters by Cederroth and Antlöv in this volume).

The failure of the Islamic parties can also be perceived as a reflection of a widespread political opportunism characteristic of the New Order legacy among those who claimed to be Islamic figures or 'leaders'. This was noticeable not only among urban and modernist Muslim communities but also among traditional Muslims. Among the modernists, former chairmen of *Himpunan Mahasiswa Islam* (HMI, or the Islamic Students' Association) seemed to be competing with one another to form Islamic parties, as reflected in the appearance of the PUI (led by Deliar Noer), Masyumi Baru (led by Ridwan Saidi), and the PPIIM (led by Abdullah Hehamahua).[6] At the same time, among the *nadliyins* (radical religious leaders), other independent NU parties were established. The PKB, which was regarded as the 'official party' of the NU, was formed around a group with a nationalist-religious orientation which refused to establish a directly Islamic party. Several other competing NU parties were, however, established by radical adherents, including the PKU, the PNU and Partai SUNI. The NU's vote was thus split between at least five parties.

The idea that was behind the multiplication of political parties in 1999 was that every citizen had the right to establish a political party based on the fundamental principles that he or she chose. At the Justice Department 141 parties were formally registered, out of which forty-eight were found to be eligible to contest the election. However, the establishment of so many Islamic parties, a total of seventeen contesting the election, became futile since, as we have seen, there was no principle that could distinguish the programmes of one Islamic party from another. Whether we like it or not, it seems probable that the establishment of such a mass of Islamic parties was the result of a very strong appetite for power among the various Islamic leaders. They were trapped in the euphoria of reform that provided such broad political opportunities, but failed to take into account the mass base of support that they needed in order to implement their policies. They also failed to anticipate the changes that the Muslims were going through, both internally and externally, as a result of the thirty-two years of social–economic transformation under the New Order, including globalization and Westernization – and interestingly, a stronger solidarity with western Asia.

This tendency among the Islamic political elite towards political opportunism and orientation toward power is not a new phenomenon. In fact it can be seen as a product of the policy of corporatization and political co-optation that characterized the Suharto regime. During the New Order, Islamic leaders from almost all levels seemed to compete with each other to become instruments of the state authority as a means to ensure the status quo and access funds and power. Ironically, after Suharto stepped down, there were still a lot of Islamic leaders who did not have the ability and the willingness to keep a distance from the ruling power. The Habibie regime, which was in fact, as I have argued extensively elsewhere, only an extension of the Suharto regime, was regarded and treated by these leaders as if it were a representation of Islam. Consequently, some elements of Islam were trapped as 'instruments of the authority' in order to defend the status quo. It appeared as though Habibie's transitional government had really cared for Islamic aspirations, while, as a matter of fact, during his presidential period Habibie turned a blind eye to the killings that the military was committing in Aceh, a region where the majority of the people are faithful Muslims. The tendency to serve as tools for those in power was also evident when groups of Muslims were mobilizing the masses in the name of PAMSWAKARSA (paramilitary civilian guards, often including hooligan elements), groups that were designed to hold back student demonstrators.

Polarization of politics and leadership

A polarization of the political orientation among the Muslim communities was already evident during the formation period of Indonesian nationalism, decades before Indonesia became independent. Despite efforts to unite the various Islamic movements under the Majelis Islam A'la Indonesia (MIAI) during the Japanese occupation, as well as within Masyumi after independence at the end of 1945, unity lasted for only a very short time. In 1947, Sarekat Islam withdrew from Masyumi, followed by NU in 1952. During the New Order era, as discussed earlier, NU exited from the PPP and declared a return to its 1926 *khittah*. This constantly recurring phenomenon of divisions among the Islamic parties not only exposed the sharp differences in political orientation among the elites who wore the Islamic banners, it also revealed leadership conflicts among the Islamic figures themselves.

The tendency among Islamic leaders with different cultural backgrounds to maintain a constantly suspicious attitude towards each other seems to have been an important factor responsible for the political and leadership polarization of the Islamic parties. Despite the general agreement that the Muslims were politically marginalized during the New Order regime, this low level of consensus among the parties with Islamic claims can also be used as a parameter to indicate the fragile cohesiveness among the Islamic leaders. There had hardly been any serious efforts to build political cooperation, not to speak of an alliance with an inclusive orientation among the Islamic elites and Islamic politicians, whether before or after the 1999 general election. After the election, an agreement to combine the remainder of the votes (*stembus accord*) was reached among eight of the Islamic political parties. However, this was not accepted by the Indonesian Election Committee (PPI) as a basis for counting the remaining votes, because there was insufficient support from the other Islamic parties who did not give their approval during the voting at the Commission for General Election (KPU). Meanwhile, the idea of forming an 'Islamic Fraction' in the DPR, which had emerged among some of the elites of the Islamic parties, was aborted even before it was explored because of deep-rooted distrust among the Islamic leaders themselves.

As a preliminary conclusion, I would argue that the decline in the total number of votes received by the Islamic parties from 43.9 per cent in 1955 to 29.3 per cent in 1977 and 17.7 per cent in 1999 is a consequence of the impact of the above-mentioned sharp political and leadership polarization among the Muslim communities in Indonesia. Even if the PAN (7.1 per cent) and the PKB (12.6 per cent) had been considered and categorized as Islamic parties – or at least as 'secular' Islamic parties, since their voters mainly consisted of Muhammadiyah and NU supporters, the total number of votes obtained by all Islamic parties would still have been smaller than what it had been in the 1955 election. Altogether, with the PAN and the PKB included, all the Islamic-oriented parties received 37.4 per cent of the votes, a figure which was much lower than the total number of votes that the then Islamic parties – Masyumi, the NU, the PSII, Perti and a number of smaller parties – received in the 1955 election.

The phenomenon that was observed among the modernist Islamic parties could perhaps assist in outlining clearly the sharp political polarization between Islamic leaders of various beliefs and orientations. Islamic parties, such as the PBB, Masyumi Baru, the PPII Masyumi and the PUI, for example, had no choice but to compete for the same mass base, which consisted of supporters, partisans, members and extended families of Muhammadiyah. Meanwhile, unofficially, the PAN, which had refused to call itself an Islamic party, shared an identity with Muhammadiyah since it was founded by Amien Rais, Muhammadiyah's chairman. In addition, Muhammadiyah and 'urban Muslims' in general were also the resource for supporters of the PPP, one of the two officially permitted New Order political parties, that after the demise of the New Order returned to its foundation as an Islamic party and again chose the *Ka'bah* as its party emblem (previously it had not been allowed to have Islamic symbols, since all social organizations during the New Order had to be based on *Pancasila*, which was secular in character. This restriction was lifted in 1998).

Islam, politics and the New Indonesia

After the 1999 election, and ahead of 2004, Islamic leaders should perhaps allow themselves some time for evaluation and introspection by pondering the question of what actually was wrong with their understanding of the relationship between Islam and the state. Why has Indonesian Islam, which is a social majority, never succeeded in also becoming a political majority? In other words, why did the majority of Muslims decide to give their support to secular political parties rather than to the Islamic parties? One immediate result of this is that in 1999 and 2000, fundamentalist Muslim organizations have been forced to operate outside of the parliamentary system, taking quite radical steps with street actions, demonstrations and extreme verbal attacks on the government.

The non-performance of the Islamic parties in the 1999 election should have been predicted by the Islamic political elites who chose to form their own political parties rather than to become part of a larger political grouping. The bitter experience that they had during the 1955 election and the political secularization that the Muslim communities have gone through as a direct impact of the social, economic and political restructuring during the New Order era seems to have eluded the founders of these new Islamic parties. All of these changes were also exacerbated by a major shift in the Muslim communities' political orientation from 'political Islam' to 'secular Islam', a shift which had been underway since the 1970s (Ali and Effendi 1986; and Effendi 1998). This shift in orientation was reflected, among other things, in the ineffectiveness of the official announcements made by MUI leaders and the Central Committee of Muhammadiyah urging Muslims to vote only for Muslim legislature candidates – a call which was actually an effort to reduce support for the PDI-P. It was also reflected in the victory of the PDI-P in pockets of Muslim communities, despite the fact that a majority of the party's legislature candidates were non-Muslims.

In light of these facts, are the Islamic political parties still relevant? I would argue that any party, regardless of its ideology, as long as it is founded to provide a forum wherein the members can articulate and aggregate their interests, can be relevant. In the Indonesian context, what matters is not the use of the philosophies, labels and symbols of Islam. Furthermore, if the Islamic political parties wish to modify the foundation of the state, there will be no problem as long as any change meets the objective needs of a majority of the Indonesian people.

Therefore, the problem lies more in the misguided outlook and self-perception among the Islamic leaders concerning the relationship between Islam and the state on the one hand and the relationship between Islamic leaders and their followers on the other. These attitudes eventually resulted in the choice of wrong solutions, as reflected in the formation of such a large number of Islamic political parties with hardly any differences in vision, programmes and political platforms.

Some of the Islamic parties were born out of political prejudice and distrusts that were frequently not entirely correct. Others were established on the basis that their leaders could use them to obtain new sources of income, and thus they were orientated more towards worldly possessions and positions. Yet other Islamic parties were established without any clear objectives; they were born out of a political euphoria that empowered previously timid Islamic leaders who happened to be alienated in the midst of the confusing reform movements.

This reality depicts clearly that the era has ended in which the Islamic leaders could order their followers around. It is time for them to do some introspection and began to see that the Muslim communities, which constitute the majority of the Indonesian nation, not only have highly diverse political aspirations and orientations, but may also have views, discourses and self-perceptions that may not be congruent with those who claim themselves to be 'Islamic leaders'.

The inclusive spirit and diverse political aspirations of the Islamic communities by no means imply a disaster for the future of Islam or, for that matter, for the future of Indonesia. On the contrary, the political pluralism of the Muslims should be regarded as a blessing to this nation as it seeks to find a New Indonesia which is more open, tolerant, just, able to respect differences, civilized and democratic. Without such an attitude, Islam and the Muslims will continue to be treated as tools and even commodities that those who often brag and call themselves 'leaders of Islam' will use in their political struggles. An honest, clear and imaginative reaction to the new challenges can serve as the basis for a fresh harmony in the relationship between Islam and the state in a New Indonesia – something that Muslims and secularists alike have been yearning for.

Notes

1 Islamic political parties in the 1955 election were NU (16.9 per cent) Masyumi (20.9 per cent), PSII (2.9 per cent), Perti (1.3 per cent), PPTI (0.2 per cent), and Akui (0.2 per cent). For details on the result of the 1955 election, see, among others, Feith 1957.
2 For the politics of accommodation adopted by the New Order regime in handling the forces of Islam, see Bachtiar Effendi 1998.
3 It is interesting to note that one of the *kiais* in Pekalongan accused Golkar and the Habibie group (Habibie was still the president at that time) of being the provocators behind the mass clashes between the PKB and the PPP. See Sri Januarti, 2000.
4 Consider the initiative of the *ulamas* in collecting gold to help bail Indonesia out of the economic crises of 1997 and 1998 that can be perceived as an effort to provide justification for the corrupt power of Suharto, himself the source of the crisis.
5 Observe the actions of Soemargono, KISDI's chairman, who would readily speak on behalf of Islam in defending the actions of the repressive power of the state. This eventually affected the image of Islam and the Muslims themselves.
6 At the same time, Akbar Tanjung, also a former HMI chairman, was now leading the Golkar party – a party with a relatively secular orientation – as its chairman.

References

Ali, Fachry and Bahtiar Effendi (1986) *Merambah Jalan Baru Islam: Rekonstruksi Pemikiran Islam Masa Orde Baru* [Looking for a new Islamic path: reconstruction of Islamic thoughts during the New Order.] Bandung: Mizan.

Arief Afandi (ed.) (1996) *Demokrasi Atas Bawah: Polemik Strategi Perjuangan Umat Model Gus Dur dan Amien Rais* [Democratization from above and below: the polemic over Gus Dur and Amien Rais's strategy to build Islamic constituencies.] Yogyakarta: Pustaka Pelajar.

Dhakidae, Daniel (1981) 'Pemilihan Umum di Indonesia: Saksi Pasang Naik dan Surut Partai Politik' [General elections in Indonesia: witnessing the waves of political parties.] *Prisma*, no. 9.

Effendi, Bachtiar (1998) *Islam dan Negara: Transformasi Pemikiran dan Praktik Politik Islam di Indonesia* [Islam and the state: the transformation of Islamic party discourse and practice in Indonesia.] Jakarta: Paramadina Press.

Feith, Herbert (1957) *The Indonesian Election of 1955.* New York: Cornell Modern Indonesia Project.

Gaffar, Afan (1992) *Javanese Votes: A Case Study of Election Under a Hegemonic Party System.* Yogyakarta: Gadjah Mada University Press.

Kuntowijoyo (1997) *Identitas Politik Umat Islam* [The political identity of Muslims.] Bandung: Mizan.

Madjid, Nurcholish (1987) *Islam, Kemodernan, dan Keindonesiaan* [Islam, modernity and the state of being Indonesian.] Bandung: Mizan.

Noer, Deliar (1988) 'Islam dan Politik: Mayoritas atau Minoritas?' [Islam and politics: majority or minority?] *Prisma,* no. 5.

Samsuddin, A. (1972) *Pemilihan Umum 1971: Seri Berita dan Pendapat* [The general elections 1971: news and views.] Jakarta: Lembaga Pendidikan dan Konsultasi Pers.

Sri Januarti (2000) 'Pertikaian PPP dan PKB Kasus Pekalongan: Antara Luka Lama dan Politisasi Bahasa Agama' [Conflicts between PPP and PKB, in Pekalongan: between old wounds and the politicization of the religious language.] In Hermawan Sulistyo (ed.), *Pemilu 1999 dan Kekerasan Politik* [The general elections of 1999 and political violence]. Jakarta: PPW-LIPI.

Syamsuddin Haris (1991) *PPP dan Politik Orde Baru* [PPP and New Order politics.] Jakarta: Grasindo.

5

TRADITIONAL POWER AND PARTY POLITICS IN NORTH LOMBOK, 1965–99

Sven Cederroth

Ben Anderson (1972) has argued that we seldom encounter descriptions of a complete indigenous political theory. Rather, the analysis is abstracted into bits and pieces from many different historical sources and then supplemented by insights gained from field experiences. Despite this lack, it is obvious, says Anderson, that there exists such a political theory which offers 'a systematic and logical explanation of political behaviour quite independent of the perspectives of modern political science and in many ways in fundamental opposition to them' (Anderson 1972: 2).

A central concept for understanding an indigenous political theory refers to the view of power and its use, which in many ways is quite opposite to the Western view. Anderson has summarized the Javanese view of power as 'something concrete, homogenous, constant in total quantity and without inherent moral implications' (1972: 8). Given this view, the main concern with power is not how it is exercised but how it should be acquired. Since there can exist only a given quantity of power, this has to be concentrated and its diffusion prevented. Power is not, as in Western political theory, seen as something morally ambiguous, the use of which must always be verified to make sure that it is legitimate.

One consequence of this view of power is that history is seen not as a linear process but as consisting of recurrent cycles, an oscillation between periods with a high concentration of power and periods of order on the one hand and periods of disorder when the power has been diffused on the other. Power is concentrated in the hands of a ruler who personifies the unity of society and the administrative structure modelled on this idea of power gives rise to a patrimonial state.

A prominent feature of such an administrative structure is that it is composed of stratified clusters of patron–client relationships. All the way from the ruler in the centre down to low officials in the peripheries, the administration consists of clusters of personal dependants, whose destinies are linked to that of their patron. The more powerful the patron, the larger the size of his clientele. Traditionally, the economic base of this patron–client structure was found in a system of *appanage* in which the ruler and his clients could distribute in various degrees the rights of cultivation to a piece of land. Thus, on the way down in the hierarchy, favours were continually distributed and redistributed in smaller portions. Everybody in the system was dependent on the favours of his superior and each in turn redistributed downwards to his own clientele. In Indonesian, those within the system are referred to as the *tokoh*, the leaders, the big people, while all those without any position are the *rakyat*, the common people. Local languages have their own concepts.

One example of such a polity is found on the island of Lombok, in the petty kingdom of Bayan. This traditional kingdom was built on a model that closely resembles what Max Weber (1964) termed 'the patrimonial state'. In such a state power is exercised on the basis of tradition, it is handed down as it 'has always existed' from generation to generation and the authority is based primarily on personal loyalties. The person in the authority position, whether a king or a petty chief, may bestow positions according to his personal will, not necessarily according to any formal rules. Those recruited will then be bound to the chief by ties of personal loyalty. Usually there is no fixed hierarchy among the officials, but positions often become permanent and traditionally stereotyped. The officials do not receive any fixed salaries but are granted benefices, often in the form of a piece of land.

In this chapter, I will attempt to show how the present political system in Lombok can be seen as a continuation in many ways of the above-mentioned traditional ideas of power and based on patron–client relations. These institutions have recently been coated with a thin and transparent varnish of Western-inspired democratic institutions, but behind this surface the ideas and the institutions of the patrimonial state shine through.

In contrast to the authority structure characteristic of a patrimonial state stands the rational authority of a bureaucratic administration – what Max Weber termed 'legal authority'. Under such a system there is a consistent body of abstract rules that applies to everybody within the sphere of authority. The person in authority occupies an office and his orders are impersonal and in conformity with the rules. Loyalties are towards the body of rules, not towards the ruler as a person. Offices are organized according to hierarchic principles and positions are usually salaried.

Of course, legal authority can be exercised in many different forms, but there can be no doubt that its existence in one form or another[1] is a necessary prerequisite for the existence of a liberal democracy with a functioning party system based on free, general and secret elections. What then are the attributes of a party system and elections carried out under conditions which exhibit many characteristics of the patrimonial ideal type as outlined here? Under such conditions, to what extent are the elections democratic?

I would argue that much of politics in Indonesia can be explained in terms of its political culture: patron–client relationships, traditional authority, indigenous political forms. What I will do here, therefore, is to present a story of politics and elections in a village in north Lombok that will allow us to see what happens when patronage and traditional authority are in operation but also when other political factors, such as intimidation and force, and at times also religious orientation, are important for political choices.

Traditional politics in the kingdom of Bayan

Northern Lombok was until recently an isolated and traditional region in what today has become an island competing with Bali for global tourism. The kingdom of Bayan had its own traditional leadership structure and its own religious orientation. During the past twenty years, Bayan has rapidly been incorporated into the Indonesian nation-state, and might today be most famous as a launching site for hiking up to Rinjani volcano. Transmigration, infrastructural modernization, tourism, government development programmes and state intervention have all meant that North Lombok is fast changing. But the basic texture of Bayan is intact (cf. Cederroth 1981, 1996, 1997). The immediate impression one gets when entering a village in the region is that of a traditional society. Houses have a specific style, being built of wood and bamboo and having *alang-alang* grass for the roof. They all look more or less the same. During the last ten to fifteen years this uniform picture has started gradually to change. In the village centres, some people have now built modern stone houses and more are following. In several of the villages, such as Bayan, Anyar and Sukadana, there are groups of hereditary noblemen who still dominate most resources and have a firm control over the village administration. It is above all among this group that architectural modernization has begun, but also migrants have brought new building styles with them. In most of the outlying hamlets, however, not much has changed, and even in 2002 the traditional outlook is more or less intact.

The immediate impression given by the physical infrastructure is that of a society with a relatively equitable distribution of wealth. This impression is confirmed when we learn that in the village of Bayan almost 85 per cent of the families have access to individually owned, irrigated rice fields. Most of the land holdings are small, more than 90 per cent less than 1.5 ha in size. Only one person owns more than 5 ha. Variation in access to land is of even less significance when it is realized that, until quite recently, there existed other productive resources at the free disposal of any villager wanting to exploit them. In the area there were, and to some extent still are, extensive areas of communally owned non-irrigated dry land waiting to be cultivated.

Any poor peasant whose irrigated land proved to be insufficient for his subsistence needs could gain a supplementary living from shifting to cultivation of dry rice and vegetables on the non-irrigated fields.

As long as the system of communally owned non-irrigated land persisted, its distribution was the exclusive prerogative of an age-old institution known as *tua lokaq*, the 'council of elders'. Members of this council, which still functions in respect to questions and problems regarding the *adat*,[2] belong to the older, respected villagers having a superior position of some kind in the traditional village hierarchy. This means that the council is not only made up of members of the modern government bureaucracy but also contains religious and *adat* officials. The sub-district head, who is the eldest member of the leading noble family in Bayan, the village head, who is the younger brother of the sub-district head, the various hamlet heads (most of whom are members of the nobility) and religious officials such as *pemangku* and *kiyai*[3] belong to the *adat* council. The traditional right of the council was to distribute the right to communal land among its members, who in their turn can use the land thus allotted for further distribution among their dependants.

On Lombok, Islam is the dominant religion, adhered to by the native Sasak people, but there is also a Hindu minority, mostly made up of ethnic Balinese. Most of the Sasak are now orthodox Muslims, adherents to what in Lombok is called *waktu lima*. However, besides the Hindu Balinese minority there is also a smaller group of Sasak which professes a syncretist version of Islam, known as *wetu telu* (Cederroth 1997). Whereas the orthodox *waktu lima* Sasak follow the Islamic fundamentals as taught to them by their religious teachers (the *tuan guru*), the *wetu telu* practice a religious syncretism in which there are traces not only of Islam, but of Hinduism and pantheistic beliefs as well. In sum, *wetu telu* may be characterized as a syncretism in which aspects of pantheism and Hinduism are mixed with Islamic beliefs, glossed lightly over the older belief systems. The Muslim elements are in no way dominant, however, and resemble more a thin varnish through which the older beliefs are still clearly visible. In many aspects of their belief system, the *wetu telu* confessors show close affinity with the Javanese syncretist Muslims, the *agami jawi* (Koentjaraningrat 1985).

Until about a century ago this syncretism was dominant all over Lombok. Today, the Bayan area is the major stronghold of the *wetu telu* religion, although there are also smaller groups of adherents in other parts of the island, especially in the south-central areas. In all the remaining areas, orthodox *waktu lima* Islam, propagated by the charismatic *tuan guru* teachers has completely captured the minds of the Sasak. For the orthodox Muslims, their *tuan guru* is regarded as a person above ordinary human beings. He is close to Allah and because of this cannot do anything wrong. All his words are transmitted directly from Allah and are therefore the law for his followers. In other words, the *tuan guru* possesses extraordinary qualities which are, to his followers, of a similar kind as those ascribed to President Sukarno by his syncretist followers, or for that matter the stories about the arrival of a just kingdom which attracted the communists in the early 1960s.

Since the Bayan area is one of the few remaining parts of Lombok where there is still an abundance of uncultivated land, it has attracted a continuous stream of spontaneous migrants. These are mostly poor, landless villagers from the central overpopulated parts of the island who settle in Bayan in hope of finding a better living. The first migrants came in the 1950s, and right from the beginning they did not mingle with the native population, whose lack of a 'proper' Islamic faith and religious education they despised. Instead, they settled in a hamlet of their own located some 2 kilometres from the central parts of the village. All of them were orthodox Muslims. Ever since the migrants began to arrive there have been conflicts between adherents of *waktu limu* and *wetu telu*. The *waktu lima* regard the *wetu telu* confessors as 'immature' Muslims who have to be taught the fundamentals and learn to practice the religion the way it should be done. The *wetu telu* for their part maintain that the migrants have forgotten their heritage, they have no culture, no *adat* and therefore their lives are no better than animals. Although ethnically both religious groups are Sasak, religiously they have little in common (Cederroth 1996).

Party politics, 1945–65

Party politics first entered Bayan in the early 1950s, as it did in the rest of rural Indonesia. It was the sub-district head who introduced the Nationalist Party, the PNI, that soon gathered a massive following and organized some 90 per cent of the Bayanese population, all of them followers of the leading noblemen. It is not surprising that when the political parties began to recruit members among the rural masses in the early 1950s, the choice of the PNI was a natural one for the Bayanese. First, there was the immense personal popularity of President Sukarno. Second, the nationalists were seen as staunch defendants of traditional ways of living, in comparison to the communists and the Muslims. For the conservative Bayanese noblemen these were important facts in favour of the party. In addition, it was culturally appropriate for them to associate with the strong and state-bearing government party.

There were two exceptions to the complete dominance of the PNI. The people in one of the commoner hamlets refused to join their traditional patrons and instead chose to associate with the PKI, the Communist Party. This was not an independent choice of the commoners, but they followed the advice of a religious official, a *kiyai*, who disassociated himself from his noble fellows and began to build a group of followers of his own. It should be emphasized that when recruiting the extremely traditional villagers of

Bayan, the PKI organisers did not use any Marxist arguments, which would not have been understood anyway. They never mentioned concepts such as class conflicts, but instead concentrated their arguments around the need for mutual co-operation[4] and on the return to a just society where the rights of everybody were secured and nobody was oppressed. The choice between the PNI and the PKI, as it was presented to the Bayanese, was less of a choice between two different political alternatives than between two charismatic leaders using messianic arguments to appeal to the same type of traditionally oriented villagers. Sukarno, being a great orator who could spellbind his listeners, possessed immense charismatic qualities. His rhetoric, to make Indonesia a state of Marhaens – where justice would be offered to the little man, who was no longer to be exploited by foreign or domestic oppressors – greatly appealed to the Bayanese. But so did the similar rhetoric of the communists, evoking memories of the *datu-datuan* movements of the past, heralding the arrival of a just king who would come to establish his kingdom and make an end of all injustices.[5] To the Bayanese communists, the establishment of the party was a presage to this just kingdom, the arrival of which had so often been promised by the ancestors and which was now finally to see the light of day.

The Islamic parties in Bayan were less well organized. The only party with some following was Masjumi, sometimes characterized as a radical, 'modernist' Islamic party, a staunch proponent of the transformation of Indonesia to an Islamic state based upon Koranic law. The support came mainly from the migrants and was based on the charismatic *tuan guru* Haji Zainuddin, who with his 'extraordinary qualities' had a strong following. Nahdlatul Ulama (NU), Sarekat Islam and other Islamic parties who often were heavily 'Java-centric' in leadership and mobilization, had virtually no following. Thus, in the Bayan sub-district all three parties with a certain following – the Muslim Masyumi, the communist PKI and the nationalist PNI – were, regardless of religion, ideology and class, solidly based on patron–client relations. Among the native population it was the leading nobility who dominated all but one of the commoner hamlets, whereas among the newcomers it was the *tuan guru* who exerted a similar influence.

Given this set-up, it was no great surprise that in the elections of 1955, the PNI could capture close to 90 per cent of the votes in the sub-district. This was quite predictable, as the syncretist noblemen had such a dominant position in village affairs. Soon thereafter, however, national developments, over which the Bayanese had no influence, were to shatter the established party structure. The first unruly signs came when Masjumi was banned in 1960 on the pretext of having been involved in a rebellion against the central government and President Sukarno. In the course of events, the rivalry between NU and Masjumi hardened. Therefore, when Masjumi was outlawed there was no automatic overflow to other Islamic parties. Instead, the *tuan guru* who had supported Masjumi recommended that his followers should not join any other party. Consequently, most of the orthodox newcomers in Bayan were to stand outside party politics for almost a decade and a half to come.

During and after the *coup d'etat* in 1965, members of the communist hamlet were rounded up and taken into custody for a few weeks. The PKI leader disappeared, never to be heard of again. When freed again the communists returned to a very different world. No longer were they free to handle their own affairs, and they had to report daily to the local military. In this way, the attempts of the inhabitants of the communist hamlet to free themselves from their traditional dependency on the Bayanese nobility ended in tragedy. It also provoked a backlash from the nobility who used this opportunity to further strengthen their grip on the local administration. Since the hamlet leader had disappeared, the office was offered to a young member of the local nobility who had emerged as an unofficial leader of a group opposed to the leading faction of the sub-district and village heads.[6] Offering this post to a member of an opposing faction was obviously an attempt by the village leaders to close ranks ahead of external attacks on their leadership.

Party politics, 1965–95

As a tiny syncretist minority on an increasingly orthodox Muslim island, the lifestyle of the Bayanese nobility has long been under attack. Their association with the syncretistic President Sukarno and the PNI should be seen in this light and was an attempt to forge close ties with the legitimate government and its administration to better withstand disruptions from orthodox 'educators'. The events in 1965 dramatically changed the preconditions for this strategy. Although not outlawed, the PNI was nevertheless regarded with the utmost scepticism by the new power holders who set out to create their own quasi-party, an amalgamation of the so-called functional groups, *Golongan Karya* or Golkar for short.[7]

In Bayan, the orthodox Muslim newcomers had grasped the opportunity offered by the national events to try to change the heretical habits of the Bayanese. In the official Indonesian rhetoric, communism was equated with atheism. For some time members of syncretist religions such as the *wetu telu* were seen as a type of atheist and thus as potential communist traitors. In 1967 an official decree forced every citizen to choose one of four recognized religions: Islam, Buddhism, Hinduism or Christianity. Since syncretism was not among these, and since they were already nominal Muslims, the Bayanese felt compelled to choose Islam.[8] This enforced conversion was the perfect excuse for the orthodox Muslims to start a wave of 'education', which led to a tense situation and even clashes between the groups.

After a few syncretist sanctities, among them a *wetu telu* mosque, had been deliberately destroyed by mobs of orthodox fanatics, the situation grew very tense. But for the time being the syncretist nobility continued to cling to the PNI, nurturing hopes of a revival for the party. When elections were ordered by the New Order government in 1971, the PNI even managed to get one of their own officers, Anggirta, a young nobleman leader of one of the internal factions, nominated as a candidate for the Dewan Perwakilan Rakyat Daerah (DPR-D), the local House of Representatives.

Some months before the elections, however, an official decree suddenly and unexpectedly – for the Bayanese at least – changed the rules of the game. In this decree it was stated that all civil servants had to take an oath of loyalty to Golkar (or so it was interpreted), the so-called *mono-loyalitas*. Almost all the leading persons in villages all over Indonesia suddenly found themselves members of Golkar. And with them came their followers. In this way a Golkar victory in the coming elections was almost self-evident. Nevertheless, for the Bayanese nobility the decree was welcome. They could now leave the increasingly discredited PNI without losing face and simultaneously gain an affiliation with the new power holders.

There remained one problem, however. That was Anggirta, the young DPR-D candidate who was also the leader of one of three nobility factions in Bayan. He simply refused to desert his party in this way, shortly before the elections. This refusal cost him his position in the administration since everybody who refused to join Golkar was automatically dismissed. Among the orthodox newcomers a similar dismissal took place when the hamlet head insisted upon remaining a member of NU.

Anggirta and his followers were now in opposition to their fellow nobility from the two other factions. Anggirta was a bright and daring person who had always been outspoken and straightforward, and when injustice was done he had always offered his help to those in need. In this way he had become very popular and had gained a widespread following extending far outside his own hamlet. Now he felt that he himself had been unjustly treated. He had to take revenge and therefore set out upon a vigorous campaign for the PNI.

On the other hand, for his fellow (now Golkarized) noblemen, a good showing in the coming elections was essential in order to gain the confidence of the administration. They mobilized their network of followers and within a short time the membership of the PNI had fallen from close to 90 per cent of the villagers to only five individuals, the remaining PNI members being only Anggirta and his close family members. Since there remained a few members of other political parties as well, Bayan could not be declared as a village which was *bebas parpol*, 'free from party politics', which happened in many other villages where the entire population had declared their loyalty to Golkar. Indeed, the election results showed that the influence of Anggirta over his nobility faction was considerable. Despite the fact that only five members remained in the party, the PNI achieved a very good result in the elections. It turned out to be a close second, after Golkar. Because of the enforced Golkarization, however, Anggirta, who ran for the PNI, was not elected to DPR-D. The events also caused a severe rift in the ranks of the nobility, an open wound that was to prove difficult to heal.

During the following years, the New Order regime ordered a 'simplification' of the party system as part of the preparations for the next general elections that were to be held in 1977. This decree forced all old political parties to combine into two parties. First, there was the *Partai Demokrasi Indonesia* (PDI), which came to consist of some Christian parties and the old PNI, with the latter playing the leading role, and second, the Muslim *Partai Persatuan Pembangunan* (PPP), an amalgamation of some Muslim parties dominated by the NU. Golkar, which was not officially a political party but a 'socio-economic organization', remained intact.

In Bayan, some changes in leading positions had taken place in the time between the two elections. The sub-district head had died and the village head who had held the post for almost twenty-five years had resigned. These posts were filled by the two eldest sons of the sub-district head. Anggirta remained outside Golkar and joined the PDI together with his fellow PNI members. Therefore no reconciliation took place, rather the mutual feelings of distrust deepened even more.

The 1977 elections saw a new Bayanese candidate for the DPR-D, namely the new village head, who was chosen as a Golkar candidate. This time it was therefore essential that the two nobility factions that stood behind him achieve an overwhelming Golkar victory. The entire government apparatus was united behind this task. The campaign of the PDI was obstructed in numerous ways, ranging from petty things to outright sabotage. A few years later Anggirta complained to me, half jokingly, that he could not even go to the river to take a bath without someone following him to spy on his undertakings.

During the campaign, not only were the virtues of Golkar emphasized, but much intimidation and many serious threats were also used to scare people away from voting for the PDI and PPP parties. The most serious, only thinly veiled, threat of physical abuse was made when the Golkar campaigners claimed that a vote for the PDI would be considered by the government as equal to a vote for the PKI, the communists, and any person guilty of this would be treated accordingly. In a similar vein it was also said that anybody who did not vote for Golkar would be thrown out of the hamlet and forced to leave Bayan. Such punishments, known locally as *selong,*[9] were formerly practised against criminals.

In addition to these implicit threats of corporal punishment, it was also implied that administrative measures would be taken against those who did not vote for Golkar. Thus, it was argued that when a person had been found to vote for any of the political parties, he would be refused necessary approval letters by the government (see Antlöv 1995: Chapters 4 and 8 for a fuller description of various forms of intimidation in a village on Java). Such letters are necessary for many purposes, and without them a person can, for instance, neither travel nor marry. It was also clearly spelt out that persons who had voted for any of the political parties would be refused communal land when it was to be distributed, or, if they already had such land, it would be taken back. Vast tracks of communally owned land were now in the process of being turned into private property and this distribution was handled by the village civil servants, above all the village head and the associated hamlet heads. The land was obviously not distributed democratically.

Finally, a threat of a somewhat different character was brought forward. During the campaigning it was maintained that anyone found guilty of having voted for the PDI would be refused the services of religious leaders (*kiyai*) when necessary for religious ceremonies. In fact this was the most serious threat of all, since among the *wetu telu* a *kiyai* is the main link with God. The *kiyai* acts on behalf of ordinary citizens and he is responsible, among other things, for guiding the soul of a deceased to the realm of the dead. If such services are not provided the soul of the deceased person will remain forever in this world, wandering aimlessly.

Strictly speaking, all of these threats were illegal. The fact that they were brought forward nevertheless tells us something about the system of traditional loyalties and the desperate need of the Bayanese noblemen to ally with the pro-government forces and their great irritation with the traitors – as they saw the non-Golkar voters – in their midst. When the votes of the 1977 election were counted, however, the result for the PDI was even better than what it had been for the PDI in 1971. The two parties, Golkar and the PDI, had received an almost equal number of votes. As a result of this, the candidacy of the village head failed and he was not elected as a member of the DPR-D. Because of this humiliation the village head started shortly afterwards to try to take revenge upon known PDI sympathizers. For instance, the members of one small hamlet where all the votes had been cast for the PDI were set to perform forced labour on the road outside the village office. Before this they had been insulted and forced to run around the central village hamlets, cupped hands above their heads, shouting '*aku sampi, aku sampi*' (I am a buffalo, I am a buffalo).[10] In taking this action the village head went too far, however; such a provocation could not remain unanswered. As soon as Anggirta, the PDI leader, heard of the events he ordered his followers to stop working and return home. It is of course, a serious matter to take open actions against the orders of a superior, especially in such a conservative and hierarchic community as Bayan. But Anggirta did not stop at this. He went straight to the sub-district head to forward his complaints about the illegal actions. He also threatened to bring the events to the knowledge of the central party authorities so that the village head would be punished. Hearing this, the sub-district head tried to mediate and asked the two enemies to shake hands and forgot about the incident. Anggirta, however, refused to do this until he had received a public apology. And indeed, after some time, and probably after pressure from the sub-district head, who, it should be remembered, was the older brother of the village head, the apology came. The incident was, therefore, never brought before the higher authorities.

This dramatic incident marked the low point of the internal relations between the two Bayanese nobility factions controlled by the village head and the Anggirta faction. From then on things slowly improved. To be sure, there were some more incidents of a less serious character, but each time the sub-district head stepped in and mediated. Finally, shortly before the elections in 1982, Anggirta was asked by the sub-district head to leave PDI. In return he would get a job in the village administration. He refused to take such a step before the elections, but promised to refrain from any active campaigning on behalf of the PDI. Much to the satisfaction of the authorities, Golkar won a comfortable victory this time, whereas the votes for the PDI were less than half of what the party had got in the previous election.

Soon after the elections, Anggirta left PDI and was immediately rewarded with the job promised to him. In 1985, two years before the next elections, he accepted the nomination as chairman of the village Golkar branch (we will return to his story later). Shortly thereafter he was promoted to a position as leader for the Golkar sub-district organization. In the 1987 and 1992 elections, the entire Bayanese nobility was thus united behind Golkar which each time received almost 90 per cent of the votes. This was about the same number that was cast for the PNI during its heyday. The PDI presence was very low-key; the party held only a few campaign meetings and, with the exception of a few hamlets where they were still dominant, they got only a few stray votes. The only PPP votes were cast in some of the transmigrant hamlets.

Thus, in sum, the campaigning and voting in the period 1971–77 can be characterized as giving a strong position to the PNI/PDI, followed by a decline in the 1982 election and, thereafter, an almost complete Golkar dominance. Only a few traditional hamlets remained loyal to the PDI. The main reason for this shift from the PDI to Golkar has to do with the change of allegiance by Anggirta described here. With the exception of a few hamlets he was followed by almost all voters in the hamlets that by tradition had belonged to his sphere of influence. His own decision to quit the PDI in favour of Golkar was achieved through an appeal to their common interests as the joint noble family of Bayan. The appeal was made by the sub-district head, the leading member of the dominant nobility faction to Anggirta, the leading member of the second nobility faction, who also happened to be his own brother-in-law. After this deal had been struck there was simply no room in the village for any other party, and every attempt made by these to gain votes was severely repressed. The village leaders and other authorities did not refrain from threats and intimidation to prevent people from voting for any of the two political parties. Although in a formal sense the elections were free and multi-party, in practice they were not, since for the ordinary villagers there was simply no choice.

The 1997 election

Having briefly sketched the local party politics in Bayan up to the mid-1990s, we shall now proceed to take a closer look at the campaign which took place during the 1997 election, the last before the fall of Suharto. On the national scene, there had been some dramatic incidents indicating the pending changes. Among these, the enforced removal of Megawati Sukarnoputri from the PDI was perhaps the most important, dealing a severe blow to the PDI nationally, where the party received only 2.3 per cent of the votes. In Bayan, however, nothing of this counted; even those who knew anything about the incidents could not care less. For all but a few hamlets, the PDI was not an alternative anyway and Golkar continued to be the only available choice for almost all the villagers. Since the PPP and the PDI were not present in Bayan, we will need to look more closely at Golkar campaigning to learn more about how Golkar could win more than 97 per cent of the votes in Bayan.

During April and May of 1997, Golkar held several campaign meetings in various parts of the village. These events were always accompanied by a popular entertainment of some kind such as *cupak grantang*,[11] a *joget* dance or a film show. During the meetings it was important to show the support of all locally important persons such as the sub-district head, the village head, in Bayan also that of *pemangku adat*, the representative of the customary law, while in more orthodox communities it might have been a religious teacher, a *tuan guru*. One after the other they were therefore asked to take the stand and say a few words to those who had assembled. This showed that they all stood united behind Golkar and they urged everyone to vote for the party.

The leading role, however, was taken by the *jurkam*, the 'campaign expert' (*juru kampanje*). In Bayan he was none other than Anggirta, the former PDI leader, now totally 'Golkarized'. After the people had listened to the short speeches of the local leaders, Anggirta started his speech by telling the people that they did not need to be afraid or hesitate to choose Golkar, since the whole government apparatus, from the hamlet head to the president, as well as the ABRI (the military), were all Golkar. Since this was the case, why should they hesitate? Golkar was identical with the New Order, while politics (here meaning the political parties) belonged to the Old Order. Anggirta continued:

> During the 'political era', Indonesia declined and became passive. Politics was only talked about, and there was no time for development. Compare this with the present situation during the

Golkar-sponsored New Order. Look at the developments, look at education and look at the observance of religious duties. From the cities to the furthest corners of our land, everybody can see and feel the differences. During the Old Order not even the bridges were taken care of, clothing was insufficient, food was scarce and we were even eating bulgur, food for horses. But since the New Order took over, all the bridges from Mataram have been rebuilt with more durable materials; the road has 'hotmix' [tarmac] all the way. To go to Mataram now only takes a few hours; it is no longer necessary to wait for one or two days while the trucks are loading and then ride to Mataram on top of all the goods. Formerly, there was only one market in all of North Lombok, but now the government has built market-places in every village. No longer is it necessary to travel for a full day or more to reach the market, now there is one around the corner, which is held at least once a week.

What is important is that when you enjoy the fruits of development you must always remember that they have come about because of Golkar. Every new bridge, every bit of asphalt, every school and all the new clinics are there because of Golkar. They are all the ideas of Golkar, and in the election you must give credit to this by voting for Golkar. Take care not to return to the Old Order with its political squabbles; give your votes to those who have achieved all this and who will continue to work for development.

Anggirta went on like this for some time, promoting the virtues of Golkar and denouncing the 'political parties' (meaning the PPP and the PDI). Someone commented that he sounded very much like a medicine hawker, talking smoothly and promising that his medicine was the perfect cure for every possible disease.

In his speeches Anggirta also made a point of the fact that it was well known all over the sub-district that he had formerly been a leading PDI cadre. Here is an excerpt from another speech:

Come, let us ensure together that Golkar wins a huge victory here in Bayan. Why? Because Golkar cares for the welfare of the entire population, not just for some individuals. I myself can serve as an example of this. When I was campaigning for the other political party I had no success. I was forced to quit my post as village secretary and I was even estranged from my family and my friends in Bayan. My life was not happy. When the party leadership needed my assistance I was approached but as soon as the election day had passed everything was forgotten. Working for the party gave the same reward as when you assist in pushing a car that won't start. Once the machine comes to life, the car drives away and all you get is the dust it leaves behind. My strife was not rewarded. All the PDI people thought about was their own fortune – once the peanut has been shelled, the shell is forgotten [*kacang lupa kulitnya*]. I noticed what happened around me, all the developments that were taking place: roads, bridges, markets, new irrigation dams etc. Little by little the welfare grew and it was welfare for everyone, not just a few. All this convinced me that Golkar was the right choice and therefore I was persuaded to leave the political party.

Another campaign technique was to open a dialogue with some selected people from the crowd. A man from a mountain hamlet which had recently received piped water was brought up to the front and asked:

Is it true that you now have easy access to clean water?
Yes, that is correct.
And who has arranged that you got this benefit?
It is the Golkar people of the government who assisted us in getting the water running.
If that is so, will you then vote for Golkar in the election?
Yes, I will vote for Golkar.
Are you sure?
Right (*betul*).

Also, former members of either of the two political parties might be called upon to explain why they had left the party and joined Golkar. The answers always evolved around the development which had taken place, the improvements in communication being a specifically favoured subject. Golkar was portrayed as the defender of the people, securing development for everybody.

On another occasion, a young boy, a student of SMA, the senior high school, was called to the stage by Anggirta and asked whom he would vote for. When he answered 'Golkar', the campaign leader asked him why he would vote like that. The boy answered:

Formerly there was neither an SMP [junior high school] nor an SMA [senior high school] in the sub-district of Bayan. But after Golkar came to power both schools have been built. It is no longer necessary to leave Bayan and stay in Mataram to study. For this I am very grateful and will vote for Golkar.

Besides the large campaign meetings, Golkar also made use of a door-to-door campaign in which all lower civil service cadres, hamlet heads (*kadus*), neighbourhood heads (*rukun warga* and *rukun tetangga*) and neighbourhood guards (*hansip*) were engaged. These staff were ordered to visit all the households in their neighbourhood to instil into them, through personal persuasion, the necessity of voting for Golkar. It was above all in these more informal, personal settings that intimidating tactics as described for earlier elections seem to have been used. According to many reports, whoever did not vote for Golkar would be denied all government services, etc. as described earlier.

If such threats were to be carried out it would mean, for instance, that boys could not be circumcised, no one could marry off their children, and souls would be denied entrance into heaven after death, since there would be nobody there to perform the necessary rites and escort them on the journey. Although such threats were not only illegal but also untrue, in this traditional, hierarchical society with its deeply ingrained respect for authority and habits of trusting the *kiyai* for their salvation, such arguments were nevertheless forceful and no doubt frightened many potential PDI or PPP voters into making Golkar their choice. The frightful events of thirty years ago and the fate of the PKI voters still lived vividly in the memories of many people, further adding to the force of arguments stressing the need to give support to the government and those in power.

According to official regulations, the local military staff and the police were not allowed to take any part in the election, except through supervising it. They were not allowed to vote; their family, wives, children, servants, etc. were, however, expected to vote for Golkar. Thus nobody could doubt where their sympathies lay. Furthermore, whenever there was a Golkar campaign, whether in the village centre or in the mountain hamlets, the *koramil* (regional military commander) participated. Usually, he was given an opportunity to deliver a speech in which the Golkar concept was forcefully brought forward, and he would also announce that the whole military family stood united behind Golkar. Since the government and military were behind Golkar there was absolutely no need for the people to be afraid or hesitant.

Targeting the 'Parpol' hamlets

Those hamlets that in the 1987 and 1992 election had had an above average percentage of votes for the PPP or the PDI were in 1997 selected for specific, intense attempts to convince the people to abandon their old allegiances and make Golkar their new choice. Comparing the 'bad old times' with the present 'good times' and urging people to remember who had achieved all this was a constantly recurring theme in the campaigns all over the sub-district. Especially in PDI or PPP hamlets, locally important issues were also brought up and promises for the future were made, provided that the hamlet would vote for Golkar.

To give an example, in the mountain hamlet Torean of Loloan village, the PDI had received almost as many votes as Golkar in the 1992 election.

There was a strong dissatisfaction in the hamlet with the local leadership and especially the way in which a water-sharing issue had been handled. Close to Torean there is a spring which had always been a source of clean drinking water. In the late 1980s this resource had been exploited: a canal had been built with the result that a large area could be transformed into irrigated rice fields. All this had been given to a newly established community of transmigrants from East Lombok that had settled nearby, while the local Torean villagers had received nothing. To add further to the injustice, the transmigrants had settled on land that by tradition had always been used for the cultivation of dry field crops by the Torean population. This used to be community-owned land which was distributed for use among the inhabitants. Now it had been removed from the hamlet without compensation.

Because of the large number of PDI votes, the sub-district head and Golkar chairman decided to make Torean the target of a special campaign in the 1997 election. The village head therefore invited Anggirta, who travelled together with the local Golkar candidate, a Bayanese nobleman, the youngest son of the leading noble family, to Torean for a day of campaigning. First, all the locally important people were collected and instructed to make sure that all inhabitants turned out. The campaign started with a *joget* performance, an immensely popular form of entertainment in which one or two professional female dancers invite selected people from among the onlookers to come to the stage and dance opposite them.

After some hours, the dancing was interrupted and the campaign speeches began. To begin with, the same general development-orientated issues as shown earlier were promoted, but slowly more local issues began to be dealt with. As always in Bayan, the question of transportation surfaced first. Torean, which is some six kilometres up the mountain, had had no passable road connection at all until quite recently. 'Look at the road', Anggirta said: 'formerly no four-wheel vehicles, not even Honda motorcycles, could come to Torean, but now, thanks to the untiring efforts of the government, even trucks can come here.'

Then another issue was brought up. 'Together with the road', Anggirta said, 'the government has also put a lot of resources into promoting tourism which, as you know, has given many among you a chance to work as porters and guides, earning quite handsome sums of money'.[12] Anggirta continued:

> Is this not something with which all of you can be happy? Please answer me.
> *Syukur dan terima kasih* (God be praised and thank you).
> If this is so, what will be your choice in the coming elections? Will it be Golkar?
> *Ya, betul, betul* (Yes, right so, right so).

> Yes, I heard your answers with my own ears but the words were
> heard not only by me but also by the almighty God. If you did
> not speak the truth, you were hypocritical and will be cursed by
> God. Are you afraid of being cursed?
>
> *Takut* (afraid).
>
> Well then, together with Golkar, the government, the New Order
> and God we shall win the election. *Insyhallah*.

After the public meeting was finished, Anggirta and the candidate
met with the local bigwigs to discuss the water-sharing issue. In these
discussions the government representatives promised that if Torean
returned to the Golkar fold, they would make sure that in the future, the
water resources were shared differently, and not everything would go to
the transmigrants. The road was also a point of discussion. Although
much had been done, several bridges still needed to be built and the road
had to be asphalted. This was considered by the Toreans as a high priority issue, not only because of the tourists but also, and perhaps above all,
for the Toreans themselves for transporting goods to and from the
market places.

Another hamlet where there had been a high percentage of PDI votes
was Teres Genit, a mountain hamlet of Bayan village. A few days in
advance of the campaign, the village head called the hamlet head and made
sure that all locally important people were specifically invited and that
word about the arrival of the campaign was spread in the hamlet and its
surroundings. The day began as usual with a few hours of entertainment,
this time a drama performance, the immensely popular *Cupak Grantang*
story performed by a local ensemble. Consequently, almost everyone was
present when the campaigning began with a short speech by the village
head. He welcomed all those present and introduced the concept of elections, which were to be general, direct, free and secret (*umum, langsung,
bebas dan rahasia*, the government's slogan, no, mantra). Everyone over
the age of 17 had to participate and cast their vote on election day according to their own choice. 'However', he continued, 'if you want to behave
like a responsible citizen and want to support the government and its
development efforts you have to choose Golkar'. Before finishing he
rhetorically asked if everyone was responsible and wanted to support the
government and thereby also Golkar. Of course, he was answered with a
resounding 'yes'.

Then it was Anggirta's turn, and he began by telling his own story and
reiterating the usual reasons, as described before, why he had left the political party and joined Golkar. He had found that Golkar was the means by
which his aspirations could be fulfilled. In another rhetorical question he
asked the people if they all supported his conclusions and whether
they were to be seen as supporters of party politics or of Golkar. When

he had heard that they were all Golkar supporters, he led the crowd in slogan-chanting:

Golkar – *menang* (winning)!
Pancasila[13] – *Jaya* (victory)!
Pembangunan (development) – *Jalan terus* (continue straight)!

As usual, when campaigning in hamlets that were, or could be suspected to be, pro-PDI, the main thrust of the speech was to emphasize local developments, pointing to improvements which were obvious to everyone and of importance for the people in their daily lives. These were then compared with the situation that had prevailed during the 'bad old times', the time when party politics ruled. The next, obvious step was then to give Golkar and the government the credit for the improvements. The people were urged to make sure that the developments could continue, which they could do only by voting for Golkar and preventing a return to party political bickering. In the case of Teres Genit the improvements specifically mentioned were: the new road, the permanent irrigation canal, electrification through water power and the new school. Until some ten years ago, Teres Genit had been completely without any road connection to the rest of the island; now there was not only a road, it even had a layer of asphalt in some difficult spots. Formerly, the hand-dug irrigation canal had often been damaged by heavy rains, but after it had received a coating of cement it was safe. Similarly, during the same period, a school had been built, as a result of which the children no longer had to walk to central Bayan every day, a distance of more than 10 kilometres back and forth. Finally, and this was the pinnacle of development, electricity had now also arrived in Teres Genit after water power from a nearby river had been utilized.

After having their attention brought to these and other developments that were all declared as manifestations of Golkar's development concept, the people were told that everybody should be happy and make the right choice in the election. To make sure that nobody made a mistake, the people were now taught how to cast their vote. The ballot used in the election contained three symbols, one for each of the three contesting parties. The Golkar symbol, a banyan tree, was in the middle, surrounded by the symbols of the two other parties.[14] The voter was to cast his vote by punching a hole through the symbol of his choice. The campaign leader now showed a ballot where the two other symbols had been erased and called two elderly voters to come to the stage to practice. They were taught how to punch, right in the middle, how to fold the paper and how to make sure that the right voting paper got into the right voting box.

Having made sure that everybody knew, in practical terms, how to cast their vote, Anggirta recapitulated the importance of the election and the necessity for everyone to come to the voting place. Before finishing, he once again led the crowd into a show of solidarity with Golkar. He reminded them that God was witness to their promise to vote for Golkar and that whoever did not adhere to his promise was sure to be cursed by God.

It is interesting to note that although most of his followers accepted his arguments and also switched to Golkar, a few refused. A majority of these came from the hamlet of Kebaloan where there had been a conflict about the registration of former communally owned land as individual property. During the Old Order this area was 100 per cent PNI and these loyalties were then transferred to the PDI so that during all the elections held after the establishment of the New Order this was the PDI stronghold in the entire sub-district. An important reason for this involved the actions of Anggirta. The commoners of Kebaloan were traditionally attached to his nobility group, so they are his followers. When they saw what he did and heard his daring defence of the PDI, they became convinced and dared to follow the PDI under his leadership. Even after Anggirta himself had left the PDI and was campaigning for Golkar, many of his followers continued to stand by the PDI. No arguments whatsoever, no promises, not even offerings of money or gifts could induce them to change their minds. All attempts were met with the answer '*pemaliq tulak manuk kulon*' (forbidden with supernatural sanctions). Although the number of PDI voters dropped somewhat in 1997, Kebaloan still remained its strongest support base in the sub-district. When asked about their reasons for remaining with the PDI, they did not mention the land issue but rather invoked the concept of *maliq*.[15] A breach would incur divine wrath. References to *maliq* therefore take precedence above all other concerns. Thus, they felt compelled to take refuge in an argument which referred to sanctions from the supernatural. Since it is *maliq* not to do as one's forbears have done they had to continue to support the PDI (however, Anggirta had not been able to protect their rights properly, at least those who were dissatisfied thought so).

Campaigning for the PPP and the PDI

While Golkar held a number of public campaign meetings, the two political parties were much more anonymous. Except for some transmigrants, the PPP had no adherents in the area, but as already mentioned the PDI had received quite a number of votes in earlier elections, and had a following they could depend upon. In 1997 the Bayan party branch was severely weakened since its former leader, who had once replaced Anggirta, was a supporter of Megawati and had, together with most other cadres, left the party after her ouster. This time the party held only one campaign meeting, in the house of its local leader and with some fifty people participating. Campaigning on behalf of the PDI carried out in Bayan was done on an individual basis, from person to person, much like traditional *mendea* trading.[16] The PDI campaign was directed towards those hamlets where the party by tradition had had a strong position. The discussions centred mostly on *adat* (tradition) and the need for upholding and strengthening the customs. When *adat* is strong, there will be welfare for the people. In Bayan, messianic *datu-datuan* movements have regularly occurred among the tradition-minded segments of the people. During the colonial time there were several such movements, which caused considerable consternation among the Dutch (Cederroth 1977). After liberation, these have continued.

The prominence of such movements can be explained by reference to the native concept of power as consisting of oscillating periods of concentration and disintegration. In times of disorder a renewed concentration is imminent and must be prepared for. When it arrives it is essential that people attach themselves to this new emerging centre of power. It seems that the PDI specifically targeted the leaders of such movements, obviously in hopes of influencing them, and thereby also the followers, into seeing in the party as such a new emerging centre of power. The PDI people also portrayed themselves as the champions of the poor and promised to fight for their rights.

The PDI cadres made a habit of searching for people who had some kind of conflict with the local leadership and promised their assistance in solving the conflict provided that they voted for the PDI. An example that can be mentioned is the former *pengulu*, the highest-ranking religious official of Bayan, who was now one of the leading PDI cadres. During the campaign he approached a farmer from the hamlet of Teres Genit who had a conflict about landownership with the local hamlet head. The farmer owned a piece of land that he had worked for several years. For some reason the necessary ownership certificates had never been arranged and the land was still officially classified as *tanah desa*, village land. Finally, the hamlet head lost his patience and declared that the land had to be confiscated unless everything was speedily arranged and the land taxes paid. The *pengulu* came looking for the farmer and promised his assistance in solving the problems with the hamlet head if he voted for the PDI. In Bayan, where there was a large amount of communally owned land that was now in the process of being distributed to individual owners, there were many similar problems and this situation was now utilized by the PDI to gain the confidence and votes of the people concerned. During his visit the *pengulu* told the farmer that if afterwards the hamlet head or the village head came around and asked about the reason for the visit and what choice he would make it was important that he should declare that he was a Golkar supporter in order to protect himself. The hamlet heads and the neighbourhood heads had been ordered to check the movements of known PDI cadres. Whenever a known PDI sympathizer had visited the house of someone in their area, they afterwards checked with the household head about the reason for the visit. If no satisfactory reason was provided, the household was regarded as suspect. In every hamlet there was always some Golkar cadre who had the task of reporting such suspected cases to the village head and, if necessary, to the sub-district head. There were allegations that during the voting, the suspect would receive a ballot with some kind of code on it, so that later it would be possible to tell how he had voted.

Therefore, if the PDI campaign was low key and semi-secret, so were the adherents. Except for the local leadership, most of the supporters would never admit their inclination. They were afraid of being intimidated. I have already mentioned that in the Golkar campaign the hamlet heads and other local office holders went from house to house in the areas under their supervision to convince people of the necessity of voting for Golkar. During such visits, the PDI supporters never admitted their true preferences but assured the officer that they would vote for Golkar.

As we remember, during an earlier election in 1992, the number of PDI votes in Anyar, the sub-district centre, had been far above the average for the sub-district as a whole. This annoyed the *camat*, the sub-district head who had asked how it could be that exactly in the centre itself, where there were so many civil servants and therefore presumably influential Golkar members, the political parties could find so many supporters. These Golkar cadres had been ordered to convince as many as possible to vote for the party, but despite this massive campaign, the political parties had fared very well there. There was one schoolteacher in particular of whom the *camat* was very suspicious. He was a close friend of the PDI leader and they were often seen together. According to the *camat*, Golkar cadres were not permitted to associate that closely with the opposition during the weeks preceding the elections. In other words, despite strong surveillance by Golkar, traditional ties worked to upset the results.

In sum, the 1997 campaign was characterized by the continuing control of the three nobility factions over the votes of almost all their followers among the commoners, and in this it showed a continuation of the pattern of the pre-1997 elections. Through such campaigning and supervision, the sub-district of Bayan always received among the highest percentages of Golkar votes in Lombok. After the 1997 elections, when all over the sub-district more than 90 per cent voted for Golkar, the sub-district was officially, and proudly, declared *lumbung Golkar*, 'the storehouse of Golkar'. In one of the neighbouring villages, Senaru, in the 1997 election Golkar received 3,038 votes out of a total of 3,132 cast, which amounts to 97 per cent! The PDI got fifty-three votes and the PPP forty-one.

The 1999 election

After the fall of Suharto in May 1998, new democratic elections were scheduled to be held little more than a year later. This time, not 3 but 48 parties competed in the election. However, of all these parties only a few were visible in the Bayan area and Golkar was still the party that had the highest profile. During the campaign period leading up to the first real multi-party election, the situation facing Golkar – now relabelled as *Golkar Baru*, the new Golkar – was quite different. The party no longer had the unlimited support of the entire local state apparatus: all government employees were free to vote for whatever party they liked. Furthermore, Golkar now faced competition not from two other parties but from forty-seven. Nevertheless, unlike most of the other parties, Golkar still had many resources at its disposal, and in the Bayan sub-district the party staged a huge campaign event on 3 June, four days ahead of the election.

Also during this election all three nobility factions continued to support Golkar. One of their leaders, the son of a former village head, appeared as a Golkar candidate for the local parliament and was placed high on the list with good chances of becoming elected. This was without any doubt the major factor in explaining the victory of the party. In most of the hamlets the traditional authority of the nobility was still strong enough to convince most people to follow their choice. The former campaign leader, Anggirta, who had played such a prominent role in the 1997 election, was a member of the village administration, and as such not allowed to take any part in the campaign for this election, but even without his active participation the authority displayed by the local nobility elite was still strong enough for them to retain their grip over most of their followers.

The evening before the campaign, the arena where the campaigners would congregate became the stage for a *wayang kulit*, a shadow play performance. In Java and Bali the plays are drawn from the *Ramayana* or the *Mahabarata*, two Hindu epics, whereas on Lombok the performances are from *Amir Hamza*, a large Muslim epic. For the event, Golkar had hired a *wayang kulit* troupe from Gerung, a village in South-western Lombok (thus the troupe is popularly known as Wayang Gerung). This was easily the most popular and well known of all the Lombok *wayang kulit* groups, and wherever they went they invariably drew large crowds of spectators. Its founder and acting *dalang* (puppet performer), *lalu* Nasip had from the early 1970s been engaged in campaigning for Golkar, and although he told me that he was neutral this time, he was still engaged in the Golkar campaign.

An hour before the performance was about to start the arena was already crowded and when the gamelan orchestra finally struck up the first tones, some 5,000 people had congregated to watch the performance and listen to *lalu* Nasip. Before beginning the actual performance he invited all those present to come back the next day to attend the Golkar campaign 'and maybe', he added, 'you will then be attracted by the Golkar message. If so, please pierce number 33. You do not have to be confused or afraid; if you think that Golkar is good, pierce Golkar.' The performance he now staged was much shorter than a traditional *wayang* performance – by one o'clock in the night it was already over (it usually lasts until daybreak). The narrative parts taken directly from Amir Hamza had been severely reduced in length. Instead, *lalu* Nasip made frequent use of the funny figures, the clowns. These are always a favourite with the public and when they appear, interest focuses intensely on what happens on the stage. While the acts of the main characters in the narrative parts are predetermined and identical each time the play is enacted, the appearances of the clowns are spontaneous and adapted to suit local circumstances. Thus, the clowns are not only funny, they also comment, often critically, on whatever is taking place at the time, which is certain to engage the spectators. This time, of course, it was the upcoming election that was the central topic for the clowns. The clowns were not actually urging the spectators to vote for Golkar; rather, they talked in allegories such as the following:

> Don't be quickly satisfied with a new road – wait until you know if the road is straight and that it does not lead you into a ravine. What is wrong with following the old road which has already a strong layer of asphalt, where you know that the bridges are strong and wide and you already know exactly where it takes you.
>
> When you enter a car, do not just consider the condition of the car. Look at the driver, too. Is he experienced and does he know the road and how to take his passengers safely to their destination? A new car with an inexperienced driver may take you quickly to your destination, but often the trip ends in a ravine or in a collision with another vehicle.
>
> Do not just choose another person because he looks sweet. After some time you may realize that the sweet look was merely a mask which is torn off, and you are left with the original ugly face.

Finally, before leaving the spectators to return home, *lalu* Nasip once again urged them to come back to the arena to participate in the Golkar campaign show. The next day early in the afternoon, the arena began to be crowded once again, and when the campaign meeting began, about 6,000 people had congregated. This was a giant show with several different orchestras playing, people dancing and shouting, lots of snacks, drinks and other things being sold, people meeting, talking, joking and enjoying themselves. The show lasted some 3–4 hours, after which people slowly began to drift back home. In between the partying there was also some serious action on the stage; the Golkar candidates were presented and lots of speeches were made. Only a few were listening, however; most people, and especially the young, could not care less. Basically the message was very similar to the one preached by *lalu* Nasip the evening before, only a little more straightforward this time. Instead of allusions to roads and cars, Golkar was now held up as the only reliable alternative. 'You know what you have, Golkar stands for stability, progress and will always continue to work on behalf of the ordinary people. All those who now smear Golkar, talking about corruption and manipulation, do so only because of selfish motives, you do not know how they will perform if elected. Therefore, come, let us together make sure that the New Golkar wins. God is with us and if the people stand united we can together assure *keadilan dan kemakmuran* (justice and welfare) for everybody.' More specifically, three issues were emphasized, first, the need for stability and continuity which was represented, of course, by Golkar, second, the need to fight against crime to keep Indonesian society *aman* (calm and peaceful) and finally, the third constantly recurring issue was to continue *pembangunan*, to develop the country and especially to do this on behalf of the poor.

Apart from this huge public event, very little local campaigning, as described before for the 1997 election, was undertaken this time. This was a single mobilization, centrally organized and directed; any local initiatives like those taken before were almost completely absent.

But it was not only Golkar that was hardly visible during the campaign period preceding the 1999 election: the other political parties were also largely absent in the Bayan subdistrict. Only 5 of the remaining 47 participating parties were registered for campaigning in Bayan: namely, the PDI-P, the PPP, the PAN, the PKB and the PDR, and of these only the three first were at all visible. Of these, only one, the PDI-P, had a local cadre capable of some independent campaigning. This was carried out as a door-to-door campaign, visiting the households in selected hamlets, trying to convince the members to vote for the party. Two other parties, the PPP and the PAN, both held one campaign rally each at which most of the participants came on trucks, cars and motorcycles from outside the area. Besides this there were no other campaign activities in the area. None of the political rallies in Bayan included a parade of trucks and motorcycles (*pawai*), events that were so prominent in the campaigns in other parts of the country (see the chapter by Antlöv). Participants were brought to the campaign arena by bus and truck, and when passing by there was some flag-waving, but that was all.

I visited the PPP and PAN rallies, and except for the number present – maybe five hundred at the PPP rally and two hundred at the PAN meeting – they were similar to the huge Golkar rally. On both occasions an orchestra played, people were dancing and shouting, candidates were presented and short speeches were given. Unlike the Golkar campaign, however, it was not the need for stability and continuity that was stressed but the need for change and reform. At both occasions much fire was directed towards Golkar, which was accused of everything from nepotism and corruption to causing an irreparable division of the country. Characteristically, very little was said, except in very general terms, about their own programmes and what politics they would follow if they came to power. Local issues were not touched upon at all. Again, unlike the Golkar rally, which almost turned into a popular festival, both these occasions were very tame.

The PAN rally was almost sad to see with a very small group of devoted participants assembled in one corner of a huge deserted field. Almost all the participants had been bussed in from outside the area.

The PDI-P also held a public rally. Unfortunately it took place before my arrival, but I have been told that this drew a larger number of participants, some said a thousand, others two thousand. It followed the same basic pattern as the other rallies, containing entertainment mixed with the presentation of candidates and short statements. Here as well the main issue seems to have been Golkar-bashing, but unlike the two other parties, the PDI-P also possessed a well-known front figure, the immensely popular Megawati Sukarnoputri. During the rally she was presented as the only able politician and the obvious next president of the country. People were urged to come to Praya, the main town in Central Lombok, a few days later to meet Megawati during her only appearance in Lombok.

Given the imbalance in campaigning and resources, it came as no surprise to people when the result was announced. In the sub-district as a whole Golkar received a small but secure majority of 52.9 per cent as against a national total of 22.5 per cent. The PDI-P came in a clear second with 19.6 per cent (national total 33.8) and the PPP came third with 5.5 per cent of the votes (national total 10.7). All the remaining parties received only a token vote, in most cases far below 1 per cent. The only notable exception was that the PDI, the PNI and the PNI Masa Marhaen received a few hundred votes each, in most cases probably misplaced PDI-P votes.[17]

Interpreting the election results for 1997 and 1999

After having described the structure and preliminaries of the two elections in Bayan, let us now try to understand the election results – the almost complete dominance of Golkar during the latter part of the New Order period and the fact that even afterwards the party could continue to win an absolute majority. We must begin by taking a look at some specific features of the social structure of Bayan society: the traditional hierarchy system and the accompanying loyalties of the patron–client relationship.

Comparing the position in 1997 of Golkar and the two so-called political parties, we find a striking imbalance in favour of the former. Not only could Golkar muster large economic resources, it also had the complete and undivided support of the entire local nobility which also controlled most of the government apparatus. All people with a position of some kind, that is, all those with a following and an influence were automatically and by definition members of Golkar. Therefore, during the 1997 campaign, the party was able to stage an impressive show. Practically everybody who matters in the sub-district took an active part in the campaigning at one time or another, at least to the extent that they turned up to make a short speech urging the assembled people, many of whom were already among their close associates and followers, to cast their votes for Golkar. Although this automatic and straightforward support of all local power holders had disappeared in 1999, the party still had the financial and personal resources to stage an impressive campaign rally, but it could no longer continue to hold meetings all over the sub-district as it had been done before.

Until the democratic transitions, the situation for the PDI and the PPP was very different from that faced by Golkar. Not only were they almost totally without resources – they had almost no staff, could muster no important persons for their campaign – they could not even carry out an open campaign at all. With the exception of the one, small and unimpressive campaign meeting of the PDI in 1997, neither of the two parties had any public activities at all during the official campaign month preceding the 1997 election. It seems that the PPP was not able to stage any activities at all in Bayan, and any campaigning that was done on behalf of the PDI was, as we have seen, semi-secret and on a strict person-to-person basis.

In fact, the presence of the two parties was barely tolerated at all in the sub-district. Since they were official parties, the authorities were unable to ban them outright, but apart from that every possible measure was taken to prevent them from gaining any influence. The movements of the campaign staff were tracked and the people whom they visited were later questioned, and, if necessary, threatened more or less openly by the local Golkar representative. Known, and also suspected, PDI and PPP sympathizers were socially ostracized.

Even during the first real multi-party election in 1999, the situation was not very much different. Although political parties were now free to stage whatever activities and campaigning they wanted, in practice only 4 of the 48 participating parties managed to hold even a single campaign rally, and of these only the Golkar rally was of any substance. Of all the parties only the PDI-P had a small local organization; all the other parties were totally absent. The rallies held by three of them were centrally organized and except for the Golkar rally most of the participants came from other parts of the island.

To sum up, during the New Order period the situation was, in many different ways, so skewed in favour of Golkar that, in practice at least, there was a one-party system in this part of Indonesia. Theoretically there was a multi-party system, but since in practice the political parties were prevented from becoming real alternatives, it cannot be seriously treated as such. Even after Suharto's resignation, a similar situation continued; in fact, Golkar was the only party with a strong enough party organization to offer something viable in Lombok and in many other parts of outer Indonesia. In Bayan itself the traditional politics of the nobility still held sway and they managed to mobilize their followers in support of Golkar and their candidate.

Power and the party system

Benedict Anderson (1972: 20ff.) has argued that the Javanese concept of the past, expressed in contemporary popular thought as well as in the rich doctrinal literature, makes a sharp distinction between a golden age, a *jaman mas* and a mad age, a *jaman edan*, expressed as an oscillation between times of order and times of disorder. When order prevails, the power is concentrated, during the mad age it becomes diffused. My analysis of local politics in Lombok shows that a prominent feature of campaign speeches during the New Order was to show how the Suharto government represented a period of order and harmony and from this state of things flowed with an almost automatic logic all the impressive developments to which the campaign pointed. Thus, since this was a golden age, there was development which was at the same time proof that the power was concentrated, just and legitimate. This state of things was then contrasted with the confusion and chaos, the mad age, which reigned when politics ruled during the Old Order. As long as Golkar and the New Order apparatus could continue to make such an impression credible they could keep their *wahyu*, their divinely inspired legitimacy to rule.

According to this view, it is inevitable, however, that sooner or later the concentration of power will begin to disintegrate. When this happens it is due to *pamrih*, 'the wasting of concentrated Power on the satisfaction of personal passions' (Anderson 1972: 21). What happened in May 1998 when the New Order crumbled can then be seen as the culmination of such a process of diffusion. Suharto struggled to retain his *wahyu* but in vain, since once the process has set in, it is irreversible.

An analysis of the campaign speeches in 1997 reveals a number of prominent themes (see also Voionmaa's chapter in this volume). First, and above all, there is the theme of *pembangunan*, development. Golkar was identified with the New Order regime, which was portrayed as the source of all development. It was not development in general or in some abstract sense which was emphasized, but very concrete examples of what happened in the immediate vicinity of the voters – thus developments which mattered for them in their daily lives. It was also striking that all the examples concerned infrastructural improvements in one sense or another: a new road, bridges across the rivers, water pipes to bring water to the fields or drinking water to the hamlets or the installation of electricity. The message was clear, simple and very powerful: look, we have brought you all this and we are prepared to continue to deliver the goods. Do not spoil your chances for a better future by voting for a political party that will only bring back the conflicts and the chaos of the Old Order. Similar features were enlarged upon during the Golkar campaign in 1999 as well, only this time the party also had to put some effort into defending itself against accusations of corruption and mismanagement from the other parties. In principle, however, the message was the same; the reformation had brought no changes to the Golkar campaign in Lombok.

Another prominent feature of the 1997 campaign speeches was the association of Golkar with the government, a legitimate and divinely inspired authority. In all the campaigns it was stressed again and again that Golkar was the only legitimate authority. Representatives of all the local power holders, the civil servants as well as police, military and *adat* or religious leaders (depending on whether the meeting was held in a native community or among the transmigrants) were parading on the scene to give an impression that everybody was united behind Golkar. Since the campaign leader Anggirta was the youngest son of the established ruling family, the traditional authority and loyalty vested in him was also utilized in the campaign. Who else but a descendant of the Bayanese *datu* (king) would be able to fight for the area and make sure that the development would continue? When, on top of all the other imposing authority figures, a member of the royal family was displayed to the commoners as a Golkar supporter, who could then withstand the message from this powerful entourage? The message was the same in 1999 with the Golkar DPR-D-candidate still coming from the old royal family.[18] Apart from the fact that there was no local campaigning as in earlier elections, the message was the same and Golkar was still identified with order and development.

The political history of the Bayan area gives ample proof of the success of the recruitment strategy, which has its roots in the theory of power analysed in the introductory paragraphs. During the Sukarno period, the area was overwhelmingly PNI and shortly after the emergence of the New Order the Bayanese attached themselves to this new power centre, to the extent that they were officially portrayed as the *lumbung Golkar*, the 'storehouse' of Golkar. Even after the reformation, the strategy seemed to continue; Golkar and the PDI-P were the only two parties that received a substantial share of the votes. Most people still clung to the old powerhouse, but the situation was very uncertain and the votes for the PDI-P may be seen as the beginning of a new power centre replacing the crumbling New Order.

In order to clarify the way loyalties operate in Bayan politics, the first questions to be asked are what the parties actually represent for the villagers and how they function. From the foregoing description of the role of the parties, it is obvious that there is one factor which takes precedence above everything else when determining political loyalties – and that is the tendency for people to associate themselves with a locally important person, to become part of his following. In fact, the political system can be seen as consisting of layers of patrons and their clients in concentric but also partly overlapping circles – from petty officials on the hamlet level all the way up through the village, the sub-district, the district and the provincial levels.

This is an old principle for structuring administrative and political loyalties. Patron–client relationships have, in fact, been one of the leading organizational principles in Lombok society for several hundred years. In the old kingdoms, the *datu*, the kings and their relatives were constantly involved in manipulation and intrigues with each other in a quest to win the minds and hearts of the population.[19] What has happened now is that the same principles have been brought into the party system. Instead of being ideologically grounded and based on democratic selection criteria, the struggle for power between the parties is a more or less direct continuation of earlier methods and practices. The mode of power struggles characteristic of the petty kingdoms continues within the guise of modern political parties.

In past times there were no clear-cut geographical borders between the kingdoms. Instead there was an ongoing quest and competition to win as many followers as possible. These kingdoms had a central core of undisputed influence, but after that the supremacy faded away into a grey zone, perhaps with some bright spots but without total control. In those extensive border areas, alliances often shifted and zones of influence were intertwined. Such instability created a sort of power balance between the elite and the general population. The villagers could put pressure on their masters if they felt unduly exploited. If this happened, another competing *datu* would be only too happy to extend his protection to them, thereby enlarging his own sphere of influence at the expense of his rival. This constant manipulation often led to warfare among the competing petty kingdoms.

Undoubtedly, similar processes are at work when political loyalties are staked out among the villagers today. In the villages, the alliances that were created have, in rather vague words, been described as 'factional politics'. A more appropriate terminology would perhaps be to use the Indonesian phrase '*bapakisme*', implying the existence of a powerful, dominant father figure, a *bapak*, who controls everything and who is never openly contradicted by his subordinates (*anak buah*). Relations between a *bapak* and his *anak buah* that have their roots in the old kingdoms form the basis for politics and the jostling for power and influence on the village level today (Cederroth 1991).

This pattern has put its stamp on politics not only locally but also on the national level. In his work about the Indonesian Nationalist Party, Joel Rocamora wrote that

> In the pre-election period, political parties should not then be seen as hierarchical entities with roots deep in Indonesian society, fiercely fighting each other on the basis of mutually exclusive ideological claims, but rather as factions within a definable national elite divided on the basis of more mundane differences in personal experience and outlook.
>
> (Rocamora 1974: 5–6)

According to Rocamora, the parties during the late 1950s and early 1960s slowly began to define themselves on the basis of ideological and cultural differences (1974: 6). Although this might perhaps have been the case among party leaders and intellectuals in or near the centre, ideological subtleties have, as yet, not filtered through to the voters in the villages.

In the case of the Bayan area many of the elements from the old social structure at the time of the kingdom have survived until this very day. Anderson (1972) has argued that in traditional Java a just ruler gained his legitimacy by being powerful, in control, and having a certain radiation of divine authority. The Lombok kingdoms, which were founded by Javanese migrants in the fifteenth century, (Goris 1936) were based on the same principles. When the political parties appeared after independence they were incorporated into the old pattern as a new element, handy to use as an instrument for the power games in the social arena. On the one hand party politics became an instrument with which a traditional ruling syncretist nobility, who felt their power basis being eroded by a rapidly growing community of orthodox Muslim newcomers, could associate themselves with an omnipotent *bapak*, at first Sukarno and later Suharto, thereby gaining the blessings of the state apparatus. On the other hand, the parties could also be useful in the internal power game between different elite persons aspiring to the position of leading *bapak* in the sub-district administration or in one of its villages. This intra-elite wrestling for power and influence is, in principle, identical with that which took place in the old kingdoms.

To the Bayanese nobility, the parties might be a new toy, but this toy is used to play the same old game. The mass rallies organized by Golkar during the campaign can be seen as power legitimating ceremonies. By displaying power absorbed from various sources, from persons who possess an exceptional amount of power, be it worldly, through prominent civil servants, the police and the military, or spiritually, either through *adat* leaders (*pemangku*) or religious leaders, *kiyai* or *tuan guru*, or through the use of catchwords that are filled with an innate power (*pembangunan, Pancasila, Orde Baru*), the ceremony is intended as a public show of the amount of power concentrated within the Golkar party.

Even if the parties constitute nothing but a new element in an old power game, it is obvious that there is at least one great dividing line between the parties as they are seen in Bayan. Ethnic parties have never found much support in Indonesia, neither during the Sukarno period nor today. The claim by Rocamora that in the 1950s and 1960s the political parties began to define themselves on the basis of cultural differences can be seen to be the case for our area only if the concept of cultural differences is taken in a broader sense and refers to the two religious and social communities of syncretists and orthodox Muslims, that is, a phenomenon similar to the religious typology developed by Geertz (1960), and said to be characteristic of Indonesian politics in the late Sukarno period.

In addition to the patron–client relations, the party system also contains elements of strife among faction-like power groups. These factions manipulate and use the party system for their own purposes. In the description of the campaign technique used in 1997 it was repeatedly noted that Anggirta, the Golkar leader, often referred to his own personal history, how he had switched from the PDI to Golkar and how his luck had changed as a result of this. The fact that he so often stressed this can be understood in light of what has been said here about the periodic concentration and diffusion of power and the necessity of attaching oneself to those circles where a concentration of power re-emerges. Because of his position as head of one of three major nobility lines he has a considerable local influence. His noble bloodline has traditional dependants in several hamlets with several hundred families as his direct followers.[20] Therefore, as long as he stayed with the PDI and campaigned on behalf of that party, it had a strong position in the area, its number of votes almost totalling those of Golkar. The leading figures of the two other noble lineages had quickly realized, however, that the rise of the New Order demanded new loyalties and within a few years they had all switched to Golkar. The fact that Anggirta remained for some time with the PDI was due not only to stubbornness. There were also elements of an internal power struggle with the two other aristocratic lineages in his decision. Some details of the conflict were discussed earlier, and without going into further detail here,[21] it should just be noted that it was for some time a severe threat to the position of the nobility and it was solved only after mediation by the eldest member of the dominant noble lineage.

After Anggirta switched from campaigning for the PDI to Golkar he also had to convince his past followers, especially when campaigning in pro-PDI hamlets. An analysis of the speeches in which he tries to justify his shift of party loyalties shows that his arguments were expressed in terms of concentration and diffusion of power. The PDI had now lost its concentration of power; it could no longer protect and support him. Instead, the power had passed to Golkar, as could be seen from all the impressive developments that had taken place. Therefore, he also became convinced of the need to support this new power centre. Furthermore, he referred to the need for internal unity and harmony, which would be the result of his support for the new power holders.

I would finally want to argue that parties in 1999 are once again defining themselves on the basis of ideological and cultural differences. There are the parties that are seen as proponents of a traditional, *adat*-bound lifestyle, that is, formerly the PNI and the PKI and now Golkar and the PDI-P, and then there are the Muslim parties, formerly the NU and Masyumi, until the reformation the PPP and after that also the PKB. Among the parties in each group there are certain differences, but to shift, for example, from the PDI to Golkar and vice versa would not be really problematic. To take the corresponding step from the PNI to the NU in 1971, or from the PDI-P to the PKB in 1999, would be something quite different. It would amount to nothing less than a shift of worldview (see Endang Turmudi's chapter for a similar argument for East Java). Such a shift cannot take place overnight and absolutely not by force, as the example of Bayan demonstrates. During the last twenty years, there has been a large migration into the Bayan area, mainly consisting of orthodox *waktu lima* Sasak who have moved from the densely populated central parts of the island. They have settled separately and seldom mix with the local population. Almost all the votes for any of the Muslim parties came from the hamlets where the new-comers had settled, whereas among the local population there was a reverse situation: here it was Golkar or the PDI-P who received almost all the votes, while very few went to a Muslim party.

Thus, we have found in the case of Bayan more or less similar structures and motivations in all observed cases of party affiliation. The common people look to the most powerful local person, with whom they attempt to associate and from whom they expect help and protection. This person, in turn, is attracted by the charismatic qualities of an extraordinary leader on either side of the great dividing line in the society – that between syncretist traditional-ists and orthodox Muslims. The political parties are seen primarily as defendants of either the *adat*, the traditions, or of the only true religion, Islam. For the villagers, the differences between the parties on each side are of a non-ideological nature and have to do with internal factional politics, that is, conflicts between leading syncretists on one hand and between com-peting *tuan guru* on the other. The parties are the vehicle through which they show their allegiance, and in this respect the democratic reformation has brought about no changes. If the PDI-P is seen as the legitimate successor to the PDI, it can also be seen that it is still the same three parties that existed during the New Order through which the factions compete. The other forty-five parties were simply non-existent as far as the Bayan area was concerned. Thus, the change from controlled New Order elections to democratic elec-tions has meant very little; local politics continues in the same way as before.

Notes

1 Both the patrimonial state with its traditional authority as well as the legal authority with its rational bureaucracy as described here are ideal types. In prac-tice, real societies may resemble the ideal type more or less closely and may well exhibit a mixture of forms of ideal types.
2 *Adat* is customary law or tradition.
3 A *pemangku* is a kind of pre-Islamic medium who handles relations with the spirit world. A *kiyai* is a kind of Muslim priest who handles relations with Allah on behalf of the other villagers. They perform the prayers, officiate at cere-monies, etc. For more information on the position of respective officials see Polak (1978) and Cederroth (1981).
4 At that time *gotong royong* (mutual help) was a word of honour in Indonesian politics, frequently evoked by Sukarno himself.
5 Similar stories are found on Java, known as *Ratu Adil*.
6 The Bayanese nobility is internally divided into three faction-like groups, coin-ciding with the hamlet's borders. They all intermarry frequently and are all closely related, however. Despite the internal controversies, external solidarity is therefore strong and they always attempt to stand united against outside threats.

7　The history of Golkar is described by David Reeve (1985).

8　Some *wetu telu* in another part of north Lombok chose differently and were registered as Buddhists. See Cederroth 1996 for more details about these conversions.

9　Selong is the name of a district town in East Lombok. During the Balinese period this was a place to which people were exiled.

10　The buffalo is the symbol of PDI.

11　*Cupak grantang* is a masked theatre performance staged by the villagers themselves.

12　Torean is the last hamlet on the slope of Mount Rinjani and one of three possible starting points from which to begin the climb to the crater lake, Segara Anak, and the summit itself.

13　The five basic principles of the Republic of Indonesia: belief in God; national unity; humanism; social justice; and sovereignty of the people.

14　Golkar was always place number two in the elections, the moderate in between. The number two also made for a convenient symbol: two fingers in the air, symbolizing 'V' as in victory.

15　The term '*maliq*' is used to describe anything and everything which is either absolutely compulsory or absolutely forbidden. *Maliq* thus connotes severe, but unknown, supernatural consequences if what is forbidden is nevertheless carried out or, alternatively, if that which is required is ignored. In Indonesian *maliq* is always translated as '*tidak boleh tidak*'; absolute and unquestionable.

16　Before the system of weekly markets was established in the early 1980s, an informal exchange of surplus products was the only way of trading. If someone had a surplus of maize for instance, he took as much as he could carry and walked to some relatives or friends in another hamlet where he knew that, say, a lot of coconuts were grown, and the products were then exchanged. There was no haggling, it was all done on a basis of mutual understanding, and of course the *mendea* sessions also offered excellent opportunities for an exchange of views and the latest news.

17　The confusion between these very similar parties even led to one candidate appearing on the lists of two parties, PDI and PNI. He was a candidate for the local parliament in the district of West Lombok and appeared as no. 9 on the PDI list and as no. 5 on the PNI list. He subsequently withdrew from the PNI list. During the Sukarno period he had been a PNI adherent and later he had continued to support PDI, but when asked about the programme of the two parties for which he was now a candidate, he had no answer.

18　Of the three sons, the oldest was the sub-district head, the middle the Bayanese village head and the youngest was, in 2001, the Golkar representative of the DPR-D. Even though there now are elections, so far the posts have been hereditary, kept within the family. For many generations it has had a virtual monopoly on all locally important civil servant posts. Nobody has ever contested its authority in an election.

19　An excellent description of the power game in traditional Balinese kingdoms is found in Geertz 1980.

20　Traditionally, the hamlets were attached to one or another of these three noble lineages. The noblemen controlled the distribution of communal land and in turn they expected, and got, corvée labour on their own land, assistance with their ceremonial obligations and loyalty in matters of power and influence. Although these patron–client relations have been somewhat undermined by the recent transfer of the communally owned land into private ownership, they are still intact to a great extent, especially with regard to ceremonial and loyalty obligations.

21　See Cederroth 1981: 142ff. for a discussion of these conflicts.

References

Anderson, Benedict R. O'G. (1972) 'The idea of power in Javanese culture'. In C. Holt (ed.), *Culture and Politics in Indonesia*. Ithaca: Cornell University Press, pp. 1–69.

Antlöv, Hans (1995) *Exemplary Centre, Administrative Periphery: Rural Leadership and the New Order in Java*. Richmond: Curzon Press.

Cederroth, Sven (1977) 'Religiösa Reformrörelser på Lombok' [Religious reform movements on Lombok]. *Historisk Tidskrift*, no. 4, 350–373.

——(1981) *The Spell of the Ancestors and the Power of Mekkah. A Sasak Community on Lombok*. Gothenburg Studies in Social Anthropology, no. 3. Gothenburg: Acta Universitatis Gothoburgensis.

——(1991) 'From PNI to Golkar. Indonesian village politics, 1955–87'. In M. Mörner and Th. Svensson (eds), *The Transformation of Rural Society in the Third World*. London and New York: Routledge, pp. 265–294.

——(1996) 'From ancestor worship to monotheism. Politics of religion in Lombok'. *Temenos*, 32, 7–36.

——(1997) 'Return of the birds. Revival of Wetu Telu religion in the village of Bayan, Lombok, Indonesia'. Unpublished paper.

Geertz, Clifford (1960) *The Religion of Java*. Chicago: University of Chicago Press.

——(1980) *Negara. The Theatre State in Nineteenth Century Bali*. Princeton: Princeton University Press.

Goris, R. (1936) 'Aaanteekeningen over Oost-Lombok'. *Tijdschrift voor Indische Taal, -Land- en Volkenkunde*, 76, 196–248.

Koentjaraningrat (1985) *Javanese Culture*. Singapore: Oxford University Press.

Polak, A. (1978) 'Traditie en Tweespalt in een Sasakse Boerengemeenschap (Lombok, Indonesie)' [Tradition and duality in a Sasak farming community (Lombok, Indonesia)]. Proefschrift (unpublished PhD dissertation), Rijksuniversiteit te Utrecht.

Reeve, David (1985) *Golkar of Indonesia. An Alternative to the Party System*. Singapore: Oxford University Press.

Rocamora, Joel (1974) 'Nationalism in search of ideology: the Indonesian nationalist party, 1946–1965'. PhD Thesis. Ithaca: Cornell University.

Weber, Max (1964) *The Theory of Social and Economic Organization*. New York. The Free Press.

6

NATIONAL ELECTIONS, LOCAL ISSUES

The 1997 and 1999 national elections in a village on Java*

Hans Antlöv

When the local branch of the Golkar party decided not to campaign in the village of Sariendah in West Java ahead of the 1999 elections, it came as no great surprise. Although the party only two years earlier – in the last election under the authoritarian Suharto regime – had received more than 75 per cent of the votes in the village, the last few years had been dramatic. Nationally, President Suharto had been forced to step down and new democratic elections were announced. In Sariendah, Golkar had come under fire for corruption and abuse of power – the village headman had been reported to higher authorities. The local Golkar branch therefore decided to hold a very low-key campaign and build their vote recruitment on a personal basis. However, the real surprise came after the election, when Golkar ended up the second largest party in Sariendah (and in Indonesia). To understand this result we need to go beyond a study of political ideologies and party programmes to look at how political parties are organized in the country-side, and what sentiments and attitudes make people vote for particular parties. Different parties draw on different emotions. Some political parties in Indonesia are able to depend on long-lasting loyalties, past achievements and traditional bonds, while others build on sentiments of joint action, mass mobilization through ritual and powerful symbols. Others again recruit votes based on religious values and sacred representations.

* Research done in 1997 was part of a comparative project at Göteborg University on Discourses and Practices of Democracy in Southeast Asia funded by the Swedish Sida/SAREC. Research in 1999 was done while working in Jakarta for the Ford Foundation. I am grateful to these institutions for encouraging my academic curiosity. I greatly appreciate the comments made on this chapter by Sven Cederroth, Robert Cribb, Stefan Eklund, Olle Törnquist, Anders Uhlin and Joakim Öjendal.

The local and cultural dimension of politics is often neglected or simplified by political observers. I argued in the introductory chapter (Chapter 1) that fascinating details about democratic and political ideals are revealed in the mix of the local and the national. It is impossible to understand voting behaviour (and thus election results) without taking into account the local setting and common political sentiments, the everyday issues that matter to people. This might be true of many countries, but is accentuated in Indonesia where personal relations and communal feeling are still strong. Politics in Indonesia are much more than ideology and party programmes. A lack of knowledge about deep sentiments, symbols and political culture might explain why the political reform movement came as such a surprise to many commentators in 1998. This chapter sets out to understand the local politics and sentiments that motivated political behaviour in the 1997 and 1999 elections in a village in West Java. I will look at these elections as mirrors of political and social dynamics at the local level. Since other chapters in this book have outlined the national scene, I will only briefly sketch macro-level developments and focus instead on how national elections were interpreted and enacted in the countryside, far away from the corridors of power in Jakarta. The main analysis is of the local meaning and practice of the 1997 and 1999 national elections in Sariendah, a semi-urban village of some 10,000 people outside Majalaya in West Java.[1]

The 1997 elections

The 1997 election was the last under the New Order, and characterized by a controlled and engineered (and yet violent) campaign. Political developments had already started to get out of hand, with the killings at the PDI headquarters in July 1996 and regional violence in a number of areas around Indonesia. More than ever it was important for the central government to display to the world that they controlled the country and that the election was one large *pesta demokrasi*, a democratic festival. The country was still heralded by the World Bank, ADB and others as a model of governance that could be exported to other countries. But this could only be maintained if the image of Indonesia as a safe country to invest in was preserved.

As has been the case with all elections under the New Order, the formal structure of the election was closely circumscribed. Only three political parties were allowed: Golkar, the PPP and the PDI (cf. Haris's Chapter 2 in this volume). Formal campaigning was allowed only four weeks ahead of the national elections (it had been shortened by one week: in earlier years there had been five weeks of campaigning). But for all practical purposes, the campaign for Golkar was a continuous effort, as it was the only party allowed to organize itself in the countryside. Village officials seldom missed an opportunity to mention Golkar in speeches, and the closer the elections, the more visible this 'Golkarization' became. Economic development was a cornerstone for the legitimacy of the New Order, and material progress was always ascribed to the government and to Golkar (again a conceptual conflation of state, government and party). Village and hamlet meetings in 1996 and 1997 seldom failed to mention the upcoming 'democratic festival'. During a village meeting on family planning in February 1997, for instance, the sub-district official talked for half an hour about the New Order's achievements, of course including President Suharto's award by the UNDP (for successful family planning) a few years before. Golkar's 'pre-campaign' was done in a variety of forums: village meetings, mosques, rituals. Indonesia has a lot of official days: Teacher's Day, Armed Forces Day, Woman's Day [*Hari Kartini*], Youth Oath Day [*Sumpah Pemuda*], etc. These events were part of Golkar's campaign. The message was repeated over and over: Golkar is the only guarantee for growth and stability; Suharto is the leader who developed Indonesia; the New Order must continue to grow strong.

Six months ahead of the election, Golkar began formally to recruit voters. As we have seen, civil servants were *ex officio* members of the Civil Servant's Corps (*Korpri*). Since *Korpri* was, together with the armed forces, part of the greater Golkar family (*Keluarga Besar Golongan Karya*), *Korpri* members were expected to support Golkar (Reeve 1985: 326). This also extended to their families. Wives were organized in *Dharma Wanita* and children were encouraged to join the *Karang Taruna*, the state-backed Association of Active Youth. In November 1996, in accordance with national policies, the Golkar chairman in Sariendah appointed some 300 *dasa wisma*, loyal Golkar cadres, each of whom was responsible for recruiting ten voters in their immediate neighbourhoods. The recruitment was done along lines of patronage and political loyalties, the patrons (in this case the Golkar leadership) using promises of power and privileged treatment in exchange for political loyalty. This form of personal campaigning proved to be very effective. The cadres, who were local power-holders, could use all of their resources and power to persuade or force people into signing up for Golkar. Each hamlet chairman kept a membership book with photos and signatures of all members. The membership drive was carried out by the *dasa wisma* in collaboration with village officials and members of the hamlet-based paramilitary Civil Defence Corps (*Hansip*). The local leaders went from house to house, asking people to join Golkar. The arguments they used were strongly developmentalist: that Golkar and the New Order (the two were inseparable and interchangeable) had brought paved roads, health care centres, schools, television, even telephone lines to the village. Very few had the initiative or courage to resist the arguments of their leaders. When I asked the Golkar chairman in Sariendah why only 90 per cent of villagers had been signed up, he smiled to me knowingly and said that 'it would be a bad democracy if Golkar won all the votes'.

Why did people join Golkar? Fear was certainly a reason. A refusal to join Golkar could be interpreted as an anti-*Pancasila* activity and become subject to disciplinary sanctions. But more importantly, the intimacy of social relations and the strength of local leaders were convincing reasons. Or in the words of Syamsuddin Haris in this volume (Chapter 2): 'Long before they started the campaign, and long before people put their ballot in the box, the political system was construed so as to make it virtually impossible for the PPP and the PDI to obtain any substantial support'. It is important to remember that one never really saw the military march on the streets in New Order Indonesia. Compliance and support were gathered in more sophisticated ways. Most people simply said that they supported Golkar because they 'followed their leader', the powerful figures who talked with an authoritative voice. They joined Golkar in order to reduce personal interests and conform to village standards. The cadres who urged people to join Golkar were not urbane politicians or state officials from faraway places but local patrons and advisers, even relatives. To say 'no' to their request – perhaps in the presence of a village official – would be to reject the authority of those one trusts and those with whom one shares a living. People had been told over and over again by their leaders that the New Order was the only possible regime, and that Golkar was effectively their only choice. By joining Golkar, they submitted to the authority of their leaders and maintained public harmony. If they did not join Golkar, there would always be the threat of disciplinary action by their patrons, the village leadership. This is not to say that many people did not willingly join Golkar. The membership fee was very low and the material benefits possibly great, through development programmes. Golkar was not an unpopular party.

To be sure, some people were dissatisfied with features of the New Order, and especially the political and economic manoeuvring of the first family and other high-ranking officials. But the economic benefits and political stability that the New Order brought balanced and transcended this. Promises of immediate benefits have always been important aspects of Golkar's campaign. In many cases a hamlet or village leader would directly approach the sub-district branch of Golkar and suggest a project to be initiated if Golkar won by a certain percentage. One such promise in Sariendah involved the continuous effort by Cilembur, one of the poorest hamlets in Sariendah, to build a new mosque. The hamlet chairman had ever since the elections in 1987 been bargaining for a new mosque if Golkar obtained more than 90 per cent of the votes. So far, they had not reached the target, and no mosque had been built. The sub-district office in Majalaya promised again in 1997 to build a mosque in the hamlet if Golkar won by this margin. Other promises were less specific: that economic growth would continue under Golkar, and that political stability might be challenged if other parties grew too strong.

Submit to Golkar's authority, yes, but to a degree. A building company owned by Suharto's daughter Siti Hardijanti 'Tutut' Hastuti Rukmana bought a large piece of land in another neighbouring Majalaya village in

1995. Four hundred simple townhouses were built on the land, primarily for retired army officers from the Siliwangi Division in Bandung. In April 1997, Tutut herself came by helicopter from Jakarta to inaugurate the estate. Most people in Sariendah went there to have a look at this famous personality (and for the food which was freely distributed). When I asked them, people approved of her diverse economic ventures (several construction workers in Sariendah benefited directly since they were employed in the townhouse project), but they also said that Tutut should not try to replace her father, as the media had speculated that she might. A minister, perhaps, but not president, people said.

There was a generation and gender gap here. Young men were definitely more vocal in their critique of the New Order, especially those young men with some education but without proper jobs. Youth unemployment was a major problem in Indonesia, and much of the campaign violence in 1997 has been attributed to this group of lower- and middle-class youth who could not find jobs to match their education. Some frustrated adolescents in Sariendah told me that Suharto was a dictator, and put their hopes on Megawati Sukarnoputri, the new chairperson for the reform wing of the PDI. Women, especially married women, were quieter in their critique. But they, too, were critical and had harsh words to say in private, for instance about the contraceptive injections that village leaders told them to take.

The campaign

Let us now turn to the actual campaign in Sariendah, which covered four weeks in April 1997. Only Golkar held regular campaign meetings: orderly, strictly arranged and lavish. The party had immensely more (state) money at its disposal than the other two parties. In Jakarta and other cities, the media reported that Golkar distributed money to participants in its political rallies. Neighbourhoods were asked to contribute with at least five participants, who were paid a few thousand rupiah to join the Golkar rallies. In smaller cities such as Majalaya, instead of money, thousands of yellow T-shirts and caps were distributed. Some of the more active cadres were given yellow sports jackets. During parades, all the constituent organizations of Golkar were mobilized, such as the *Angkatan Muda Siliwangi*, a support group to the provincial army command, and the *Angkatan Muda Pembaruan Indonesia*, a Golkar youth association established in the late 1960s. The *Pemuda Pancasila* was the most awe-inspiring. This is a group of youngsters generally believed to have been the storm troops behind the raid on the PDI in Jakarta in July 1996.[2] They opened a village branch in Sariendah in 1993 and recruited the most die-hard New Order kids: a mix of hooligans, petty criminals and hardcore Suharto defenders. Their paramilitary uniforms, boots and berets were fearsome. In some cases they were present during Golkar cadre visits to hesitant households. I myself did not see or hear of any direct intimidation, but in this culture of fear, direct threats are not always necessary – power exists, in the words of George Simmel, in its mere possibility. The *Pemuda Pancasila* was active again during balloting, monitoring voting stations, possibly ensuring that people put their votes as they had enlisted.

Marches were organized by Golkar and its support organizations in Sariendah and Majalaya on several occasions. These were highly orchestrated events, with banners stating that 'Golkar brings development', 'The armed forces are the protector of the nation' and the like. A school brass band would play music, and members of a traditional dance group joined the celebration. On one of the main occasions, the district chairman (*bupati*) arrived in a horse-cart parade from Bandung, with hundreds of two-wheeled carts crowding the streets of Majalaya. These parades lasted for hours. Golkar's campaign did indeed live up to the epithet of being a Democratic Festival. People left their houses and watched the parades at the roadside. They waved yellow Golkar flags and gave the 'V' sign – V as in 2, the official number of Golkar in the election (and its number on the ballot), in the middle, in between the two extremist parties.

The PDI was hardly to be seen. The party had been severely weakened by the July 1996 events, in which police had stormed the PDI office in Jakarta, and forced Megawati to step down as chairperson (see Chapter 1). The propaganda around the PDI events was that it was an internal party dispute. The rhetoric went something like 'how can a divided party be trusted to rule the country?' Many people in Sariendah accepted this explanation, but even those who were critical would not support the PDI since the party officially had ousted Megawati Sukarnoputri. Sukarno's daughter retained her strong appeal, and when a movement started in Central Java and Jakarta among Megawati supporters to join the PPP campaign, PDI supporters in Sariendah followed suit. '*Mega–Bintang*' as it became known, ('Mega Star', the star as the symbol of the Islamic PPP party and Mega short for Megawati, also meaning 'superstar') soon became extremely popular in Java, and during campaigning, the PPP rallies were by far the most intense. More than one PDI rally in Majalaya had to be cancelled. The *Mega–Bintang* message filtered through to each and every village. Not many people in Sariendah read newspapers, and TV news in New Order Indonesia was highly partisan, not providing much information about (positive) developments within the PPP and the PDI. But the message from Megawati's supporters to join the campaign of the PPP, rather than their own 'illegal' campaign, was heard loud and clear.

One of the most visible campaign techniques in Indonesia is the *pawai*, the carnivals of trucks, cars and motorcycles covered in party colours driving through the major roads. As has been the case for decades, young men dismantled the mufflers on their motorcycles, painted their faces red (PDI), green (PPP) or yellow (Golkar), and drove at high speed through Sariendah, and onwards on the paved roads to neighbouring villages and on to the town of Majalaya, and back again, over and over, for many hours.

In the PPP rallies (now spiced up by *Mega–Bintang*), many drove only in neighbouring villages, where no one would recognize them; others covered their faces, perfectly well aware of the possible sanctions that could result from supporting a non-government party. There was no village organization behind the PPP rallies, since in accordance with the floating mass policy it could not organize itself in the village – the PPP leadership came from a strongly factional family. People knew by rumour on what days there would be PPP rallies, and joined in. Not all participants lasted to the final campaign meeting in the late afternoon, held at the main Majalaya square, with drum bands and speeches. There were no party-political platforms to be seen during the rallies: pictures of Sukarno and his daughter were forbidden, and no one carried any posters or brochures with campaign issues. It was the *forza* that counted, the *esprit de corps* that was infused to participants. The main topic of village talk was whether Golkar or the PPP had more lively rallies, not whether Golkar or the PPP had the better programme.

The PPP has had an ambivalent relationship with organized Islam (see the chapters by Endang Turmudi and Syamsuddin Haris in this volume) but in Majalaya it was seen as the party for the more conservative Muslims. Much of its internal campaigning was done through NU mosques. In an interesting turn of events, the Bandung government questioned the overtly Islamic message of the PPP in early 1997. In campaign meetings, the issue of '*Islam fanatik*' was raised, with the obvious intention of causing disapproval (without mentioning any party, however). Majalaya and other areas south of Bandung had in the 1950s been the scene of a violent Islamic rebellion in support of an independent nation, the *Darul Islam*. The memory of the fanatic Muslims who burnt many hamlets in Sariendah still lingered on. On a national scale, Islam in Indonesia had become more politicized during the early 1990s. Many Islamic boarding schools had been built, and it was common for girls to wear the Islamic shawl in public schools. But people in Sariendah were still apprehensive about political Islam. Religious orthodoxy is stronger in West Java than in most other provinces, but taking the step towards believing in an Islamic state or even voting for the moderate PPP was still too large for many. One additional problem for the PPP in Sariendah was that during the previous decade the party had been headed by a fractional and isolated family. They had their own small Islamic boarding school, with pupils mostly from outside Sariendah. The family had never been fully accepted by the village community, and joining the PPP would mean an association with this family. This prevented the PPP from recruiting many of the young pro-Mega activists, the 'secular nationalists' as Ramage (1995) calls them. The dilemma of the pro-Mega activists was whether to join the 'Islamist' PPP, and thus take an active part in the campaign, or simply remain inactive (to support the state party Golkar was never an option). As we have seen, most chose the former, both in Sariendah and in the rest of Java (but less so in the outer islands; see Cederroth's chapter for the case of north Lombok, where *Mega–Bintang* was unknown). Here we can see the emergence of religiously based political sentiments, an issue that will become more prominent as we proceed.

What were the ideological issues raised during campaigns? Clearly, Golkar pointed towards its achievements over the past decades as the main reason for supporting the party. Campaigns were organized to highlight order and development. The overall message was that Golkar was the only choice: without the party and Suharto, the country would not survive. The PDI and the PPP were not allowed to say anything different; they could not question the sovereignty of President Suharto, whose presidency was never a campaign issue. Even criticism of his family was seen as subversive. Obviously the July 1996 events played a crucial role for the PDI; it demonstrated that the PDI was not an independent party and therefore not an alternative. Suddenly, with the *Mega–Bintang* coalition, the PPP became the centre of attention. It remained a Muslim party, and this was clearly visible during campaigning, but this was also accompanied by the view that the PPP was the only party that could challenge Golkar for power (within the New Order system, of course).

Voting

The actual balloting was held on 28 May 1997. I observed the balloting closely in one of the twelve polling stations in Sariendah (Leumahcai) and visited several others briefly. I then joined the village officials in their office until well into the next morning. The night before the election, the Civil Defence Corps (*Hansip*) and *Pemuda Pancasila* had stayed up all night to guard the polling stations. Rumour had it that one polling station in another part of Majalaya had been burnt down during the early evening (allegedly by *Mega–Bintang* supporters) and more guards were put on duty during the night. The polling stations had been built the day before from blueprints distributed by the Department of Home Affairs well ahead of time. A detailed manual with precise regulations for the voting procedure and how the station was to look had also been distributed. Several times during election day, the hamlet chairman, who was in charge of the election, consulted the regulations. For instance, one of the questions was whether voting could be closed at noon, ahead of the regulated 2 p.m., since no new voters had arrived. After consulting the book, the hamlet chairman decided to keep voting open until 2 o'clock. By and large, it was a lively and festive event. Vendors were selling food outside, and most villagers were hanging around waiting for the station to close and the counting to begin.

Actual voting was fairly straightforward. The polling station consisted of a fenced yard of some 20 by 10 metres. It had three small ballot booths, two large tables (one for registration, one for the officials), one ballot box with three slots, and one small bench and a small desk for the election observers from the three political parties. There were also some thirty chairs for voters to sit in while waiting for their turn. Chairs and tables were shaded. Sariendah had twelve such ballot stations, divided by hamlets.

At 6.30 in the morning the seven officials and two of the official election observers arrived at the polling station in Leumahcai. The sub-district branch of the PDI had the evening before distributed an official letter to all village headmen in Majalaya stating that no PDI observer would be present. No reason was given in the letter, but the unofficial reason was that they were simply unable to mobilize enough observers. Because of the letter, there was no need for replacement. The Golkar observer in Leumahcai was the local chairman of the Civil Defence Corps while the PPP observer was the youngest brother of the PPP village leader, from another part of the village. The PPP had election observers in eight polling stations. In the remaining eight hamlets, a Civil Defence Corps representative replaced the PPP observer. There were thus two observers in all polling stations.

The ballot papers had been sent from Bandung a few days earlier. They were kept in a sealed box, opened under some pomp at 7.30 a.m., after a short speech by the hamlet chairman. There were 683 eligible voters in Leumahcai, and thus 683 ballots for the national parliament, 683 for the provincial parliament, and the same for the district parliament, each having a separate colour. The ballot was a rectangular piece of paper with the three party symbols: a bull's head for the PDI, a banyan tree for Golkar and a star representing the PPP. The voter made a hole with a nail in the picture of choice (hence the Indonesian name for voting, *coblos*, 'to pierce'). After the observers had counted the ballot papers and toured the premises, they formally acknowledged that voting could start at 8 a.m. The two observers sat down at a separate table between the officials and the ballot box. Hundreds of women and children had already gathered outside. Twenty voters were allowed in. They showed their registration card, and sat down to wait. When their names were called, they went forward to the official's desk, exchanged their registration card for three ballots, and went to the booth. Each booth was 1.5 square metres, wrapped in cloth from rice sacks. It was, as far as I could tell, impossible to look in. After having pierced the ballot, the voters folded the ballot into an envelope, walked outside and put one ballot in each slot in the sealed ballot box. They then left the enclosed area, often to take a snack. Traders of soup, ice cream and other snacks were making good business.

Women voted first. When one impatient young man joined the line of women, people laughed and said that he should wait. After perhaps two hours, more and more men arrived, and by noon most registered voters had visited the polling station. In the early morning it took perhaps forty-five minutes of queuing to vote; by 11 a.m. there was hardly any queue at all. At noon the officials started to look through their lists to see which voters had not yet arrived. The names were called out in public, and the crowd gave their version of why the person had not arrived. It was mostly young men who did not show up.

As we shall see, there was in Sariendah no organized campaign not to vote, or to vote blank, as had been the case in other parts of Java. Pressures for voting were strong. Voting was compulsory in New Order Indonesia. Polling stations were physically located close to where you lived, manned by people you knew. Absentees were noticed. The whole 'festival of democracy' notion made it difficult to stay at home legitimately. It should also be noted here that not everybody was allowed to vote. Even in 1997, the seven persons in Sariendah who had been accused of being communists in 1965 were banned from politics. They had received a general amnesty in 1994 (ahead of Indonesia's fiftieth year anniversary), but this decision had not been honoured by all village governments.

The polling station closed a little bit after two in the afternoon. A joint lunch had been served to the officials at 1 o'clock (the PPP observer chose to have his snack in one of the stalls). The ballot box was opened under supervision of the two observers, and the hamlet chairman started to count the votes. He did so by holding up the ballot in public and announcing the party's name. The two observers sat just opposite the chairman, and replied *sah*, 'valid', for each vote. A member of the Civil Defence Corps registered the vote on a blackboard. The PPP observer and several people in the audience also kept independent records (which later turned out to correspond with the official count). It took about an hour to count each of the three rounds. When the first PDI vote was registered, after some fifteen minutes, the chairman took a breath and shouted in an extra loud, somewhat biting voice, 'PDI'. People cheered ironically. Since the PDI was no threat to anyone, their few votes could be appreciated. The votes were collected by the Leumahcai vice-chairman who put them in three separate large envelopes. The official result was signed by the hamlet chairman and the two observers. The result was taken to the village office and the envelopes with the votes were sealed and sent to the sub-district.

The result

Of the 683 registered voters in Leumahcai, the PPP received 144 (21.1 per cent), Golkar 498 (72.9 per cent) and the PDI 13 votes (2.3 per cent) (see Table 6.1). Twelve votes were invalid, and sixteen persons did not vote. It was a comfortable Golkar victory, with results very similar to the national ones, where Golkar received 76 per cent of the votes, the PPP 18 per cent and the PDI 2.3 per cent. In Majalaya sub-district, Golkar received 66.4 per cent

Table 6.1 Election results, 1997 (as percentage of registered voters)

Party	Leumahcai	Nationwide
Golkar	72.9	76
PPP	21.1	18
PDI	2.3	2.3

of the votes, ranging from 50.1 per cent in one urban ward to 79.4 per cent in a typical rural village. For the third time in a row, Sariendah had the second largest Golkar vote in the sub-district.

I did not hear any allegations that the results at hamlet, village and sub-district levels in Majalaya had been manipulated – although this of course does not mean it did not happen. During a previous election I had observed, in 1987, one hamlet chairman in Sariendah claimed that he knew exactly how people had voted, through a magic mirror in a tree (Antlöv 1995: 177). This year there were no suggestions by anyone in Sariendah that the voting proce-dure as such was anything but secret. The hamlet official could possibly have marked ballots before he handed them over to voters, but no one claimed that. The campaign, as we have seen, was anything but fair, and many observers were deeply concerned about how the result from the sub-district was handled at the district, provincial and national levels. Away from the public, sub-district and district officials could report whatever result they wanted (or were told). But in the polling stations in Sariendah, the actual voting was fair and the election report to the sub-district was accurate, as far as I could tell. This is quite a different story from the very real cases of election fraud and voting coercion that were reported in both the domestic and foreign press. In one sub-district in East Java, the entire balloting had to be redone. In many other places there were newspaper accusations of fraud. Even such a loyal friend of Indonesia as the United States criticized (via its ambassador) the result in pub-lic. It could perhaps be argued that Golkar was so sure of winning in Sariendah that there was no need to manipulate the result!

If we read the literature on voting patterns in general, and the literature on voting in Indonesia in particular, we sometimes get the sense that voters (people!) are mindless marionettes who vote as authoritative figures or party programmes instruct them to do. In the Introduction (Chapter 1), I criticized Benedict Anderson's article on Indonesian elections, which dismissed New Order elections as being engineered. On one level, as we have seen, the elec-tions were indeed highly organized. But where there is domination, there is also resistance. I would thus want to argue, carefully, that in spite of the pressures from officials, some villagers displayed a greater sense of autonomous electoral behaviour in Sariendah than one would expect from reading the general literature on political behaviour in New Order

Indonesia. I shall recount one small example. One local leader told me that he of course had joined Golkar, as was expected of a man in his position, but that nobody could tell him how to vote. When he was in the polling booth, it was his right to vote as he wished – as he put it, *bebas rahasia* 'freely and secretly'. He was not afraid of intimidation, he said, because no one knew how he had voted. He did not passively accept or embrace the government's pressure to vote for Golkar. He showed a degree of political maturity, accepting the presence of Golkar but also critically examining its ideology. He might have voted for Golkar (knowing him, he probably *did* vote for Golkar!), but the important thing for us to recognize here is that he felt that he had a political choice. There is always a balance between agency and structure, choice and authority, rationality and power. The electoral process and campaign in New Order Indonesia were indeed organized to bring electoral success to Golkar. The reason why elections were held in Indonesia in the first place was to legitimate the New Order, internationally and domestically. Strong pressures and grand incentives were used to induce people to vote for Golkar. But my point here is that not even Golkar could fully control electoral behaviour. Since balloting in Sariendah was relatively free (if not fair) – voters were not physically intimidated, the ballot papers were correct, the counting procedure was transparent – people could in secret give their vote to the party of their choice. There was a democratic awareness in 1997 that anticipated what was to happen a year later.

There were surprisingly few blank ballots. Ten days ahead of the elections, Megawati Sukarnoputri announced her decision to vote blank. This was criticized by several ministers, and received wide attention in the Jakarta press. But while the *Mega–Bintang* campaign was clearly adopted in Sariendah, Megawati's decision to vote blank was never heeded there. Many people said that it was a 'waste' to vote blank because the blank votes were not counted in the official result. This is a good internalization of the official New Order message. In the province of East Java, on the contrary, close to a quarter of the voters either voted blank or not at all.

In spite of the independent voting behaviour that characterized at least some people in Sariendah, a great majority of villagers still ended up voting for Golkar. Why? We remember that people became members of Golkar because of a combination of intimacy and intimidation. Peer-group values (as well as common sense) told them to join the strong party.

Normative issues also assisted Golkar. Political order has always been highly valued on Java, and disorder is frightening to people. Voting for Golkar was opting for stability and continuity, a sentiment not necessarily based on well-informed political convictions. Having lived through poverty, violence and calamities, stability, growth and peace suddenly become attractive alternatives. The New Order and Golkar had an impressive track record. It was tangible. Almost everyone in Sariendah had been able to raise their living standards over the previous twenty years. This was appreciated.

Golkar also made clever use of patronage. They recruited local leaders and let them handle the local campaign and vote recruitment. In a community where solidarity is still high and in which you need your neighbours and patrons, it is difficult to go against the will of your uncle, teacher, cleric or landlord, who asks (rather than explicitly demands or forces) you to vote for the government party. And if that was not enough, there was always the threat of disciplinary reprisals silently residing in the back of people's minds.

Given the government's promises, track record, control over leadership, threats and lack of viable political alternatives, why is it that not everybody voted for Golkar? The former Golkar chairman in Sariendah – a frank and intelligent civil servant working in Bandung – made the most intriguing comment. When we met in the village office in the evening after election day in May 1997, he said that Golkar had lost voters in the hamlets where the village officials lived. This was meant as a joke but no one laughed. It carried some truth. The hamlet with 96 per cent Golkar votes was Cilembur, the poor hamlet where Golkar had promised to build a mosque. Voters had heeded the enchanting Golkar summons, and done as the hamlet chairman, a popular spiritual teacher, had asked them. He had even promised to sell his own house to build the mosque if Golkar did not meet its promise. The PDI did not receive a single vote, and the PPP only nine votes. In the neighbouring hamlet, Golkar received only 59 per cent. The hamlet chairman there was unpopular, being accused of corruption and authoritarianism, a chairman of Golkar's Board for Islamic Revival. Three other prominent village leaders also lived in the hamlet. What seems to have happened is that people voted against the local leadership of Golkar and other state clients. Villagers were dissatisfied with Golkar's local leadership style. They were prepared to support Golkar at the national level, but were sceptical of the party locally because of arrogant and dishonest officials. One way of interpreting the result is that PPP votes were mainly votes against money politics and against Golkar, rather than pro-PPP. Since the ideological difference between the parties was so small, other factors – such as leadership and morality – made the difference. Good leaders, and those they represent, should distribute goods and prove themselves to be service-minded. They should not be corrupt or try to influence village affairs in their personal interest. People felt that Golkar had not mobilized enough financial support for the hamlets. Village leaders had made some promises, but these were too uncertain.

Most of the non-Golkar votes were thus votes *against* Golkar, not pro-PPP or PDI (which is also a conclusion I drew in my study of the 1987 election, see Antlöv 1995: Chapter 9). Although not so intensely as in 1987, in 1997 many people still believed that Golkar was the best party to run the country. A local leader, highly critical of Golkar for its local performance and leadership, told me that if he had been the village Golkar representative, he could easily have mobilized 90 per cent of the votes for Golkar. There was never any serious talk about joining another party. For most people in Sariendah, Golkar was equivalent with the New Order. As we have seen, this was a strong ideological message, and most people accepted it. That Golkar received less than all the votes in Sariendah was due more to local factors than national issues (although issues of the corruption and greed of the Suharto family were rapidly becoming more prominent). During the post-election analysis in Sariendah, it was only the percentage of Golkar votes that was counted. It is as if a natural state of affairs would be that Golkar received all votes, and deviations from this norm must be explained. That deviation, I would argue, was local leadership – what was seen as the arrogant and corrupt local leadership of Golkar and the village government.

The 1999 election

In February 1998, eight months after the 1997 national election, a unanimous People's Consultative Assembly re-elected President Suharto for a seventh term. The vote was 1,000 to 0. But only three months later, the same individuals, under intense domestic and international pressures, were forced to decide that Indonesia would do best without Suharto. It was a turbulent period. I was evacuated under dramatic conditions to Singapore, and thus was not able to follow first-hand developments in Sariendah. But on subsequent visits to the village, I learnt that people there had in a sense been just as far away as I was from the centres of activity. Bandung was relatively quiet and there was no rioting or uprising in Majalaya. Most people saw the whole process on TV. And they could not believe their eyes. The inaccessible and invulnerable Suharto had been forced to resign! Not that people were sorry. As I think the story about the 1997 elections highlights, the president of Indonesia had become a less and less likeable figure, as his and his family's kleptomania grew.

The sheer fact that the president of Indonesia could be replaced, all of a sudden, was something new.[3] During the previous decades, it had hardly been possible even to replace a disliked village headman. Suddenly, new horizons were opened, new concepts of what was possible. After more than three decades in what could be likened to a political prison, people were now free to express their thoughts and views. People in Sariendah had obviously done this already in private in the past; but now the street-side discussions became much more explicitly political. Not only the president but also the village headman were discussed. A headman election in December 1998 in Sariendah – six months into *reformasi* – led to intense debates and conflicts within the village (to which I will return later since it affected the 1999 national elections).

Much has been written about the national election result and the many problems of counting the votes nationally and approving the final result, and I will not reiterate that story here. What I propose to do is again to interpret the national election as mirrored in Sariendah. Why did people vote as they did? How free and fair were the campaign, voting and counting? What were the symbols and sentiments used by the many new parties to recruit voters? Was the local meaning and practice of the 1999 elections very different from 1997? And given the fact that Sariendah was an 'exemplary' New Order village, with Golkar in one hamlet (Cilembur) even winning 96 per cent of all votes in 1997, we would also want to know how successful Golkar was in the 1999 election. And we can already now reveal the secret: in Leumahcai Golkar received 15 per cent of the votes and in Cilembur even less, only 13 per cent.

This was the 'first free and fair election' in Indonesia for more than four decades. But it was only two years since the last election was held. And the way the election was organized was fairly similar to the 1997 election: campaigning, voting and counting were done in similar ways in the two elections. But also there were obviously a number of crucial differences: the political parties that participated, how campaigning was organized, who oversaw and counted votes and reported the result. Within the context of local politics, the political space provided in 1999 made local politics less relevant for the national election. During the New Order elections, local issues were the main avenues for expressing national sentiments. 'The Political' was a closed sphere, only for the initiated. Ordinary people thus had to use local sentiments and issues to air disappointments and grievances (such as was the case with the leadership issue in 1997). In 1999, on the other hand, almost anything was allowed, and national issues were important conversational topics. And yet, as we shall see, local issues continued to play a dominant role in 1999 for the way politics played out locally.

A major innovation in 1999 was that the election was no longer conducted under the auspices of the Indonesian executive branch (in Sariendah that would be the village government) but by the political parties themselves. Each polling station was managed by three party representatives, selected among the contesting parties, in theory so that each party would have the same number of representatives in each village. The village election committee consisted of all the parties registered in the village (in Sariendah seven). The sub-district election committee consisted of the political parties registered in the sub-district, etc, all the way up to the KPU, the National Election Commission with its 48 party representatives and 5 government representatives. But old habits die hard. Since the Sariendah Village Election Committee was headed by a PSII representative (*Parti Sarekat Islam Indonesia*), 7 of the 12 polling stations were headed by PSII representatives. But this was never an issue, and it was not a problem: people only laconically noted the similarities with the New Order. In the atmosphere of festivity and transition and strong public pressures, villagers were fairly sure that there would not be any misuse of that mandate.

Another new regulation was the short Presidential Decree 5/1999, soberly stating that civil servants were no longer allowed to join a political party. This decree literally signified the end of the *mono-loyalitas* of civil servants which in the past had forced them to support Golkar. The political opposition had been pressing hard for this regulation as a means of neutralizing Golkar, and in the end, even Golkar itself approved of the law, as a way of showing that the 'New Golkar' (as it now called itself) was serious about political reforms. In practical terms, this meant that the village government and their 'clients of the state' could no longer support Golkar. And it was really astounding that people knew about this short decree, and made sure that there were no abuses. Supporters of the PDI-P in particular made public statements that they would report any interference or abuse of power by village officials to higher authorities. A national network of election monitors was in place by early May, and newspapers ran frequent stories about reported campaign abuses, such as 'money politics' and use of government facilities for Golkar meetings. In a few cases on Java, village offices were burnt down by dissatisfied villagers protesting the involvement of village officials in the election. No need for that in Sariendah. The headman and his staff stayed out of the campaign altogether, even to the extent that the local Golkar chairman complained to me that he was getting no support. There were no reports from other parties of foul play. It was, almost everybody in Sariendah agreed, a free and fair campaign and election.

The most important innovation in 1999 was the political freedom to say whatever you wished and be organized in any party. Long before the elections had been announced, already during the second half of 1998, political parties were being established. In February 1999, around 140 parties had been officially registered with the Department of Home Affairs. Of these, 48 were found eligible to run for election by an independent commission.[4] Of those, 7 parties were registered in Sariendah and allowed to campaign in the village: the PPP, the PKB, Golkar, the PAN, the PDI-P, the MKGR and the PSII. The first five were the main contestants nationally, with the PDI-P coming out on top both in Sariendah and nationally. To understand the presence of the MKGR and the PSII – parties that nationally received only less than 1 per cent of the vote – in Sariendah we need to look at local issues. The MKGR (*Musyawarah Kekeluargaan Gotong Royong*) was one of Golkar's original functional groups when it was established in the early 1960s, but became a separate party in October 1998. Its chairman in Sariendah was a popular former headman and chairman of the PNI during the 1971 election. He himself decided to return to what in his view was a crucial original Golkar component, and one that was not as discredited as Golkar. The party's campaign built singularly on the popularity of the former headman – and quite successfully so. The PSII (*Partai Sarekat Islam Indonesia*) had its supporters among more modernist Islamic villagers. The south Bandung area has a long tradition of support for Sarekat

Islam, ever since it was established in the 1920s. In the 1950s, Sarekat Islam had been a fairly prominent party in Majalaya. The party readily renewed its old networks of mosques and religious teachers. However, the modernist Islamic votes also went to the PAN, with a former chairman of Muhammadiyah as leading figure. The PPP and the PKB competed for voters from the more traditionalist Islam.

The PDI-P ('P' standing for *Perjuangan*, struggle) was Megawati Sukarnoputri's new political vehicle, after the PDI's split in 1996. The old PDI also competed in the national elections, although they did not have a Sariendah branch. Nationally, the PDI-P catered to two very different categories of voter: the young restless radicals and the older supporters of the PNI and Sukarno. The old PNI had been led by a popular and rich member of the village elite, who during both the 1950s and 1980s had been elected headman. He later became head of the Sariendah Golkar branch. When he in 1999 decided to quit Golkar, there were strong pressures on him from fellow villagers to join the PDI-P, his 'old' party. However, when he decided instead to support the MKGR, a young radical could take over and turn the PDI-P into a vehicle for the *anak fabrik*, 'the factory kids'.

The campaign

From mid-March 1999, Sariendah was full of party symbols and flags, often two or three different flags on the same pole and several stickers on the same window. There were no apparent conflicts in displaying more than one flag; people were generally very liberal about allowing the free flow of information and opinions, and proud that they could do so. This was different from the political situation in other parts of Indonesia, which were hit by campaign-related violence.[5] But there were no such stories coming out from Majalaya, in spite of the fact that the population to a very high degree is made up of young factory workers. Many of these half-educated young men and women were supporters of the PDI-P, and they took all opportunities during the campaign to display their emotions. In other parts of Java, these groups of young men from different parties clashed with each other. But except for a small skirmish at the Majalaya market, nothing serious happened. This came as quite a surprise to some political observers in Bandung who knew Majalaya's history and the social tensions that exist between different villages and between the rich and the poor.

As mentioned in the introductory paragraph, the former state party Golkar was one of the least active parties in Sariendah. We have to remember that Suharto until he stepped down was the chairman of Golkar's board, and that Habibie was also chairman for a time. Nationally, many people blamed Golkar for the political and economic situation and there were even nationally based arguments that Golkar should be banned. This obviously did not happen, but that was only because some changes in leadership took place within the party. It also changed its name to Partai Golkar, sometimes with Baru ('New') as an added adjective.

Golkar experienced serious setbacks in Sariendah. Because of Presidential Decree 5/99, the village headman could not remain as chair of the village Golkar branch. More seriously, Golkar also lost two of its more prominent leaders to other parties (one to the MKGR, the other to the PDI-P). There was an acute leadership crisis in the Sariendah branch of Golkar. No one really wanted to chair what was seen as a bleeding party. The question was solved only when one of the retired village officials was more or less forced to take on the chairmanship. Given the odds, he did a fairly good job. Golkar had very little public support. The demise of the *mono-loyalitas* of the Civil Servant's Corps meant that Golkar no longer could use the government machinery in its campaign. No village government facilities were used by Golkar during the campaign, not even the village auditorium, which is available to everyone.

There was another reason why the village government hesitated to support Golkar. Just a few months earlier, in December 1998, Sariendah had elected a new headman. One of the first things he did was to dismiss all village officials. He was immediately challenged by a group of fired officials, who brought the case to the attention of higher authorities, filing reports to the district chairman (*bupati*) in Bandung, the local army commander and six other district authorities. The dismissed officials alleged that the new headman had been involved in various corrupt practices when he was village secretary. They contacted a journalist living in Bandung who wrote for a small, progressive tabloid in Jakarta. The paper was closely related to the PDI-P and ran a lot of stories about official corruption and abuse of power. The journalist loved the story. It was exactly what his readers wanted to hear, and he wrote two articles, one published in February and the other in April 1999. The stories were used as examples of the corrupt character of village administration in Indonesia, and the headman was indirectly tied to Golkar (as part of the on-going election campaign). What the journalist failed to see was that the fired village officials, previously on the other side of the fence, had been equally corrupt while in power, and that they only wanted a chance to regain their power. But it made for good stories.

In March 1999, three months ahead of the national elections, the Majalaya sub-district chairman organized a major village meeting in Sariendah. He talked about the violence in Maluku and the village offices that had been burnt to the ground in West Java during the past months. *Demi keamanan* (for the sake of security), he asked that the conflict over the dismissed officials in Sariendah should not be intensified. He was worried that the case would be politicized, worsening a growing tendency for inter-group violence. He told the audience that nothing would happen with the case until after the election – it was simply put on ice.

Although the case of village corruption and abuse of power in this way never was a public issue during the campaign, it obviously was a major topic of conversation. And it probably influenced the outcome of the elections to the detriment of Golkar, although only to a degree. All those involved were former Golkar leaders. People were fairly sober about the issue, realizing that it was also part of the infighting of the political elite – no one really believed that the fired village officials were any less corrupt.

Since Golkar could not mobilize the village official leadership during its campaign, it instead took *karya* as its focus. *Karya* means 'functional' or 'functionary' (as in Golkar's full name Golongan Karya, functional groups) but also 'work' and 'devotion'. Through *karya*, Golkar wanted to show its real achievements and commitment, having brought economic development and political stability to Indonesia for the past three decades. In Sariendah, the local interpretation of this national strategy meant that Golkar arranged a number of *gotong royong*, joint labour parties, working together to improve the economic infrastructure of the village, cleaning roads, maintaining irrigation channels, etc. One of Golkar's official slogans captured this ideology well: *Golkar Baru: Bersatu untuk Maju* (New Golkar: united for development). This was the reformed way of describing political stability and economic development, the slogan of the New Order.

But it did not work very well, at least not during campaigning in Majalaya. When it was Golkar's turn to campaign, a large crowd of young men had assembled and started to throw stones.[6] After around an hour, Golkar decided for security reasons to cancel the parade of trucks that is an inseparable part of political campaigns in Indonesia that had been scheduled to travel around Majalaya. All the frustration of what these young and angry men saw as thirty-two years of New Order rule was channelled against Golkar (I am not saying that their perception mirrored reality; in fact most people in 1999 strongly undervalued the material achievements of the New Order). Because of the deep economic crisis, it was difficult for Golkar to get through with the *karya* message; what people were actually experiencing was a deep economic recession. Textile factories in Majalaya had been forced to shut down, since they depended on imported raw materials. Unemployment figures during 1998 and 1999 rose drastically. And Golkar became the object of this frustration. Among the vocal young men, it was as if Golkar had done nothing right. On a national level, there were attempts by non-governmental organizations to disband Golkar and bar the party from the elections. They failed, but the efforts proved how strong anti-Golkar sentiments were. And to some extent, these emotions were mirrored in Majalaya.

It was no great surprise that Megawati Sukarnoputri's new party, the PDI-P, was able to profit from this and exhibited the most massive show of force. Just about all the young men in the village went on motorcycles and trucks around Sariendah and surrounding villages. Six trucks were hired in

Sariendah. Each filled up with some forty to fifty persons, all clad and painted in red, shouting and screaming for six hours. Somewhat later on a Sunday that officially was a public holiday with no campaigning allowed, PDI-P trucks from surrounding villages and Majalaya passed through the village. PDI-P supporters in Sariendah demanded of the local PDI-P leader that he hire trucks. But he had no money. The group managed to collect some 100,000 rupiah ($13), but this was far from enough. The chairman knew that no campaigning was allowed, and thus tried to dissuade the young men from creating a political situation. After a few hours, the road-side crowd dispersed, disappointed, but at least they had cheered on many *pawai* trucks passing through Sariendah from the PDI-P branches that did not heed the regulations.

Just as in 1997, there were no great ideological discussions or political debates. During previous elections, there had always been a kind of public show of ideological debate – the three political parties had been encouraged to present their programmes during allotted days. In 1999, even this pretence was discarded. As has been noted by many commentators, there was a focus during the 1999 campaign on personalities instead of issues, on normative categories rather than rational choice, and it was not really viewed as a major political exercise of free choice and democracy. In this way, the 1999 election was similar to elections in other neighbouring Asian countries, such as the Philippines and Thailand. People in Sariendah saw elections as a chance to get rid of some of the excesses of the New Order, especially the corruption and abuse of power, but it was not a question of ideological choices.

Voting

The formal process of casting ballots during 1999 was very similar to that in 1997. Even though previous elections had been organized by Golkar and its supporters, the infrastructure for a free and fair election was in place. Although the 1999 election was in non-government hands, the actual process was very similar. People started to gather in front of the ballot station in Leumahcai at six in the morning. The station opened at 7 a.m., and women were encouraged to vote first. They entered the compound, got their ballots – now obviously much larger and complex since 48 parties were competing – and sat down and waited for their turn. The booths were designed quite similarly to those of 1997. A major innovation was that each voter's fingertip was dipped in black ink. They could thus not go and vote again, a practice that had been reported during previous elections, where civil servants (i.e. supporters of Golkar) were encouraged to vote both at work and at home. In 1999, voters could only go to the polling station once.

New also was the presence of independent election monitors. In 1997, representatives of the political parties had supervised an election organized by the government. This time it was the political parties that organized the elections, supervised by independent election monitors. There were some 120 accredited national organizations and 20 international election monitoring institutions in Indonesia (Benedanto *et al.* 1999: 31). In Sariendah 21 organizations had been accredited, and 3 of these were present in Leumahcai. They did not do very much more than observe: at one stage an administrative issue arose in Leumahcai (whether the ballot station could keep open longer than stipulated, since there were still people waiting to vote). The committee chairman consulted with the three monitors before they decided to be pragmatic and keep the station open for another fifteen minutes.

The results

The voting station in Leumahcai closed at 2:15 pm. The counting procedure was very similar to that followed in 1997. The three boxes (one each for national, provincial and district government) were opened under some festivity. The counting started with the votes for the national government. There was a bit of a hustle, since everybody wanted to be involved in this historical movement. Finally, the local election commission chairman in Leumahcai managed to get people to sit down. He opened the box, and began to pick up the votes one by one. He held them up in the air in front of himself and shouted out the result. The three monitors acknowledged the vote with a *sah* (valid) or *benar* (correct). The vote was then noted on a large piece of paper on a blackboard with the names of the political parties. Just as in 1997, the large audience was active in commenting on the result: votes for the PDI-P were greeted with a cheer and for Golkar with a hiss. Since it was a slow process to mark the votes on the large white paper, it took more than an hour and a half to count the 614 votes in Leumahcai.

The result was a surprise to everyone, even Golkar. The PDI-P won 51.9 per cent in Leumahcai, the PSII 16.4 per cent, Golkar 14.8 per cent, the PKB 4.6 per cent, the PAN 2.9 per cent and another 17 parties less than 2 per cent of the total votes. In the village of Sariendah, the votes were shared among 40 parties, 21 of which received less than 10 votes each. The six largest parties shared 92 per cent of the total votes (see Table 6.2).

After the election, many people stayed up all night to make sure that all results were delivered in good order to the village headman. I sat in the village office until 3 a.m., when the final result from two remaining hamlets had not yet been delivered: there was an inconsistency of three votes in the various tallies. Many of the election observers also sat in the village office, supporting the inexperienced Village Election Committee in their struggle to finalize the official result. It took them three more days to sort things out. There was seemingly not any manipulation or fraud; it was simply difficult to get all the votes properly counted and tabulated (a fact that I think many election officials in Florida would agree upon).

Table 6.2 Vote distribution in Leumahcai and Sariendah (1999)

Party	Leumahcai		Sariendah		National
	Votes	Percentage	Votes	Percentage	Percentage
PDI-P	339	51.9	2,441	43.6	33.7
PSII	107	16.4	419	7.5	0.25
Golkar	97	14.8	1,023	18.3	22.4
PKB	30	4.6	729	13.0	12.6
PAN	19	2.9	315	5.6	7.1
PPP	11	1.7	202	3.6	10.7
MKGR	11	1.7	92	1.6	0.25
Others	39	6.0	381	6.8	12.9
Total	653	100	5,602	100	100

Interpreting the results: patronage, mobilization and local meaning

We have so far recorded the story of two general elections in the same village, just two years apart: the first under a declining authoritarian regime and the second after one year of emerging democratic polity. The first thing we may note is how similar the actual elections were. If one came dropping in from another planet (or from Sweden) to ballot stations in 1997 and 1999, it would at first glance be difficult to tell the difference. There were small variations, and for the trained eye the black tint on people's fingers would reveal the more democratic nature of the 1999 election. So if the main differences were not during polling, where were they? Obviously, they appear in the process leading up to the polling and the way in which the results were treated.

To account for the 1997 election result in Sariendah, I have argued that a double explanation of voting behaviour is necessary, including both campaign intimidation and vote-shaping, as well as people's actual voting behaviour – both the structure and agency. To say that people were simply forced to vote for Golkar is not true; but neither were they fully exercising their uncensored will. The main conclusion I am suggesting here is that intimidation and manipulation do not reveal the entire, or even the main, story of why people voted for Golkar.

Local leaders played a very important role in mobilizing voters and making sure that people voted the way that the government wanted. It was through their active intervention that Golkar could ensure its success. It was a clever and very conscious strategy. But it only worked as long as the image of the local leaders was acceptable to the people. The ideology of generosity and service-mindedness (*jasa*) was important: leaders must be seen as providing something good. It was thus not traditional authority in the sense of blindly doing what local leaders told you: their influence was large and the patronage power clearly tangible, but only as long as they could command prestige and authority. In the hamlets in Sariendah where unpopular leaders lived, Golkar received fewer votes.

In 1997, before the financial crisis, the New Order could still cater to the aspirations of a majority of the Indonesian population – and Golkar could win the elections. But the New Order was rapidly alienating not only the poorest (who had not benefited from economic growth) but also the critical middle classes, who demanded rule by law and more than simple material welfare. Repression increased and people (especially the influential middle class, including students) were disillusioned. This paved the way for the transition. There were in 1997 perceptions and practices among common people that – in spite of the authoritarian regime – made a more open and accountable government a plausible alternative.

Although Golkar won a comfortable victory in Sariendah, Java and Indonesia, we could also anticipate the 1998 events. For the better informed and more well-educated, the negative aspects of New Order development were becoming more visible. The censorship that academics encountered, or the lack of clean drinking water that the middle classes in Jakarta experienced, was more important for these groups than their comfortable lifestyle. What is meaningful for people will influence their political choices. For many people in Sariendah, their increase in living standard was more important than political pluralism, and this explained their votes for Golkar.

People are not undemocratic or politically inept in Indonesia, as proponents of the so-called Asian Values discourse would describe them. They know their rights and responsibilities, and I believe that the election in 1997 was an important marker of an evolution into meaningful democracy. If people were as 'ignorant' as the government liked to portray them, how could they possibly, only two years later, independently vote a new government into power, in an election that generally was portrayed as free and fair? In spite of Golkar receiving its largest victory ever, I believe that the 1997 election proved that voters indeed had some practice with critical thinking, at least in some pockets of resistance.

What about the result in 1999? Perhaps the only thing that we need to explain in Sariendah is the vote for Golkar. It is difficult to say whether 18 per cent is a case of a bottle half empty or half full. Just two years earlier, Golkar had won 73 per cent of the votes in Sariendah. And this time Golkar only managed to get a quarter of that result. Under any other circumstances, this result would have been a total disaster. But since the campaign had been such a failure and Golkar was without support from the village government, its representatives in Sariendah were surprised and delighted that they even managed to get a single vote. One year earlier, Golkar had been accused of being the main architect of the, by now heavily discredited, New Order and the mastermind behind what looked more and more like a failed national project. Under such circumstances to end up the second largest party, not only in Sariendah but in Indonesia overall, can be seen as a real accomplishment. The national result has been explained by an election system that favours outer Indonesia over Java, where Golkar remained strong (see Cederroth in this volume). During the campaign in April and May, it seemed as if Golkar had almost given up Java. They knew they would not be able to win on this populous island, and they put all their efforts into winning in cities and in the countryside, far away from the student demonstrations in Jakarta.

Thus, Golkar's 18 per cent in Sariendah came as a surprise to many. How can it be explained? The 'rational' reasons would be that supporters either thought that things had indeed been good under Golkar in the past, or that they believed that Golkar had been reformed and represented something new. Both of these explanations operated in Sariendah – several Golkar voters talked about the need for political stability. But in addition there were also questions of long-lasting loyalties and conservatism. Voting behaviour – not only in Indonesia – is quite orthodox. People do not easily change loyalties, especially from a party that has been around for more than thirty years and brought a number of benefits. I do not want to overstate it, but Golkar during the New Order was not necessarily a very unpopular party and Suharto was not an unpopular ruler, at least not until the mid-1990s. We thus have to recognize that the New Order for a long time had at least an appearance of legitimacy with quite broad popular support. In both 1997 and 1999 they could recruit voters based on long-lasting loyalties, past achievements and traditional bonds. And it was important for them in 1997, as well as in 1999, to be able to mobilize influential leaders to back them, and to use their authority to convince, co-opt and coerce.

Many people were bewildered in 1999, only just learning to live with many new freedoms. On TV there were daily demonstrations, regional conflicts, elite infighting and heated talk shows. Far away, in Sariendah, the average peasant could easily be confused, even frightened. Many villagers have lived through turbulent times: the independence war, religious conflicts, fighting communists, hyper-inflation. And in May 1998, the world was turned upside down again. Golkar (more than Suharto) represented some form of stability in this turbulent era.

Just one year after a political transition that had not involved villagers, there were thus many people to be found in Sariendah who supported the New Order and Golkar. One informant, a strong Golkar supporter, told me in 1999 that he wanted a *negara aman, tentram dan makmur* (a stable, safe and prosperous country); a return to the New Order. Members of the village elite hesitated to fully engage in the new political freedom. For these advocates of the status quo, *reformasi* meant the rule of the masses, that the *masih bodoh* ('still ignorant', one of the New Order's favourite characterizations of ordinary people) by their sheer numbers would dominate the more articulate and sophisticated members of the elite. My informant could not hide his pleasure when members of the party-political election committee in Leumahcai encountered problems with counting votes. And he just had to intervene and tell them how it was to be done – that it had worked so much better under the New Order. Political patronage was not quite as explicit as during previous elections (since the *mono-loyalitas* of civil servants was abolished), although the role of leadership and forms of village-based patron–client relations continued to be an important conduit for electoral behaviour.

Money politics is a major issue in all Southeast Asian countries. So we should not be surprised to learn that money was a major issue during the 1999 election in Indonesia. During 1992 and 1997 Golkar did not need to use money politics explicitly. Mobilization, power and repression – or the threat thereof – were sufficient. In 1999, with the new democratic space, it was impossible for Golkar to play power politics. It had to resort to other resources, and money was the most important. Golkar was by far the richest party. There were many reports of misuse of public funds for party campaigns. The national press agency Antara reported on 22 April 1999 that 'a road in the Majalaya village [of Padaulun] was asphalted with funds from the Social Safety Net programme, but the vehicles were carrying references to the Golkar party'. There were no direct reports of this from Sariendah; maybe the village leadership had learnt their lesson when the village headman in January 1999 was accused by the dismissed village officials of using development funds for private purposes. The village leadership in Sariendah was thus extremely careful not to engage in any activity that could cause them further problems.

If Golkar could draw on long-lasting loyalties and a sense of continuity, the PDI-P obviously had to use a very different strategy. In 1997 (in the *Mega–Bintang* coalition) and in 1999 the PDI-P's campaigns were built on strong sentiments of joint action, of mass mobilization through engaging rituals and powerful symbols. The PDI-P could forcefully portray a strong vision of a joint future: sentiments were extracted from participants in the mass rallies and campaigns that made for strong communal bonds and feelings of shared destiny between PDI-P followers. An imagined enemy was inferred, the 'status quo forces', represented by the village formal leadership and Golkar.

In Sariendah, the PDI-P – and to a lesser extent the MKGR and the PPP – could also mobilize informal leaders. The village officials decided not to enter into the election and other leaders were free to make their own allegiances. In 1997, the full village leadership had stood united behind Golkar. The village government and local leadership had been extremely active in recruiting voters and controlling votes. The recruitment of these 'clients of the state' was a main reason for the success of Golkar. In 1999, when they no longer supported Golkar, and local leaders were divided among a number of parties, Golkar could no longer sustain its vote. It was a more equal distribution of votes, in which factors beyond leadership also came into play.

Perhaps Indonesian politics is no more personalized than that of such diverse countries as India, the United States, South Africa and the Philippines, but leadership does provide an important clue to understanding voting behaviour. I would not go as far as some students of Indonesian political culture, who find traditional authority to be the moving force in Indonesian politics, but we still need to recognize the role local leadership plays in politics.[7] When the Sariendah branch of Golkar lost its main advocates in 1999, it was unable to mobilize voters. In the same way, the PDI and the PPP were in 1997 unable, indeed obstructed, from even having a party branch chairman in the village. Political ideologies are important in Indonesia, but not in the traditional sense of national election promises and policy priorities; it is the political ideology of the immediate public leader that plays an important part in deciding voting behaviour.

We have seen in this comparison of the 1997 and 1999 elections that politics in Indonesia operate according to community norms, local issues and patronage. These factors do not make Indonesia very different from many other countries, but perhaps they are, in the words of Ben Anderson (1990), in combination a 'unique amalgam' in Indonesia. The two elections were obviously very different in character, but it is also important to see the continuity between the New Order and what has followed; only this continuity of underlying Indonesian politics can help us to understand why it seems to be so difficult to achieve more sustainable changes towards a new Indonesia.

Notes

1 I did 12 months of anthropological fieldwork in 1986 and have returned for shorter stays in 1987, 1989, 1991, 1994, 1995 and several times per year since 1997. See Antlöv 1995 for a more thorough presentation of the village and its local politics, including the 1987 national election.
2 They were allegedly also involved in the Jakarta rioting in May 1998 and the violence in East Timor and the Moluccas.
3 Suharto had gone to great lengths in 1966 to make the transition from Sukarno at least *look* legal and formal.
4 The conditions were that the party must have branches in at least one-third of Indonesia's 27 provinces and in at least half of the districts/cities within those provinces. In the end, however, several parties that, strictly speaking, did not fulfil the conditions were nevertheless allowed to participate.
5 It should be noted that there was far less political violence in 1999 than in 1997: there were 19 reported dead in 1999 and 327 in 1997 (Benedanto *et al.* 1999: 73).
6 Each political party was assigned particular days on which to campaign. In the larger cities, where all 48 parties were active, 3 or 4 parties of the same general orientation were lumped together. In smaller towns, such as in Majalaya, each of the political parties had one or more days by itself for their campaign.
7 For a more forceful critique of the political culture school of Indonesian studies, see Antlöv, 2004.

References

Anderson, Benedict (1990) *Language and Power: Exploring Political Cultures in Indonesia*. Ithaca: Cornell University.

Antlöv, Hans (1995) *Exemplary Centre, Administrative Periphery: Rural Leadership and the New Order in Java*. Richmond: Curzon Press.

——(2004) 'The Social Construction of Political Culture and National Identity in Indonesia'. In Hans Antlöv and Jörgen Hellman (eds), *The Java that Never Was. Academic Images and Political Practices*. Berlin: LIT Verlag.

Benedanto, Pax, Ignatius Haryanto and E. Pudjiachirusanto (1999) *Pemilihan Umum 1999: Demokrasi atau Rebutan Kursi [The 1999 Elections: Democracy or Fighting for Seats.]* Jakarta: Lembaga Studi Pers dan Pembangunan.

Ramage, Douglas E. (1995) *Politics in Indonesia. Democracy, Islam and the Ideology of Tolerance*. London: Routledge.

Reeve, David (1985) *Golkar of Indonesia: An Alternative to the Party System*. Singapore: Oxford University Press.

7

ELECTIONS AND THE MEDIA

A discourse analysis of the 1997 and 1999
elections in Indonesia

Kaarlo Voionmaa

Arguably, the most important event in the recent development of Indonesia
is political liberalization. Instead of the 3 parties allowed under the
so-called New Order regime, 48 parties contested the general election on
7 June 1999. The election was a major test of whether Indonesia really had
made a turn towards more democratic rule. Freedom of speech was institu-
tionalized, and the public space grew rapidly. During the New Order,
Indonesia developed a closed political system that was based on the state
ideology of *Pancasila*, encompassing the five principles of belief in God,
nationalism, humanitarianism, democracy and social justice. They were
first formulated by Sukarno in 1945, and later accepted as key elements of
the national ideology.

The New Order reigned until May 1998. It organized elections that
have generally been assessed as anything but free and fair (e.g., Haris's
chapters in this volume). The fact that only two political parties besides
Golkar, the regime-controlled quasi party, were allowed to take part in the
elections can be taken as a major undemocratic feature of the electoral
system. People were thus not only deprived of their right to form new
political parties, but their choice was also limited to the three parties
recognized by the government. The 1945 Constitution and the 1982 Press
Law provided for nominal freedom of the press, but in practice the government applied a policy that severely restricted this freedom, for
instance, by introducing publishing licences under a 1984 ministerial
decree, and regulating the amount of advertising permitted and the number of pages allowed in newspapers. Low-key debates on sensitive topics
like corruption were printed in the English-language press, while major
Indonesian-language newspapers were more cautious in bringing up such
controversial subjects.

Towards its end, the New Order was under heavy criticism from various
democratic intellectuals in the country. Occasionally, critics were the

138

victims of violent treatment, as for instance, when government forces attacked the headquarters of the PDI (Indonesian Democratic Party) on 27 July 1996. Rioting followed the attack, and more than a hundred people were tried for participating in the riots (but none for the attack on the PDI). Cracks started to appear in the façade of the New Order. Thus, for instance, the National Human Rights Commission, which was originally set up by Suharto himself, laid full blame for the riots at the PDI headquarters on the government's excessive intervention in the internal affairs of the PDI.

After Suharto's downfall, a number of remarkable events took place. In less than twelve months, more than 140 new parties were established, although 'only' 48 fulfilled the criteria to contest the national elections. The upsurge of political parties might indicate a radical change in Indonesia's political scene, but we also have to consider what ideological lines of thought they represented. Studying their founding principles as expressed in their public presentations, we may conclude that the change from the New Order was hardly as radical as one might have expected. As many as 34 of the 48 parties acknowledged that the state ideology Pancasila was their founding principle or asas. Seventeen parties had Islam, or a combination of Islam and Pancasila, as their asas (see Haris's and Turmudi's chapters in this volume). Only two parties gave other founding principles: namely the Democratic Peoples' Party (PRD), which had 'social democracy' as its foundation, and the Indonesian Uni-Democracy Party (PUD), which had 'religious democracy'.

This chapter attempts to analyse the role of the media during the 1999 election. The aim is to look at trends by major politicians in their use of media as well as language. I will also make a few preliminary comparisons between the new democratic political discourse and the undemocratic 1997 election. In commenting on the texts, I am interested in the argumentation used by the writers: for instance, whether claims made were backed up by evidence or not; what the lack of evidence possibly indicated; and what the evidence provided did indicate. Another major focus concerns writers' lexical choices. One small example can be found in an interview with the Governor of Yogyakarta, Sultan Hamenkubuwono X, where he uses the term 'government official' instead of 'president', thus blurring the power difference between ordinary government officials and the president. Obviously, the Sultan used a vague term instead of a more precise term, and in the respective commentaries, I have examined some reasons for such and similar usage.

Previously having examined editorials ahead of the 1997 general elections, I came to the conclusion that several texts contained multiple layers of political meaning (cf. Voionmaa 1998). Roughly speaking, they would report on one level the 'official version' of the state of affairs, while on another they would indicate that there were still other ways of interpreting the matters being discussed. These other interpretations seem to have been directed at a more limited group of people, those capable of 'reading between the lines'. In general, we may note that texts obviously have many layers or, to put it in another way, texts and their readers create ever more different and varying readings and interpretations. In the case of the editorials studied for the 1997 elections, this layering was employed under the fairly restrictive conditions that the New Order regime had imposed on political discourse.

The comparison will not scrutinize in detail the political language under New Order rule; for this I refer the reader to an outstanding study by Virginia Matheson Hooker (1993) in which New Order language has been analysed in its modern and historical contexts. Studying the differences in political discourse in the two elections will, hopefully, shed some additional light on the changes when Indonesia moved from a less democratic rule to one with strong democratic aspirations. One of the tasks of this chapter is to see whether any changes have, in fact, taken place. Anticipating the conclusion, we might reveal that there were major similarities between the political discourses in 1997 and 1999, one of which was the lack of substantial discussion about public policies and party ideologies.

Political discourse in Indonesian news media has been studied before: for instance in Flournoy (1992) and Graf (1998). Flournoy's book deals with, among other things, measuring the extent to which different Indonesian daily newspapers handled issues such as war, defence and diplomacy. The present study does not discuss the amount of treatment but mainly comments on what was said in the actual political discourse.

Graf's study is a detailed analysis of the media rhetoric in Indonesia based on articles by Goenawan Mohamad, the previous chief editor of *Tempo*, which is one of the most influential political magazines in modern Indonesia. Graf's data comprise Goenawan Mohamad's influential column *Catatan Pinggir* (Sidelines) between 1977 and 1994. The study included both quantitative and qualitative analysis of the articles. In his study, Graf manages to investigate in depth the ways in which the political discourse changed under the pressure of the New Order government. Graf's analysis is interesting in various respects, not least because of its methodology, in which quantitative and qualitative approaches have been combined.[1]

Before we begin, it is necessary to establish what is meant here by the term 'discourse', which has been used in different ways in the literature. Thus, investigating democratization in modern Indonesia, Anders Uhlin defines discourse as 'speech consisting of a certain set of ideas' (Uhlin 1997: 3).[2] The meaning Uhlin gives to the term seems to comprise the social science research as a whole. In the present study, I will employ the term 'discourse' in the sense of presenting one's ideas in a public medium such as a newspaper, TV or radio. Discourse, in this sense, takes place whenever a person or a group of persons makes a contribution to a medium in the form of text or picture. Note that in using the term 'discourse' in this way, it will include linguistic interaction since, typically, a given contribution appears in a media context where it is meant to evoke reaction among the public and possibly even a response in the form of another contribution.[3]

Obviously, a political struggle has been going on since the end of the New Order to create new political discourses. While the New Order government considered anti-government information to have a negative effect on the general public and hushed up this kind of information, Habibie's government allowed much more diverse discourse. Nevertheless, the Habibie government still tried to pursue a policy of censorship, although this was less successful or harsh than under Suharto.[4]

To further refine our definition of what discourses may represent, it might be useful to look at an editorial published in the *Jakarta Post* on 22 March 1999, under the heading 'Golkar is the Problem':

> As it is, the nation is deeply polarized between those who support Golkar, and therefore endorse maintaining the status quo, and those who see the party as standing in the way of badly needed political reforms ... Another crisis is something this country can ill afford ... Next time around, the crisis would likely be even more destructive than what we have witnessed this past year.

In the editorial, the problem of political discourse faced by the Indonesians was put in clear terms. It concerned polarization of the country into two main camps: namely, those who did not wish to renounce the New Order democracy as sustained by Golkar, and those who would like to see major political reforms. The question was whether members of these camps (i.e. anti- and pro-democratic political parties and their members) could speak to one another, or whether, indeed, any communication could occur between them.

A curious reaction to the new situation was withdrawal by politicians from political discourse under more or less obvious pretexts. An example of such a reaction seems to have been the one by Megawati Sukarnoputri's PDI-P. Consider the following excerpt from the *JP* article, 'Mega Still Says No to Presidential Debate' (23 April 1999) where a PDI-P spokesperson contended that: 'This nation needs a strong, tested leader with continuous commitment to democracy and justice. Megawati has shown she possesses this quality ... the most important thing is work, not talk only.'

Laying stress on work as opposed to talk is typical of politicians and political movements that would like to present themselves as result oriented. They typically emerge in times of social and political unrest and crisis; they attract people by presenting a more or less clear plan of operation with which to manage the crisis. Often this plan means that politics can be realized without taking into consideration parties with differing opinions, especially if these parties are weak rivals. (It is always most advisable to listen carefully to what one's strong adversaries say.) These 'work-not-talk' parties typically do not trust or rely on the public political discourse as a means of attaining functional solutions to economic, social and political problems.[5]

It is questionable, however, whether a political system can become more democratic if the leading political forces are not willing to get engaged in the public political discourse. We may consider what Wimar Witoelar, a noted talk show host and public affairs commentator, proposed in the *JP* on March 7, 1999, under the title, 'Sizing Up Value of Expert Advice': 'The very people who say that punditry brings more confusion rather than solutions are probably those who contribute to the confusion.'

The consuming problem of Indonesian political discourse seems to be whether there are enough sufficiently strong parties to necessitate open, fair and problem-oriented political discourse. Contributions such as Haris's chapters in the present volume clearly indicate that there were many parties and groupings that had the competence, but it is doubtful whether they had sufficient financial and other more concrete resources to draw upon.

Data and methodology

Taking into consideration the limited time and space at my disposal, I decided to proceed in the following manner: first, I scrutinized the data in editions of the *Jakarta Post* (*JP*) in March and April 1999. The aim was to identify the topics most central with regard to the general and presidential elections. Note that the presidential election was dependent on the general elections, since members of the Indonesian parliament (DPR) formed part of the People's Consultative Assembly (MPR) that would later elect the president. The data are not presented comprehensively, but excerpted. The goal is to present different arguments on topics that had a direct bearing on the general and presidential elections in Indonesia in 1999, and subsequently to comment on these arguments.

The data on which this study is based contain 201 texts from 45 different editions of the *JP*; these texts are editorials, articles and reports. Insofar as I can tell, all these materials were originally written in English. The present study should be seen as an exploration of political discourse as represented in newspaper texts whose contents I could not determine beforehand but learnt 'as I went along'. In a sense, the study is a voyage of discovery into Indonesian political discourse prior to a major event in the country's history, the *Pemilu* or general elections of 1999.

The *JP* was founded in 1983, and it claims on its homepage to be a 'prestigious newspaper respected for its independent views and bold coverage of various national and international events'. The number of its subscribers had increased from 8,657 in 1983 to 41,049 in 1998. Nevertheless, the *JP* is quite a small newspaper given the total Indonesian population of nearly 210 million people. Its limited number of subscribers is balanced out by the fact that the newspaper has 'gone international', for it has agreements with three global database companies. The *JP* is an English-language newspaper, and for linguistic reasons only reaches a small minority in the country. Obviously, it is a news medium for the country's political, cultural and social elite. We may assume that in studying an English-language newspaper like the *JP*, we learn of the political discourse among those Indonesians who are most likely to have an influence in the political, cultural and social spheres of the country's public life. This makes the *JP* a good data source for text-critical treatment of the political discourse in Indonesia.

The focus of the present study is on the Indonesian election campaign and the general elections on 7 June 1999. More specifically, for reasons of space, I will focus on the eligibility and recruitment of political candidates, including presidential, as a case study of the language and discourse used by the *JP* during the 1999 election. Consequently, I have only considered texts[6] that relate to this main topic in the respective *JP*. In practice, this means that large parts of the papers (concerned with non-election issues, or matters outside of the candidates) will not be treated in the present study.

In a later section, I will make comparisons between the political discourse of 1997 and that of 1999, and in that connection, I will discuss changes in the approach to themes such as political violence and national cohesion in the news media in Indonesia.

Having thus established the theme, I will examine selected parts or excerpts of respective texts. In general, I studied how writers of the texts discussed the issues at hand and then commented on that discussion. I have indicated the name of the writer if it appears in the title of the respective text. Apart from comments on the contents of the texts, I will also indicate non-linguistic aspects such as the placement of text in the newspaper edition concerned (p. 1, p. 2, etc.), its length and its portion of the whole page. These pieces of information may give the reader some idea of the status of the text in the newspaper.[7]

The *Jakarta Post* on political candidates

In the general elections of 7 June 1999, the candidates contended for 462 seats in the House of Representatives. The Armed Forces were automatically allocated 38 seats to make it a total of 500. These representatives then formed part of the MPR that six months later, together with 200 regional and functional representatives, elected the country's president and vice-president. This was the reason why both the parliamentary and the presidential candidature raised heated issues during the election campaign; these two issues were always discussed in close connection to one another.

The discussion on the presidential election concerned, among other things, acting President B.J. Habibie's role in the contest. The debate on parliamentary candidature revolved around the question of whether or not government officials such as ministers were allowed to campaign for election.

On 1 March the *JP* reported that 'Parties Begin Naming Presidential Candidates' (p. 2, 4 cols, 1/3 page). The report dealt mainly with the opening congress of the National Awakening Party (PKB), one of the parties that seemed to have a large following in the election polls. According to the text, the parties' positions before the general elections and the presidential election issues were conflated. The PKB's presidential candidate was Abdurrahman Wahid, also known as Gus Dur (who was later elected president). He was determined that: 'The economic crisis will be solved by the PKB if we win the elections and we will choose qualified officials for our government ... the PKB is ready to win the elections in order to destroy collusion, corruption and nepotism.'

The former state party Golkar also got a chance to make a statement in the same article. Golkar's representative Baramuli said he was convinced that Habibie was the most suitable presidential candidate. He expressed the reason for this in the following way: 'Habibie is the best and there's none like him, which is why Golkar is firm in its decision to nominate him.'

Baramuli praised Habibie without giving any factual reason as to why Habibie was the best candidate. It was a statement charged with emotion, not an opinion based on fact. We may note that political views such as Baramuli's were hardly conducive to constructive political discourse. They built up political camps barely capable of conducting such a discourse.

As we will see later on, Habibie was very controversial as a candidate. The question is why the *JP* dealt with both Abdurrahman Wahid and B.J. Habibie in the same news report. It might be because they were bitter political adversaries, and the newspaper's policy might have been to pinpoint this state of affairs.

In times of rapid political and social change, a return to old power structures might appear promising. An example of this was the introduction of Sultan Hamengkubuwono X into the discourse concerning the presidency. The Sultan was interviewed in the *JP* of 7 March 1999 (p. 10, 2 col. photo of the Sultan, 9 cols, 1/3 page). The article presented the Sultan as one of the possible candidates in the presidential election alongside Megawati Sukarnoputri, Amien Rais, B.J. Habibie and Abdurrahman Wahid. In the interview, the Sultan was introduced as a 'servant of the people'. One of the main topics in the interview concerned former President Suharto's role on the political scene. Like Amien Rais, among many others, the Sultan was critical about Suharto's political legacy but, unlike Amien, he did not support the idea of bringing legal actions against Suharto without 'adequate evidence'. The Sultan was presented to the readers as the middleman who was able to summon people of different political camps. However, insofar as his own presidential ambitions went, the Sultan stated: 'I won't comment on that. I don't have to become a government official to serve the people.'

The choice of words in the excerpt is interesting since the Sultan used the term *government official* instead of *president*. Certainly, a president is one among 'government officials', but there is a remarkable difference in status between the presidential office and that of other officials. Obviously, through his choice of words the Sultan made the self-evident point that he was not in need of the president's status. Thus, he made it clear that he was above daily political antagonisms, which he hoped would make a positive impression on readers. Note that 'serving people' had a special meaning in the context, because the Sultan could not be told what to do by the people but had authority over them instead (since he is of royal ancestry). In this context, then, we may interpret 'serving' as 'being of help on one's own conditions'.

On 10 March 1999, President Habibie was elected to top Golkar's list of presidential candidates. However, the party was not unanimous, and there was an internal party schism that a news report highlighted in the *JP*. Dealing with Habibie's candidacy the *JP* reported:

> Earlier reports quoting Akbar [Tandjung] and other Golkar officials that Habibie was their favored presidential candidate, provoked an angry response from executives of Golkar provincial chapters, who said chapters had yet to name their candidates. (see article 'Habibie Receives More Support for Another Term', *JP*, 10 March 1999, p. 2, 4 cols, 1/3 page).

In the article, leading party officials, among them chairman Akbar Tandjung, were set against the provincial party officials. Note, however, that the article did not investigate this split but only made it observable by reporting on it. The split is also concealed in the title of the article where it is stated that 'Habibie Receives More Support for Another Term'. Drawing attention to Golkar's internal schism on this matter, the *JP* laid bare the state of the party, which was hardly flattering since the readers could learn that Golkar was not even able to agree on its presidential candidate.

Two days later, on 12 March 1999, the paper resumed the matter of Habibie's nomination under the title, 'Habibie's Nomination could Backfire on Golkar: Experts' (p. 2, 4 cols, 1/3 page). Among the experts quoted was Riswandha Imawan, an academic who claimed that

> Habibie's nomination would cost Golkar...its painstaking efforts to make amends for past faults...Habibie is beyond all doubt always linked to Suharto and the New Order regime. It's highly unlikely to expect changes in Golkar if it fails to make a break with the past.

Riswanda Imawan's statement was clear and forthright enough; he meant that Golkar would do better without Habibie as its nominee. It is interesting to note that he did not explicate what he meant by 'past faults'. Apparently, there was no need to do that since the readers of the article could be assumed to know what these were. In connection with the nomination one could expect, however, more analytical discussion of the faults especially since the Indonesians were now free to employ more democratic election principles.

On 20 March 1999, a minor report (p. 2, 2 cols, 1/2 page) stated that several parties had named their presidential candidates. The report stated that PSII had opted for Habibie. According to the PSII, Habibie was the candidate who met the following criteria: 'reformist, master of science and technology, a democrat who respects human rights as well as places the nation's interest above personal benefit.' What was interesting about this report was that it took note of what Nurcholish Madjid, a distinguished Islamic scholar, had stated on the issue.[8] He was quoted as saying: 'Several Islam-oriented parties would nominate Habibie as their presidential candidate because of his identity as a Muslim intellectual.'

As a Muslim intellectual who possessed the specified qualifications, B.J. Habibie seemed to make a very good candidate indeed. In the report, no mention was made of Habibie's previous high status in the corrupt New Order regime. Thus, there seemed to be a fairly deep cleavage between those political camps that found involvement in the New Order regime compromising and those that did not mind or perhaps even regarded a New Order background as a plus for a politician.

On 23 March, the *JP* published a news report on the presidential election game (p. 2, 3 cols, 1/3 page). In this context, Abdurrahman Wahid made the following negative comments about Habibie: 'The funny part is that Habibie admitted to me that he does not have any political insight because he's "new to ruling this country".'

Obviously, here we are witnessing a power play centred geographically in Jakarta's political headquarters where actors knew each other only too well to be able to tell what gossip they had heard and passed on to one another (cf. in the excerpt, 'Habibie admitted to me'). The intimacy of the relationships could make the play pungent. Also the statement ascribed to Habibie, cf. 'he is new to ruling this country', seemed fairly strange given Habibie's background as one of the leading figures in the New Order regime. Obviously, through this statement Habibie was trying to distance himself from his position as minister and golf-mate to Suharto, implying that even as such he did not have very much real power.

One may wonder how it was possible that ruling the country previously in the New Order regime had not given Habibie competence to run the country after the collapse of that regime. Abdurrahman Wahid also thought that Habibie's alleged incompetence was 'a funny part'. Perhaps it was the gap between the requirements for a president and the supposed incompetence of the candidate that he found amusing. Of course, his statements also reflected the tone of debate; in this case, he was scornful of Habibie's candidature.

The debate on the presidential election seemed to lose some of its vehemence over time. We may assume that the debate was simmering beyond the public arena at different political headquarters in Jakarta. However, on 23 April we find a statement by Megawati Sukarnoputri on the issue. It is worth noting that the PDI-P, represented by its secretary-general, Alex Litaay, addressed the tone of the debate (see *JP*, 'Mega Still Says No to Presidential Debate', 23 April, p. 2, 3 cols, 1/3 page): 'Popular politician Megawati Sukarnoputri reiterated on Thursday [22 April 1999] her refusal to take part in a presidential debate because she was afraid the event would turn into a mindless argument.'

Not taking part in the public debate was motivated by two things: first, that the next president would be elected by the MPR and not by referendum; second, Alex Litaay, Megawati's spokesman, maintained that 'it is likely such a debate would grow into an ugly, senseless discussion... So why waste time doing it? Megawati's refusal... would not lessen the party's popularity or harm its image.' According to the article this was a response to Amien Rais who had been calling for a debate 'among presidential hopefuls, in order to educate the public about their capabilities.'

Alex Litaay maintained that work, not talk, was needed: 'This nation needs a strong, tested leader with continuous commitment to democracy and justice. Megawati has shown she possesses this quality... the most important thing is work, not talk only.' Since politics mostly consists of talking, that is, being able to articulate oneself in political matters, Alex Litaay was prompted to augment his statements on Megawati: 'Her opinions and thoughts are very deep. And everywhere she goes, people's support for her is tremendous.'

Before the election results were known, it was hard to tell what the power positions were for each political party and political leader. Perhaps they did not know with which rivals they had to fight, even though some opinion polls indicated that there were four strong parties, namely the PDI, the PKB, the National Mandate Party (PAN) and Golkar. We may note that it was hard to predict Golkar's future position, because although the party had immense funding and the broadest infrastructure during the New Order, it was by now riddled with internal conflicts. It is also noteworthy that among the parties we do not find the Islamist PPP, one of the three parties allowed to operate during the New Order era.

In this fairly unclear political situation, it was not strange that the political debates developed into what Alex Litaay defined as a 'senseless' situation. The dilemma was that without discussing in public the many problems plaguing Indonesia, the political development of the country could easily turn undemocratic. Even if the PDI-P most strongly objected to public debates, it did not affect its popularity, since it was the party that won most votes. The chapters by Antlöv and Cederroth in this volume provide a good analysis of the other attractions provided by the PDI-P.

The most debated issue in the context of general election candidates concerned the status of government officials in the elections.[9] There had been suggestions to the effect that government officials, members of the General Election Commission (KPU) and members of the National Election Committee (PPI) should be barred from contesting the elections and from being elected. Here is an overview of the headlines of the articles on KPU.

Headlines in the JP *related to the candidate eligibility debate in March–April 1999*

1   19 March: '5 Ministers Barred from Campaigning'
2   19 March: 'KPU Passes Controversial Internal Campaign Ruling'
3   20 March: 'Elections Body to Decide Ministers' Fate on Monday'
4   20 March: 'Poll Bodies Independence Ensured'
5   22 March: 'Ministers Can Campaign, says Akbar Tandjung'
6   23 March: 'KPU Split on Letting Ministers Campaign'
7   24 March: 'KPU to Indirectly Bar Ministers from Campaigning'
8   25 March: 'KPU Bars Ministers from Campaigning'
9   26 March: 'KPU Ruling Referred to Supreme Court'
10 26 March: 'Analysts Express Doubts about KPU's Credibility'
11 26 March: 'Golkar Challenges KPU's Decision on Campaigning'
12 26 March: 'New Values vs. Old'
13 29 March: 'Expert Urges Court Ruling on Ministers in Campaign'
14 30 March: 'Habibie, KPU Still at Odds over Ministers'
15 30 March: 'A Nearsighted Ruling'
16 31 March: 'KPU Firm with its Decision on Poll Campaigns'
17 31 March: 'The Supreme Court's Ambiguous Ruling'
18   3 April: 'President May Allow Ministers to Campaign'

The discussion on the right of government officials to become candidates extended from 19 March to 3 April 1999. Habibie had the last say on the issue; as indicated in the 3 April edition, the issue was not settled but the headline stated that 'President may Allow Ministers to Campaign'.

The problem at hand was expressed in the news report of headline 1, according to which five ministers were to be barred from campaigning. This piece of news was based on an announcement from the government itself, although it remained a little unclear whether all the members of the government supported it. The announcement seemed to be in full agreement with the principle of division of power, that is, the ministers should take the executive share of the power and not the legislative one. We may put this more figuratively by saying that the players and referees should not be mixed, in order for the game to be free and fair.

Analysing headline 2, we can observe that the principle of separation of powers seems to be omitted, since we learn that through its own ruling the KPU would allow its own fifty-three members as well as those of the PPI to campaign in the general elections.

Reading the article we learn that the ruling had not been arrived at in a democratic manner but as a result of a dispute between the government and the party representatives: a majority of the party representatives in KPU threatened to boycott the commission. According to one of the five government representatives in KPU, the government officials were obliged to bow to the pressure of the party representatives.

On the grounds indicated, KPU would not be a neutral body, but an arena where party political interests would clash. The chairman of the PPI, Yacob Tobing said (see headline 2): 'Political parties have sent their representatives to the election commission in order to fight for their interests and it is not wrong if they campaign and become candidates.'

The news report under headline 3 dealt with the impending decision by KPU on whether or not to allow ministers to campaign. The reason why government officials' engagement in the election campaign was so delicate an issue drew on experiences from the New Order era, when politicians in a position of power could profit extensively at the expense of the state (headline 3; see Uhlin 1997, Colmey and Liebhold 1999). As several politicians put it in a news report: 'The New Order acknowledged a tradition which allowed ministers to use their position and state budget in their campaign for the ruling party.'

As one might expect, Golkar did not initially support the barring of ministers from campaigning. Discussing ministers of the government, Akbar Tandjung, chairman of the Golkar party, claimed the following (headline 5): 'Just because ministers held a political post and were state officials should not preclude them from the campaign process. "They should be allowed to campaign as long as there is no conflict of interest. [If so] they can take leave," he said.' The representative of Golkar did not believe that there could be any just reason to bar ministers from campaigning. He would have sounded fairly convincing in his statement were it not for the fact that he did not give any indication of how to judge whether a 'conflict of interest' really was at hand.

The news report headlines themselves indicated that KPU's line of operation was not quite fair. On 23 March ('KPU Split on Letting Ministers Campaign'), it was reported that KPU was split on the question of allowing ministers to campaign, while only one day later, on 24 March ('KPU to Indirectly Bar Ministers from Campaigning'), a solution that made the ban somehow indirect seemed to be in sight. In the next stage of this dispute,

KPU barred ministers from campaigning (*JP*, 25 March; 'KPU Bars Ministers from Campaigning'). Then, the ruling by KPU concerning this issue was referred to the Supreme Court, which in due course gave its ruling on the matter ('KPU Ruling Referred to Supreme Court'). Several analysts expressed their doubts about the commission's credibility (*JP*, 26 March; 'Analysts Express Doubts about KPU's Credibility'). The party political challenges of KPU appeared on 26 March when the *JP* reported that Golkar had challenged KPU's decision on campaigning ('Golkar Challenges KPU's Decision on Campaigning'). The tenacity of different parties in the actual dispute shows what strong interests were at stake. Of course, the mighty Golkar party would only grudgingly give up any part of its position of power and the material benefits this position brought with it.

General elections 1997 and 1999: a comparison of discourses

Based on a condensed earlier study (Voionmaa 1998), I will attempt two things in this section. First, I shall compare political discourses during the general elections in 1997 and 1999 respectively, and then I will discuss some of their linguistic aspects. We may set the scene by taking a look at the themes of the texts studied in Voionmaa (1998). Table 7.1 gives an overview of the themes.

All the texts were written in English and they were editorials or editorial-like texts. Of necessity, they gave their support to the prevailing system of the New Order. Before the general election, the news media were, however, hesitant as to whether the system would be endorsed by the voters or not, as expressed in the *Indonesian Observer*'s (*IO*) editorial 'A New 24 Million-Vote Generation' on 12 May 1997. After the election, the *IO* and the *Indonesia Times* (*IT*) heaved deep sighs of relief. The *JP* for its part reminded its readers of the violence that had erupted prior to the election, and suggested that violence had affected the unity of the Indonesian nation. While critical, the *JP* did not question the legitimacy of the New Order system, but like the other two papers it agreed that the system had been endorsed through the polls.

Comparing the election campaign discourse in 1997 with the corresponding discourse in spring 1999, we can divide the themes into three groups. First, there are those themes that no longer have any relevance; second, there are themes that are essentially similar in both the 1997 and 1999 elections; and third, there are themes that are related to one another in some respect but that have changed their character fairly radically over time. In what follows, I will discuss the issue of non-voting as an example of the first theme; election campaign violence as an example of the second theme and, finally, unity of the Indonesian nation as an example of the third kind of theme.

Non-voting was an important issue in 1997. The *IT* discussed non-voting in its editorial 'After the Assured Landslide for Golkar' on 2 June 1997;

Table 7.1 Selected themes in Indonesian English-language newspapers before, during and after the general election (1997)

Paper	Date	Title of the text	Theme of the article
IO	12 May	A New 24 Million-Vote Generation	Endorsement of the New Order through the election; ideological tenets of political parties
JP	24 May	What Went Wrong	Violence during the election campaign; unity of the Indonesian nation
JP	28 May	Non-Voting is No Problem for Govt	Non-voting: political disillusionment
IT	30 May	People Give New Mandate to Golkar	Violence during the election campaign; endorsement of the New Order through elections
IT	2 June	After Assured Landslide for Golkar	Election: assessment of Golkar's victory; fairness of the election
IO	4 June	Small Party, Narrow Mindset	Ideological tenets of political parties; endorsement of the New Order through elections

Notes
IO *Indonesian Observer.*
IT *Indonesia Times.*
JP *Jakarta Post.*

it mentioned that a number of people had not used 'their right to vote'. The *JP* of 28 May 1997 also dealt with the issue; in this case, it tried to convince the readership that 'the government need not worry about people abstaining from voting'. The paper had consulted analysts, and these people had made it clear that 'the Golput (non-voter) phenomenon...had never exceeded 10 percent of the vote'. The *JP* also pointed out that in Western democracies such as the United States, the share of non-voters could reach between 40 and 50 per cent of those entitled to vote (see *JP*, 'Non-Voting is No Problem for Govt: Analysts', 28 May 1997).

Insofar as the election campaign of 1999 is concerned, we may first take note of the fact that people were encouraged by the media to register as voters. Some of the headlines included 'People Encouraged to Register for General Election' (5 April); 'Catholics Encouraged to Vote in June 7 Polls' (6 April); 'Parties to Encourage Members to Register for Election Soon' (7 April); and '2.65 Million Jakarta Voters Register for General Election' (13 April).

In the spring of 1999, political parties were mushrooming to contest the general election. Thus, the situation was dramatically different from that in

1997 when non-voting was a political issue. There were problems connected with the new situation, too, as the *JP* indicated in its editorial 'Euphoria of Number' on 5 March 1999. There, the *JP* called the situation a 'nightmare of the status quo' caused by the large number of different parties without many ideological differences. Most parties still stuck to the old principles of *Pancasila* and/or Islam. Thus, one may wonder whether indeed the number of contesting parties was a valid and reliable sign of growing democracy. In spite of the political liberalization it could be questioned whether there really were real different ideological alternatives in the 1999 election.

Turning to the second theme, political violence, we may note that it seems to be a persistent part of Indonesian politics irrespective of the changes towards more democratic forms of political life that we have witnessed in the country. In 1997, the election campaign was very violent indeed, as the *JP* reported in its editorial, 'What Went Wrong' (24 May 1997): 'Clashes between supporters of rival parties increased in intensity as the campaign period moved toward its final days…Roads were jammed or blocked. Shops and schools were closed.' The *JP* predicted that even if the violence had ceased for the time being it had left behind 'a bitter aftertaste that will linger on for some to come.'

Insofar as the situation in spring 1999 is concerned, we have to consider the role of the armed forces (ABRI/TNI). After Suharto's downfall its role had become problematic and precarious. In the spring of 1999, the *JP* published news reports on 1, 5, 20 and 25 March in which ABRI/TNI was discussed. On 1 March, for instance, the Islamic PPP party pleaded 'stop condemning ABRI'. It might not be a coincidence that it was the PPP, one of the three parties that was allowed to function during the New Order regime that pleaded on behalf of ABRI/TNI. As the foundations of the New Order were tumbling down, the PPP felt that ABRI/TNI made an important contribution to security in the country.

At the other end of the political spectrum there were pro-democracy student groups that kept themselves vigilant concerning the role of ABRI/TNI and the military. Thus, on 5 March 1999, the *JP* reported that student groups demanded that Wiranto, the minister of defence, resign from his office, because of offences during the New Order.

On 8 March 1999, Edith Hartanto proposed that a 'Code of Conduct' should be established 'to avoid campaign violence'. Hartanto's proposal aimed at building up structures that would make resorting to physical violence ever more difficult in politics. Proposals such as the one by Hartanto were welcomed, but some feared that they would not have much immediate effect on the deep-rooted habit of campaign violence. Insofar as the *JP* itself is concerned, I would have welcomed more investigative articles on the specific reasons for violence in Indonesian politics.

The social stability during the New Order era was largely based on the efficient and effective suppression of the people's political aspirations and activities (cf. Southwood and Flanagan 1983; Maristo and Sysikaski 1997). This made for what we have called the 'legacy of political violence of the New Order'. The *JP* did mention this legacy in a number of reports. Thus, for instance, Suharto's rise to power in 1965–66 was touched upon on 12 March as the *JP* reported that the '*Supersemar*[10] anniversary passes unnoticed'. In addition, the *JP* spoke of the issue of political prisoners in its editorial of 25 March, which dealt with the 'General's amnesty'. There were also several news reports saying that the government had freed political prisoners. However, the *JP* did not treat the New Order violence in depth, critically corroborating the paper's image substantially as that of a fairly shallow news media.

On 6 April 1999, the *JP* published an editorial entitled 'Why the Violence' that dealt with tension between the PDI-P and Golkar. It contained the claim that: 'Golkar has been endeavouring...to convince...that it has repented...Unfortunately, the party's claims have not been supported by actions.' This claim was in line with the anti-Golkar course that the *JP* was pursuing during the election campaign. The question is, of course, whether political violence would lessen if support for Golkar declined. Golkar is still the second largest party in Indonesia. Perhaps the roots of violence can also be found elsewhere than in the former state-bearing party.

On 22 April, the *JP* published the editorial 'Who's Foiling the Polls?' Therein, it was claimed that: 'The real threat [menacing the general election] is the inability of the government, including the military, to contain the violence.' This statement shows once again how keen the *JP* was to attack the Habibie government for its inability to create and maintain stability in the country. Looking at the statement more closely, the *JP* seems to mean that the military should play a more important part in Indonesia. The military is reproached for being unable to contain violence. Recalling the recent political oppression in Indonesia, this sounds ominous, and the role of the military should be discussed more specifically, but to search for such a discussion in the *JP* would be in vain. Thus, the *JP* seems fairly one-sided when it criticizes the inability of the government and military to contain violence. We may wonder, indeed, whether this is a sign that the *JP* is incapable of conducting a more cogent and reasoned political debate.

Finally, there is the theme of 'unity of the Indonesian nation'. Starting with the situation in spring 1997, consider again the *JP* editorial 'What Went Wrong', published on 24 May 1997. The main topic of the editorial was election campaign violence, but after having dealt with that issue, the editorial went on to establish the following: 'We Indonesians like to see ourselves as people who value harmony. Regretfully, the events of the past few days indicate that, perhaps, our cohesion as a nation or a society is not as great as we would like to believe.'

As indicated before, the *JP* did not question the basic legitimacy of the New Order system. However, it did cast doubts on the foundations of the national cohesion. The other two newspapers, the *IO* and the *IT*, differed from the *JP* on this point. They maintained that the Indonesian people supported the political system and that the unity of the nation was not threatened. Consider, for example, what the *IT* wrote on 30 May 1997 in its editorial, 'People Give Mandate to Golkar': 'Overall performance of the 1997 election indicated that the basic format of Indonesia's political system has been overwhelmingly endorsed by the people.'

When dealing with unity of a nation in the modern era of globalization, it is advisable to see it in relation to other nations. I would argue that, in general, the national unity of Indonesia, as depicted by the news media in 1997, was concerned mainly with what happened inside the country. The New Order regime had development plans that set the aims for the Indonesian nation. This was echoed in the *IT*, which said that: 'To use Indonesia's political catch word, the national development is in fact *Pancasila* in action, or national ideology in deeds.' Indonesia under the New Order relied on its state ideology and it seems that it was not very susceptible to foreign influence. True, Indonesia played a certain role among developing and Islamic countries, but ideologically it was fairly self-contained. The fact that there was a dearth of political impulses from outside, and that this continued for such a long time, may be one of the reasons why the present political discourse in Indonesia sounds so inane.

The spring of 1999 brought remarkable changes: the future of the Indonesian nation was no longer dependent on what happened on the domestic scene but there was now a new receptivity to foreign influences. The reactions of important foreign powers, especially the United States and Australia, for example, were carefully registered. The main focus is now on the interrelationships between politics and economy. Trust between foreign nations and the domestic public was one of the key concepts. We can consider the headline of the *JP* on 19 March 1999: 'U.S. Investors to Keep Close Eye on RI [Republic of Indonesia] Polls.'

On 16 March 1999, the *JP* published in its 'Insight' section an article by Kwik Kian Gie entitled 'Investors Waiting for Legitimate Government' (p. 2, 7 cols, 1/4 page) where it was stated that 'companies will make new investments only if there is political stability and political stability can be established only if the new government can win the public's trust'.

As part of the global economy, Indonesia's position would to an increasing extent be determined by powers over which the nation had no say. (Of course, this situation is repeated in neighbouring countries.) On 15 April the *JP* noted what the International Monetary Fund (IMF) would like to see. Concerning the macroeconomic situation in Indonesia, the IMF called for 'ensuring transparency in program implementation...and the need to avoid political interference in these processes....'

In times of swift change, with far-reaching material and social effects on practically every branch of life, the role of the news media becomes critical; and diminishing national unity (defined as a common belief system) has enhanced this role. Given, among other things, that the *JP* did not independently and critically investigate issues of political importance, we may ask what difference the newspaper really made to the Indonesian political discourse in 1999.

Let us momentarily examine the language policy of the New Order and after. This will hopefully help us to understand the central role of language for the political system in question. The language policy that the New Order government exerted was oppressive, and we may assume that the structures that were then created to enhance the role of *bahasa Indonesia* are still there. With the political oppression gone, one may wonder whether the Indonesian language will continue to keep the status it had under the New Order as one of the basic elements of modern Indonesian identity.

The New Order language policy was also prescriptive. It would standardize *bahasa Indonesia* and encourage its 'correct usage'. Quoting from a study by Virginia Hooker (1993), the aim of the policy was 'to enhance a particular mode of [political] orientation'; this would be 'comprehended unambiguously by both native and non-native users of the language' (Hooker 1993: 273–274). We may also consider what Benedict Anderson says about the 'revolutionary mode of thinking' of the New Order. He states that it was characterized by 'clarity within the mystified colonial world, coherence, simplicity, and comprehensiveness *vis-à-vis* the factitious (and real) complications of racial division, *adat* [customary law] particularity, and religious schism' (Anderson 1990: 136). It seems that we might epitomize the linguistic ideals of the New Order in terms of clarity and simplicity of expression, and comprehensiveness of use. Clarity and simplicity were (and, indeed, are) important so that people could use and understand *bahasa* as well as possible. Comprehensiveness was also important, since *bahasa* was to function as the common medium of communication for the new Indonesian state.

Despite the fact that *bahasa Indonesia* has had an important role in the development of the Indonesian national identity, it is surprising that in the data of the present study, I have not been able to find any mention of the language question. One reason may be that the role of *bahasa Indonesia* is regarded as so self-evident that it is not discussed because of this. Another possibility is that given the large number of, say, speakers of Javanese, the language question might be too charged to bring up. Still another possibility is that in English-language news media, issues pertaining to language simply do not appear pertinent. For whatever reason, this lack of discussion on the language issue indicates a fairly low level of ambition in relation to the treatment of Indonesia's political situation.

In her study on Sukarno and Suharto's Independence Day Speeches, Virginia Hooker observes that in Suharto's speeches 'all the references to the audience indicate that the speaker considers that they need to be led and directed' (Hooker 1993: 279). Thus, Suharto placed Indonesians in the role of children who needed to be taught to behave themselves better. Figuratively speaking, in the speeches we exclusively hear the voice of the powerful, 'His Master's Voice'.

We may relate this to the media discourse in 1997. Addressing the election campaign violence, the *JP* editorial 'What Went Wrong' (24 May 1997) reads as follows: 'with a little more political and emotional maturity among our people, all this [violence] need not have happened... People would not have been so easy to incite, had the situation been less loaded with emotions... in the climate of mutual suspicion that prevailed, people were easily provoked to commit acts of violence.'

In this manner, the *JP* established that people behaved themselves badly because they were not mature enough. The tenor of the editorial was paternalistic, embellished with formulations that sounded wise. It was stated that 'the situation' was 'loaded with emotions' and 'the climate' was full of 'mutual suspicion', but a critical observer may wonder how the 'situation' came to be emotionally charged and how the 'climate' became as bad as it was. In the paternalist New Order style of talking down to people, questions such as these were not answered, nor was a dialogue even established.

Another example of journalistic paternalism was the *IO* editorial 'Small Party, Narrow Mindset' (4 June 1997). The PDI had lost in the general election of 1997; the editorial treats the aftermath of the election as follows: 'The troubled Indonesian Democratic Party has threatened to withdraw from the House of Representatives, a move which will likely put the political machinery into disarray.'

The PDI and its chairman Surjadi were considering a refusal to sign the election result, and the editorial commented on that possibility as follows:

> What Soerjadi and his stooges should do now is not to refuse to sign the election result, but work even harder to win the people's sympathy. He is supposed to have learned a lesson from the experience of being made a 'political pawn' by any faction at the expense of throwing out his good team-mates.

Moving to the role of language in the 1999 media discourse, we may observe that there was much less paternalism. But still, Indonesians were being instructed to learn from what they saw happening elsewhere. The *JP* editorial 'The Kosovo Tragedy' on 3 April 1999 (p. 3, 2 cols, 1/2 page) told Indonesians the following:

> For Indonesians, there is a powerful lesson to be learned from the Kosovo war... Much more even than Yugoslavia, Indonesia is a hugely diverse nation... Without wisdom and restraint, even the most innocent arguments can escalate into conflict.

An innocent observer may wonder whether people should put forth any arguments at all for fear of igniting conflict. Statements exemplified in the editorial given here were paternalist and they promoted an atmosphere in which reasoned discourse became almost impossible.

Although not representative, we may take another example of paternalistic journalism; this concerns an article by Jusuf Wanandi entitled 'Indonesia's Long-Term Objectives' (23 April, p. 4, 6 cols, 1/2 page). '[Indonesians] must realize that there is no alternative to growth and development in the future than by riding the wave of globalization.'

The instances of paternalism that we encounter in the *JP* in spring 1999 were fairly few and mild; it seems that the New Order style of language, where the people were regarded as children of the president, no longer held Indonesians in its grip. Of course, the transition from paternalist language to a usage that we may call 'coequal' does not take place overnight.[11] It will evolve gradually, as democratic usage of the political discourse becomes more and more confirmed in the country.

When reading the *JP* in the spring of 1999, one notices that informative articles on issues that matter were also written exclusively by various external writers. See, for instance, the article by Lance Castles 'Voting Pattern May Change' (*JP* 23 March, p. 3, 6 cols, 1/3 page) where he discusses the actual issue of ideological recruitment taking place among the Indonesian people. As a reader, one gets the impression that in this manner the *JP* is fanning an anti-Golkar atmosphere as much as it can, but that it does not take full responsibility upon itself in the debate. Obviously, as soon as a debate turns towards a really vital issue, the voices change. These voices do not seem to come from the editors of the *JP*, but from a number of external political commentators. I find it hard to believe that this is the way towards the more democratic and consequential political discourse that still should be expected of the paper.

Conclusions

During the period of observation (1 March through 23 April 1999), the *Jakarta Post* promoted the pro-democracy movement. It called the prevalent status quo a nightmare, and it established that this state of affairs was of Golkar's making, to a great extent. It also clarified the point that the political game was described as taking place between distinct and identifiable camps. It made the nature of the game more explicit, and it also clarified what was at stake.

Obviously, the opposing camps had been there even during the New Order era, but the pro-democracy movement had not had many opportunities to put forth its views in the media. We grant that during the spring of 1999, the *JP* did work for a more democratic political discourse in Indonesia by formulating its anti-Golkar political line more clearly. In its editorial 'New Values vs. Old' on 26 March 1999 it claimed that this line constituted 'new values'. It went on to state that there is an 'unavoidable struggle between old and new values'. By using emotionally charged words such as 'unavoidable' before the word 'struggle', the paper seemed to be very determined to advocate its pro-democratic line.

On the other hand, the pro-democracy movement did not propound clear and distinct plans as to how the country might get out of its difficulties. Instead, it launched a massive attack on the Habibie government and waited for the situation to get better as soon as the new government was installed. The *JP* put this point across as follows (editorial 'Who's foiling the poll', 22 April 1999, p. 4, 2 cols, 1/2 page).

> This country is becoming more and more difficult to govern, not so much because of the increasing ethnic and communal conflicts, but more because of the administration's inability to rule. President Habibie and his administration... are fast losing their credibility.

The editorial also pointed out that the country's recovery would depend on the elections and their result, although it reasonably added: 'Elections are only the first step in the process of establishing a legitimate and credible government.'

While promoting a more democratic political discourse, the *JP* was still lacking in a number of vital respects. There were important issues that were *not* covered by the *JP*. Most important among these were the political programmes of the parties; that is, both the parties that were contesting the election as well as the ones that were not allowed to contest it. The *JP* did not bring up fundamental ideological issues; obviously, the voter was not offered much help in choosing one party ahead of another.

To counter this one could ask whether the *JP* is to blame for the shallowness of the political discourse in spring 1999. Based on my own studies and on studies of my colleagues published in the present volume, I find it more to the point to contend that there was a genuine lack of ideological debate in the country. As I have already indicated, the dearth of externally based political impulses during the New Order era probably contributed to this state of affairs.

Most of the articles dealing with election issues focus on Jakarta, or what the Jakarta elite said or did. The *JP* did not discuss at any length the role of non-governmental organizations or other groups within a broader civil society. It was merely reporting what 'political society' was saying and doing. I have argued that these reports did not really reflect what was going on in the country. During spring 1999, we never come to learn through the *JP* about local and regional politics; for instance how religious and regional movements related themselves to national politics.[12]

The *JP* did not take the lead in the public discourse. We might expect that as the fourth power of the state, the news media would keep scrutinizing political power structures as one of its main functions. If the media just report what the people in power say, they no longer live up to these expectations but have become 'His Master's Voice'. It would seem that the *JP* missed an opportunity to take up the role of a media representative that was prepared to discuss vital political issues in a penetrating and effective manner. To put it more succinctly, the newspaper did not challenge candidates to present their views. (Less surprisingly, this was also true of other major Indonesian news media.)

We may well ask whether the *JP* had any real impact at all on the election campaign – and conclude that the political discourse of the newspaper was lacking in a number of respects. One example of this concerns the fact that articles dealing with political and social issues overwhelmingly consisted only of summaries or quotes of what political pundits had said. There is not one single article based on investigations made independently by the newspaper. This lack of investigative journalism is even more surprising given the plethora of financial and other improprieties connected with Suharto, his family and cronies.

Thus, although the *JP* did promote the pro-democratic movement during the general election campaign, it fell short in many respects as a medium of democratic discourse. At this phase the Indonesian media, and the *JP* in particular, had barely started on the road towards the accomplishment of its mission as the fourth state power of a democratic society.

Notes

1 The role of *Catatan Pinggir* in the political discourse was to give guidelines to the enlightened public; the guidelines were given in the typical Javanese mode, where allusions are made to the shadow play (*wayang kulit*). See Graf 1998, p. 156.

2 Dealing with the pro-democracy movement in the country, Uhlin distinguishes between 4 main and 10 subcategories of discourse. (See Uhlin 1997: 128–154.)

3 The literature on discourse and discourse analysis is vast. I have consulted, among others, Potter and Wetherell (1987), Mann and Thompson (1992), Fairclough (1995), van Dijk (1997) and Heikkinen (1999).

4 An instance of this policy was the investigation by the police of the tapped telephone scandal involving Attorney General Andi M. Ghalib and President Habibie. The main objective of the examination was not to discern whether there had been such a telephone call, but whether the news media had violated the law forbidding dissemination of false information which stirs up public unrest.

5 Interestingly, Benedict Anderson refers to the same distinction in his essay on Indonesian politics in colonial times. Dealing with the acculturation by the Javanese officials to the Dutch colonial bureaucracy, Anderson says: 'For the conventional colonial official, the world divided normally into two: *praters* and *werkers*. *Praters* (talkers) were the parliamentarians, editors, idealists, 'reds' and ideologues. *Werkers* (doers) were busy and practical men of affairs, who kept their mouth shut, 'ran a tight ship', had a strong sense of hierarchy and knew their place down to the last E.' (Anderson 1990: 133).

6 I will use the general term 'text' to cover any type of written material that I examine in the present study. The texts can be news reports, ordinary articles and editorials.

7 The length of given text is given in number of columns (col.); the portion is estimated in terms of fractions, that is, 1/6, 1/4, 1/3 and 1/2 of the respective page. Note that I have not made use of these pieces of information. These non-linguistic features could be used in another related study.

8 See Liddle (1997) for an essay on Nurcholish Madjid's role in modern Indonesia.

9 In Habibie's transitional government, there were 37 ministers, most of them members of Golkar. In the General Election Commission (KPU), there were 5 civil servants and 1 representative for each of the 48 political parties. In voting, the 5 civil servants' votes were equal to the 48 party representatives' votes. In addition, the National Election Committee (PPI) was made up of KPU executives (7 members), government representatives (5) and 1 representative from each political party. KPU would establish the 'electoral code of conduct', whereas the PPI would, among other things, establish the election committees across the country. All this was expected to be fully functioning before 1 April 1999, when voter registration started.

10 Supersemar (*surat perintah sebelas maret*) is an acronym for the letter by which Sukarno transferred his presidential authority to Suharto in 1966.

11 In coequal language usage, interlocutors strive after mutuality; there is two-way interaction instead of the one-way interaction seen in the style that this chapter refers to as 'paternalistic'. (See Voionmaa 1997 for the treatment of issues related to coequal language usage.)

12 The gap between the discourse of the elite and real events in 1999 is reminiscent of the situation in Indonesia before the riots of 13–15 May 1998. On 4 May, the government announced a reduction in fuel subsidies. Indonesian officials complied with Suharto's decision to slash subsidies all at once, confident of immunity from public protest.

References

Anderson, Benedict R.O'G (1990) *Language and Power. Exploring Political Cultures in Indonesia*. Ithaca: Cornell University Press.

Colmey, John and David Liebhold (1999) 'All in the family', *Time*, 153(20), 36–39.

Dijk, Teun Adrianus van (1997) *Discourse Studies: a Multidisciplinary Introduction*. 2 vols London: Sage.

Fairclough, Norman (1995) *Media Discourse*. London: Arnold.

Flournoy, Don Michael (ed.) (1992) *Content Analysis of Indonesian Newspapers*. Yogyakarta: Gadjah Mada University Press.

Graf, Arndt (1998) *Indonesiche Medienrhetorik: eine methodologische Fallstudie anhand der Kommentarkolumne 'Catatan Pinggir' von Goenawan Mohamad*. Veröffentlichungen des Seminars für Indonesische und Südseesprachen der Universität Hamburg. Band 22. Berlin: Dietrich Reimer.

Heikkinen, Vesa (1999) *Ideologinen merkitys kriittisen tekstintutkimuksen teoriassa ja käytännössä* [Ideological meaning in the theory and practice of critical text research.] Helsinki: Suomalaisen Kirjallisuuden Seura.

Hooker Matheson, Virginia (1993) 'New Order language in context'. In Virginia Matheson Hooker (ed.), *Culture and Society in New Order Indonesia*. Kuala Lumpur: Oxford University Press.

Liddle, R. William (1996) *Leadership and Culture in Indonesian Politics.* St Leonards, N.S.W.: Allen & Unwin.

Mann, William and Sandra A. Thompson (eds) (1992) *Discourse Description. Diverse Linguistic Analyses of a Fundraising Text.* Amsterdam: John Benjamins.

Maristo, Irja and Kalle Sysikaski (1997) *Indonesia!* Tampere. Suomen Sadankomitealiitto.

Potter, Jonathan and Margaret Wetherell (1987) *Discourse and Social Psychology: Beyond Attitudes and Behaviour.* London: Sage.

Southwood, Julie and Patrick Flanagan (1983) *Indonesia: Law, Propaganda and Terror.* London: Zed Books.

Uhlin, Anders (1997) *Indonesia and the 'Third Wave of Democratization': The Indonesian Pro Democracy Movement in a Changing World.* Democracy in Asia Series, No. 1. Richmond: Curzon Press.

Voionmaa, Kaarlo (1997) 'Linguistic analysis of democratic discourse: a tentative approach'. Unpublished paper. Department of Finnish, University of Tromsø.

——(1998) 'Discourses of general election 1997'. Unpublished paper, Göteborg Centre for East and Southeast Asian Studies, Göteborg University.

INDEX

Indonesian names are sorted according to first name; organizations are sorted according to acronym

162